A LITTLE WORK, A LITTLE PLAY

A LITTLE WORK, A LITTLE PLAY

The Autobiography
of H.S. Malik

BOOKWISE (INDIA) PVT. LTD.

Photographs © Harsimran Malik
'H.S. Malik: India's Grand Old Gentleman' © *Asian Golf Digest*
'Sardar Malik' © *Hindustan Times*

Typeset in 10.5/14 Giovanni Book
Jojy Philip New Delhi 110 015

Printed and bound at
Thomson Press (India) Ltd.

Foreword

I consider it a privilege to write a foreword to the memoirs of an old and valued friend, H.S. Malik. He has had, indeed, as he admits in the Preface, 'a very full and interesting life', and I am glad that he has been persuaded to share so much of it with those who will be reading his story.

My friendship with the author goes back long years. During World War One we were both officers in the Royal Flying Corps in which he served with such distinction. A few years later we found ourselves as students together at Oxford University. Here we shared a common love of games, where I must confess he gained a proficiency which I could not match, except in those, like lacrosse and ice hockey, which were peculiarly Canadian. From Oxford, we separated to serve our respective countries in various ways. We were brought together again when we both became concerned with diplomacy and international affairs. It was a great joy to me, as the Secretary of State for External Affairs of Canada, to be able to welcome to Ottawa in July 1947 the High Commissioner for India, my old friend, H.S.Malik.

While in Ottawa, the High Commissioner did much to strengthen and develop the good and close relationship between India and Canada, something which Canadians cherish and the foundations for which had been well laid out by two great men, Pandit Nehru and the Right Honourable Louis de St. Laurent.

Mr. Malik made a great many friends in Canada, for himself and for his country. He knew, of course, the customs, the ways of life of the West. He could fit easily into any part of western life, but without altering in any way the impression he always made as a proud and complete citizen of his own country and a fine representative of his race and its traditions.

I saw much of him in those days and was able to appreciate the easy skill and effectiveness of his diplomacy. One place, however, where I refused to do any business with him was on the golf course. I had my position to maintain with the diplomatic corps as a Foreign Minister. How could I do that if I golfed with one who was capable of playing the course with a score equal to his age, something which I could not hope to do unless I lived to be one hundred years old or more.

My feelings of warm friendship for the author of this most interesting volume which covers so much of the recent history of his country extends to his wife and family, whom I have had the privilege of visiting in India.

L.B. PEARSON
Ottawa, 1972

Preface

I have had a very full and interesting life and have finally been persuaded by my family and friends to write about it, though I myself am still doubtful about it being worthwhile.

Opportunities have come my way and I have, I hope, made good use of them. One of the great mysteries of life is why some people, eminently worthy in every way, seem to miss success in life while others not so worthy do much better. For lack of a better explanation, many people put this down to karma, merit earned in a previous life or lives. However, I am well aware that such success and fulfillment as have come to me cannot be due to any particular merit on my part. I can only put it down to good fortune. Moreover, time and again, when I have made mistakes— and I have made many—I have somehow escaped the expected consequences of those errors. The many tight situations I have been in, which I have survived without experiencing serious harm, the crises I have successfully faced, the successes that have come my way, all this has left me with the conviction that in some mysterious way I have been protected.

My life has been enriched by the many friendships made with fine men and women in India and in countries which I have lived in; some of them distinguished in many walks of life often exercising authority and influence in national and international affairs. These friendships have lasted through the years and have been a source of great joy and happiness to me. I have been particularly fortunate in meeting people who have become close friends even later in life when one would think that new friendships could not be formed.

These contacts have helped me grow. I feel life is a continuous process of education. I have learnt to assess the importance and significance of the great and rapid changes that have taken place in my life spanning the 20th century. Apart from the opportunity of being actively involved in World War One, my life in the I.C.S. was rich and interesting at a time when district officers enjoyed so much responsibility and authority. Service in the Central Secretariat came at a turning point in India's economic and political evolution, followed by years in an Indian Princely State during a period of revolutionary political change, and finally the fortune to serve as Free India's Ambassador in 1947 when when we were just beginning to have direct relations with other sovereign states. It has been a fascinating and rewarding experience.

A full life, rich with opportunity, service and some sense of achievement, enriched immeasurably further by having a happy family life with a wonderful wife and children, the love of friends, good health, much fun and laughter, and what has always sustained me, devotion to the noble principles and traditions of my faith, which has given my life a spiritual content without which it would have been dry and barren. It is this faith that has helped me always in discriminating between the trivial and the important.

As a young man I found myself one day dining with some friends in a restaurant in London which was a favourite haunt of artists and writers, among them were Augustus John, the great Rupert Brooke, Gerald du Maurier and others. One of my friends pointed out to me a quotation by Hilaire Belloc on the wall of the main room which was said to be a favourite of the friends who frequently met there, and I have always thought it to be as good a guide to living as any:

From humble homes and first beginnings,
Out to the undiscovered ends,
There's nothing worth the wear of winning,
But laughter and the love of friends.

H.S. MALIK
New Delhi, 1972

CHAPTER 1

I was born in the early hours of November 23rd in 1894 into a well-to-do Sikh family in Rawalpindi, West Punjab, now Pakistan, in our old family mansion. Ours was a joint family comprising my father and his three brothers, and their families along with their servants.

My most vivid recollections of my childhood are of my father and mother, but I vaguely remember seeing my old grandfather, very striking, well over six feet tall—a legend in our city—lying in state at his funeral. My father, to whom I was absolutely devoted, because I spent a great deal of time with him as a child, was a remarkable man. Powerfully built, but not very tall, his strong character inspired a great deal of respect, even awe, among his associates. He was large hearted, and his numerous friends, his children and everyone who worked for him were all devoted to him. He was known for his physical and moral courage. Enterprising and bold in his ideas, he raised our well-to-do middle class family into one of the big landowning, propertied families in our part of the country through his hard work and enterprise.

He took on major contracts for building railroads, bridges and similar projects, and with the money he earned from these he acquired and developed property, including large areas of land in the new colonies which later became very valuable. And so our family too came to own a great deal of property in Rawalpindi. He also took a very active part in civic life and was, for several years, President of the Municipal Committee. He tackled this work with his usual energy and vision, devoting himself to successfully

improving local amenities. To dishonest and laggard city officials
he was a terror, but was greatly respected by the citizens of our
city who elected him President of the Municipal Committee time
and again. In the Sikh community he directed several activities
and occupied a position of honour and respect.

The mohalla in which our house was the most prominent,
consisted of narrow streets flanked by a variety of houses,
occupied mostly by lower middle class families, both Hindu
and Sikh clerks, shopkeepers, tailors, sahukars or moneylenders.
Muslims lived in the adjoining mohalla. The houses were
generally characterless, ugly and sparsely furnished, occasionally
an owner with aesthetic ambitions put in coloured glass
windowpanes, and others decorated their gateways with crude
carvings or cement mouldings.

The paved streets were narrow with a small open drain
in the middle to carry away the wastewater from the houses.
Children used the drain often as a latrine because of the lack
of proper facilities in many of the smaller homes. In most well-
off homes, sweepers who carried the night soil to waste bins,
which were then cleared by special municipal carts, would clean
out latrines twice a day. It was a most unhygienic system, which
was certainly responsible for the frequency of typhoid and other
diseases. During the rainy season the little drains were incapable
of carrying away the water, and the narrow streets often were
flooded, thus damaging the houses.

The entrance to our house was in one such narrow street
which led to an even narrower dark galli, then to an equally dark
passage to finally arrive at our doorsteps. On the right side of the
main door was a large room with a barred window which was
never used. We youngsters were terrified of it, as we believed it to
be haunted. I used to run up the steps as fast as I could, terrified
that the ghost was going to catch hold of me!

*   *   *

Thanks to Father my boyhood years were very different from that of most boys my age in our society. Although he himself had received very little education, he realized its importance for his sons. Since education in our schools was very poor, Father had Mr. and Mrs. Morris, an Anglo-Indian couple who ran a small kindergarten, teach us instead of sending us to an elementary school.

When I was old enough to go to high school, he again preferred to arrange private tuitions by two professors of the local Gordon Mission College. Both were competent, able teachers, men of outstanding character. I owe them a great deal, for not only did they lay the foundations for my basically sound education—by this I mean the ability to apply one's mind intelligently and methodically to all problems—but in their separate ways they served as my guides in the search for knowledge.

One of my teachers was a Christian from Ceylon who had settled down in India. He was called Ponsonby—an aristocratic name. I assumed he must have had some British blood in him but he showed no signs of it for he was very dark skinned. I fear he was rather ugly but when he smiled his face transformed and his noble nature seemed to shine forth. He was a good man, a real Christian. His smile reflected his sympathetic nature. He taught me English and gave me the thorough grounding which has given me such pleasure all my life. Mrs. Ponsonby was just as fair and beautiful as her husband was dark and unprepossessing in appearance. All the college boys were in love with her, from a distance, however, as she was a devoted wife and mother of several children—a truly sweet, virtuous woman.

My other tutor, who taught me mathematics, was from a well-known Bengali family who had settled down in the Punjab. He was Professor Mukherji who, later, as Principal of St. Stephens College in Delhi, became a well-known figure in India. A fine looking man of irreproachable character, he too combined strict discipline and hard work with sympathy and innovation.

He was a born teacher and under his enthusiastic instruction, although I had no great aptitude or liking for maths, I came to like even trigonometry! It was entirely due to the excellent tuition I received from these two professors that when I left for school in England at the age of fourteen, I was up to College standards in English and mathematics, almost three years ahead of the other boys my age.*

Father encouraged my natural love for sports by having me coached in cricket and tennis by Master Sandhe Khan, a competent, enthusiastic all-round sportsman, who was in charge of sports at the Mission College. Under his coaching I became good at both games, and was able to hold my own against much older people in college and club games.

I could have become a rather lonely, reserved boy with no contact with boys my age as I wasn't going to school but luckily I organized my own teams and we boys played cricket, hockey and football against other schools and private teams, sometimes on their grounds and sometimes in our large garden outside the city.

From early childhood, I spent a lot of time with my father, so I was much closer to him than to my mother. He spoiled me thoroughly, buying me expensive toys and by indulging me in other ways. When I was ill I recall more than once taking full advantage of his fondness for me and demanding expensive gifts such as silk socks, elaborate playing cards, train sets and so on. And I always got what I wanted. I asked my mother for none of

*Note by Harsimran Malik: Many years later in Delhi we got to know Nirmal Mukherji, the distinguished I.C.S. officer, who served in many top posts in Government including Cabinet Secretary and Governor of Punjab. We got along very well and when my father died in 1985, my mother asked Nirmal to read some of Guru Gobind Singh's verses, my father's favourites, in the English translation at his bhog ceremony, which he did. It was only later that we realized that the Professor Mukherji of Rawalpindi was Nirmal's father, and there had been this old connection! Sadly my father had gone by then.

these things as I knew she would not indulge me in the same way. She was a fine, noble person, very gentle, but with a quiet strength. She was never aggressive and had a profound influence on my character. The spiritual content there has been in my life, which has meant so much to me, I owe largely to her deep faith.

I remember my boyhood as a very happy one—a mosaic of interesting events. We youngsters played certain games our parents disapproved of. One was flying kites, very popular at a particular season of the year, as it still is, and disapproved of, partly because some boys with whom our parents did not wish us to associate, indulged in this pastime. But also because there were many accidents of boys falling off the roofs of houses while kite-flying. In spite of all opposition, however, I vividly remember getting the best kites made of brightly coloured paper stretched across thin cane frames, the special cords for flying the kites coated with powdered glass. This cord would cut the cord of rival kites in our aerial combats. These demanded considerable skill to manoeuvre kites into the best position to bring down rivals! I still remember the intense tension and the thrill of these battles! Perhaps it was a forerunner of my aerial combats in World War One.

Riding was another vivid memory of my boyhood. We had a large stable with several horses both for riding and for our carriages, this being the pre-automobile age. I literally grew up in the saddle for I must have been put on a pony when I was only five or six years old. As I grew older, I was allowed to ride fully grown horses, and when I was ten or eleven Father gave me a beautiful black stallion. I grew to love him and he was a beauty, somewhat untamed. No one else was allowed to ride him, and indeed he would allow no one but his sahis, grooms, and me to mount him. He was always prancing, even with me, and when I was mounted, I showed off unashamedly to an audience!

I remember one occasion when a large crowd had gathered for a family wedding, I arrived on the scene on my black stallion, having ridden about fifteen miles. Excited by the crowd, the horse started playing up, and reared up so high on his hind legs that I deliberately slid off before he could fall on his back. I was still on my feet when I landed and my horse, instead of kicking me and bolting, pushed his muzzle into my hands trying to apologize. The crowd was thrilled and I, of course, was elated. I must have been an insufferable brat!

This early association with horses proved very useful in my service in the Punjab when riding was essential for touring the district, and in later years, in England, when, without any practice riding, except for those early years in the I.C.S., I was invited to join in a hunt or in a point to point and was generally able to perform well. My father had been a very good rider when he was young and he indulged his love of horses by acquiring beautiful ones for our carriages. I still remember the thrill of sitting with him in a carriage drawn by a beautiful, spirited pair of ponies imported from Kandahar. The coachmen and sahis immaculately accoutered. When I was alone in the carriage my greatest delight was to be permitted to sit with the coachman and occasionally be allowed to hold the reins.

When us boys went on foot to play, we often went through the bazaars, with arrays of fascinating shops and stalls. I remember the halwais with their appetizing, freshly made rasagoolas, laddoos, gulab jamuns, barfis, and jalebis and mouthwatering variety of fresh tikkis, samosas, pakoras and fried dal; the cloth shops with yards and yards of brightly-coloured cotton fabrics; the crowded shoemakers with their beautiful gold embroidered Punjabi jootis, for which Rawalpindi was famous. It was a wonderfully lively colourful scene, always exciting for us. The scents of spices, of fruits and vegetables and the manifold odours and sights of the bazaar are unforgettable memories. But we were strictly forbidden to loiter in the bazaar, or taste any of the tempting delicacies!

From a very early age I had a personal servant, Shiv Ram, who looked after all my requirements from the moment I woke up in the morning to the time I went to bed at night. He was my constant companion. He escorted me to my tutors and was present at all our games. A trusted old retainer, he had come into my father's service while still a youngster, and had travelled with Father on his far-flung projects. He had many tales to tell of Father's experiences in the wilds of the North West Frontier Province—real tales of adventure spiced up for my benefit I am sure, for Shiv Ram was a born storyteller.

CHAPTER 2

Looking back on those years before I left for England at the age of fourteen, I am overwhelmed by memories of the great affection and care Father gave me. Despite my pampered upbringing, I grew into a more or less healthy-minded youngster. And looking back I can clearly see why. For one thing, Father was a tremendous disciplinarian, with a very strict code of honour and integrity. For his children he set up the highest standards in this respect, and we knew that if we did anything dishonorable or unworthy we would have to answer to him. So while I adored him, I also held him in some awe.

While I was given a personal servant, I was also told repeatedly that being independent was one of the great virtues and that labour of all kinds was an honour, not a disgrace. Father's favourite book, although he was not a great reader, was *Self Help* by Samuel Smiles and I was made to read this until I knew it almost by heart. In those days boys from well-to-do homes were brought up to have everything done for them—even shoelaces were tied by their servants as it was considered infra dig to perform such menial tasks oneself! Therefore, the fact that we were constantly reminded to be self-reliant helped greatly to counteract any tendency towards self indulgence. There was another factor which profoundly influenced my development. As a young man, Father led a very vigorous and full life. He worked hard and was gregarious, with a large number of friends. I well remember parties where liquor flowed freely and there was much gaiety. As was customary, these parties were confined to men and none of the women in the family were present. I never saw a woman at any of these parties, although I know that in accordance with the custom of those times dancers and singers were brought in for entertainment. I suppose Father made sure that I was never present on those occasions. I can imagine what anguish the knowledge of these parties must have caused my mother as she was very religious. But she was a sweet, saintly woman of infinite patience, and eventually won over her husband to the kind of life which she wished for him.

At home there was also always an atmosphere of religious devotion and prayer. Mother recited the Sikh prayers which were a part of the daily routine and my father gradually fell into the same habit. So, even when he was very busy, he would recite the paath and shabads from the scriptures every morning before going to work, even though it meant getting up before dawn to do so. Every evening the family would sit down together and Father would recite rahras, the evening prayer, and at night before going to sleep, the kirtan sohila. Before every meal he would say an ardas, a prayer asking the Almighty for guidance and protection.

Father had a profound faith in the Sikh religion. He would stand and say ardas, before leaving the house, especially when he was about to do something he considered important. The ardas concludes with the beautiful words, *Tera bhane sarbat ka bhala*, which means 'May it please you Lord that good may come to all'. From time to time Father would bring home a sant or holy man who would conduct our prayers. When we were living in places where Father had a project, we sometimes had a sant staying with us and this meant a good deal of religious activity. I joined in as I was expected to as a matter of discipline, even if I was disinclined to do so. I can't say that I took any particular interest in religion. Sport was my chief interest.

My mindset changed almost overnight when a very remarkable personality, Sant Attar Singhji, came into our lives.

He was already well known among the Sikhs and revered as a saint. He came from a village in what was then the Princely State of Patiala in northern India. He was of peasant stock and had served in the Indian army as a jawan. Soon, however, he felt the call for a religious life, left the army, and devoted himself to a life of prayer and meditation in an isolated part of the country. Coming out of this hermit-like existence, he then took up the work of prachaar, of bestowing religious enlightenment. Our family first met him when he came to our city.

I shall never forget my first meeting with him. My mother persuaded my father to accompany her to seek darshan of this sant and they took me along. He was staying in a sarai, just outside the city along with his sevadars, his close followers. As it was the early afternoon in the hot weather he was resting in his room when we arrived. We were taken up to see him and we sat down after paying our respects. There was no one else there, just he and the three of us. Beyond greeting us he hardly said a word. There was no need for words for he seemed to emanate an aura of peace and tranquility, a kind of spiritual beauty, impossible to describe. A power seemed to flow from him created through years of prayer and meditation. It profoundly moved us all without his having uttered a single word.

Later, when I got to know him better I came to love and admire him for the true saint he was, but even at this first meeting the impression he made transformed my life. Association with him in subsequent years profoundly influenced me, and gave my life that spiritual content which has brought me such contentment. Mother, naturally, was deeply moved by this first meeting and became Santji's devoted follower for the rest of her life. On Father the effect was extraordinary, both instantaneous and profound. From that day on he gave up his parties and his drinking, and while attending to his worldly responsibilities, he took time out for religious activities, both at home and in attending dharmic diwans, the evening prayers. What a joy this almost miraculous transformation was to my mother who saw all her prayers answered.

During the few days Santji stayed in our city, we attended all the diwans and services held by him. These were simple but most impressive. They were held in the early mornings and evenings and were attended by thousands of men, women and children. Everyone joined in the singing of shabads. Occasionally Santji himself lead the singing. He never preached any sermon. Most of the time he sat in deep meditation before the Guru Granth Sahib, and when the service was over he would walk away to his room. People would fall at his feet, although he always wished to avoid that. They would persist, and every time they did this he would repeat, almost in a whisper, 'Wahe Guru', as if asking the Almighty to forgive him for what they were doing. When he left Rawalpindi I was allowed to follow him for some days. It was an unforgettable experience. I was given his kara, the steel bangle worn by every Sikh, which I kept with me always, even through my flying service during World War One.

He was a remarkable person. Although illiterate, as most Indian peasants were in those days, he seemed to understand everything that was going on in the world. It was the beauty of his soul that inspired devotion and deep respect among the tens of thousands who came to see and hear him. He had no possessions of his own and, of course, no property or money. People would offer him gifts, he would accept them and give them away to those whom he felt needed them.

Many stories were recounted about his performing miracles, although he scrupulously avoided showing off in this way. However, I witnessed a remarkable incident. He was staying in a small town called Chatwal in the adjoining Jhelum District and the Rawalpindi Sikhs were anxious to have him come and spend a few days in their city. Two of us were sent to Chatwal to invite him. There was no railway connection with Chatwal, so we went by train first to Taragarh—incidentally named after my wife's maternal grandfather—and from there on by horseback arriving at Chatwal at about 3 p.m. We were told that Santji was confined to bed, and one of the Sikhs who was looking after him informed us that he had double pneumonia with a temperature of 104°C, and that the doctor had ordered complete rest for Santji. In those pre-Penicillin days this was a dangerous illness. We were told we could not see him. Not only were we disappointed but deeply concerned.

Santji learned that we had come from Rawalpindi and he sent word that he wanted to see us. After we had paid our respects and he had talked to us quite normally, we all heard the familiar cry of the ice-cream vendor in the street below, 'Malai Kulfi! Cold Kulfi!' Santji told his attendant to ask the kulfiwalla to come up so we could all have kulfi! The attendant protested strongly saying that the doctor had strictly prohibited it. Santji, smilingly treated the whole thing as a joke, but insisted. The kulfiwalla was called and all of us, including the patient, had the ice-cream. Then, turning to the attendant, Santji told him, 'We will have the diwan, at 5 o'clock. Please make all the arrangements.' The worried attendant again protested, but he just smiled and repeated his instructions. The attendant brought the doctor who was amazed to find that both lungs were absolutely clear and the temperature normal. The diwan was held and Santji, looking on all this as quite normal, seemed very amused that everyone, especially the doctor, was so astounded.

As a result of my deep attachment to Sant Attar Singhji my interest in my religion and in the lives and teachings of our gurus grew. I also became conscious of our history and tradition. Listening to gurbani was no longer a mechanical exercise. I took real interest and got great joy out of it. I did not realize it at the time but all this was of special importance to me since I was destined to spend many years as a youngster away from my own people in foreign countries, exposed during long, continuous and impressionable years to all the various influences of alien cultures. I was fortunate to be able to participate fully in the lives of the people among whom I lived abroad—loving them, enjoying their friendship, admiring their faith, their history and traditions, without in any way weakening my love for and devotion to my own faith and traditions. I ascribe this ability to this great and wonderful man who so fortunately became a part of my youth.

As a family we had more than our share of the material things in life: a lavish house, good food, horses and carriages, servants galore and money. Yet we children, because of the atmosphere in which we lived, particularly my father's influence, were saved from becoming snobs and mere materialists. Many years later when my elder brother joined the Service of Engineers and I the Indian Civil Service, and we both occupied positions in which we could have made money, Father would still constantly remind us that complete honesty was worth more than ill-begotten wealth and that to make money in a corrupt manner was evil. This was all the more remarkable for in the contract work Father was engaged in corruption was rampant. Obscene language was forbidden in our house. This also prevented us from being abusive to our inferiors—a common failing among boys of good families in those days.

The emphasis on these fundamentals and the belief that material wealth is comparatively unimportant profoundly influenced my life as did my contact with Santji. This brought me comfort at times of crises, and gave me the ability to stay focussed in the face of success which came my way. Spiritual and religious activity was for our family a kind of uplifting exercise taking us out of the material, everyday world we lived in. It added to our *joie de vivre*—a spontaneous act of showing our gratitude to the Creator.

This has been my deep and growing conviction. Frequently in discussions with people who say that they have no use for religion,

I tell them that I don't know what they mean by 'religion'. I don't associate religion with going to church, a temple, a mosque or a gurudwara. To me religion is consciousness of the beauty of life, of the spirit which brings great happiness and satisfaction. I had a very full life but it would have been incomplete without its spiritual content.

CHAPTER 3

We had very friendly relations with the considerable Muslim community in Rawalpindi. However, religious and social differences did prevent any close, intimate interaction, and on the whole Muslims lived as a separate community with their own customs. Social contact was usually confined to occasions such as weddings and funerals when members of the two communities would get together, but these meetings friendly as they were remained formal. There was never any question of a Muslim coming informally to our homes and mixing freely with us, nor of any of us visiting Muslim homes and mixing with their families. Within these limitations, however, relations were friendly and the three main communities, Hindus, Muslims and Sikhs, lived peacefully together, often in the same part of the city.

At the same time most Hindu and Sikh families practised what I would describe as 'untouchability'. Most of them would not eat food that had been prepared or handled by a Muslim, nor would Muslim servants be serving in Hindu or Sikh homes except in jobs that required them to be out of the house such as gardeners, coachmen, watchmen, but ironically, whenever necessary, as midwives. My wife, whose father was a staunch Hindu, married to a Sikh, told me how puzzled she was as a child that on festivals their Muslim friends sent over gifts—only uncooked items—such as dry fruits and nuts. However, when gifts were sent from her family's home to Muslim friends, they were considered as prasad and were cooked food from their kitchen. Even as a young child the injustice worried her.

Nonetheless the various communities co-existed in peace and amity. There were of course occasional communal riots in India even in those early days, particularly when the timing of religious celebrations by the two major communities, Muslims and Hindus, clashed. But during my childhood I was not aware of any serious differences which were to lead to the kind of communal disturbances later.

Hindu-Sikh relations were cordial, and in many Hindu families in the Punjab one of the sons was usually brought up as a Sikh. Hindus visited Sikh gurudwaras in large numbers as they do today. While intermarriage between Hindus and Muslims was practically non-existent, it was frequent between Hindus and Sikhs. The lower castes, the 'untouchables' were completely isolated from other communities, despite the fact that Sikhs were not supposed to believe in caste discrimination.

There was little contact with the English living in our city. Rawalpindi was a cantonment where troops, both British and Indian, were stationed. It was the headquarters of a Civil Division as well as that of a district—both administrative units. The administrative head of a division was the Commissioner, and a Deputy Commissioner was that of a district. In those days all Commissioners and Deputy Commissioners were British and members of the Indian Civil Service. There was, therefore, a fairly large British colony for civil officials and their families; the officers of the British and Indian armies—all the King's Commissioned Officers of that time were also British—and a fairly large number of 'Tommies' as the British soldier was known in India.

A city with a cantonment had two parts, the cantonment and the city, two parts which as a matter of British colonial policy were kept strictly apart, managed and administered separately. The great majority of Indians lived in the city which was run by the Municipal Committee of which the Deputy Commissioner was ex-officio, a permanent President. He was assisted by a council of Indian members all of whom were nominated by him. Later, around 1910, as one of the earliest moves towards self-government, some of the Municipal Committee members had to be elected by the citizens. The cantonment area was administered by an official Cantonment Board presided over by the General Officer commanding the district. The Executive Officer of this board was known as the Cantonment Magistrate and exercised both magisterial and civil powers, and, of course, was invariably British.

The British, always referred to as 'the Europeans', were a very insular community. They had their own social and sports clubs, membership of which was not open to Indians, who the Europeans generally referred to as 'the natives'. 'The Europeans', being the rulers, undoubtedly regarded themselves as superior to the natives in every way. The two communities had no social contact apart from official ones. These occasions were always very formal, and apart from that the only Indians the Europeans got to know were their domestics who came generally from the so-called 'lower castes' and whose one aim was, naturally, to please their European masters.

While the Indian servants were mostly loyal to the Europeans, who for the most part treated them well, many servants also robbed and cheated their masters in many petty ways. One of the unfortunate results of this extremely limited association was the general impression among the British living in India that all Indians were cheats and liars. There were, fortunately, some honourable Englishmen who took the trouble to understand the country and its people.

Father was one of the leading citizens of the city being an Honorary Magistrate and Vice-President of the Municipal Committee and later its elected President. He frequently met the principal military and civil officers. However, these interactions were always very formal and Father, when he called on any official, would be ushered into a waiting room where other

Indian notables were assembled, waiting for their turn to meet the great man. Whether he was shown into the 'presence' right away or made to wait for an hour or two would depend on the whims of a man known as the 'jamadar', the chief of the army of peons, chaprasis, supplied by the Government to all important civil officials. Father tipped these peons generously from time to time, so he was generally not kept waiting unless the official concerned disapproved of something Father had done, in which case he would have to wait. On the whole, however, Father got along well with the Commissioners and Deputy Commissioners with whom he had to deal. They were generally able, intelligent, decent men, who appreciated my father's somewhat exceptional personality, and respected him in their own way. I recall hearing of only one incident which occurred many years later, after I had entered the I.C.S. and was occupying the post of Deputy Commissioner of a district not very far away from Rawalpindi. Father was the President of the Municipal Committee, and there were frequent arguments between him and the British Deputy Commissioner who was a brilliant scholar but somewhat eccentric and with very poor judgment. I was told the story, not by Father, but by one of the Municipal Councilors present at this particular committee meeting which had been specially called by the Deputy Commissioner. Some angry words were exchanged between Father and the Deputy Commissioner. Finally the D.C. lost his temper and shouted at my father, 'Malik Sahib, you cannot talk to me like this! I will have you know that I am the Deputy Commissioner!' To which my father quietly replied, 'Oh yes, Sahib, I can. I would have *you* know that *I* am the *father* of a Deputy Commissioner!' On this last statement the meeting apparently came to an end.

A number of stories circulated about some of the more eccentric British officials and the relations between them and their Indian subordinates, the senior most of whom were known as Extra Assistant Commissioners. A British Deputy

Commissioner named Bosworth Smith was the subject of a great many stories in our district. In one incident, which I particularly relished, Bosworth Smith, a generous but hot-headed man, lost his temper with one of these officials, a well respected, dignified Sikh named Khazan Singh, and abused him. He called him 'soor ka baccha', son of a pig. The Sardar was furious and asked him to apologize and Bosworth Smith, at once said, 'Never mind Sardar Sahib. I am a "soor ka baccha", my father too was a "soor ka baccha"!'

The lives of the Indians and the British were very much apart but with few exceptions. Most of the bungalows and the residences in the cantonments were occupied by the British. There would have been strong disapproval of any Indian coming to live in these areas, and it would most certainly have been disallowed, although these bungalows were all owned by Indians.

Europeans and Indians met either on official occasions or when Indians called on European officials. In those days the Indian caller was expected to, and generally did, take off his shoes before being ushered into the sahib's presence. The very few 'England returned' Indians, generally barristers-at-law, who considered this custom humiliating, refused to conform to it but they were the only exception. Much of this code of conduct was deliberate to maintain the white man's prestige, otherwise how could a handful of British rulers control millions of Indians? So Indians, whatever their status, were discouraged from riding on the horse track which was part of the Mall, the main road in the cantonment, a track said to be reserved for Europeans. Trains, compartments were at one time marked 'for Europeans only', and even after this segregationist practice had to be given up, Europeans generally did not like the idea of natives travelling in the same compartments with them. Innumerable incidents were reported from all over India in which there had been trouble between Europeans and Indians on trains leading to much ill

will and resentment. Even as late as 1919 I myself was a victim
of this stupid attitude.

We used to hear tales of the high-handed behaviour meted out
to Indians by the British Europeans in the neighbouring North
West Frontier Province (NWFP) where the question of upholding
the white man's prestige was taken even more seriously. In the
NWFP the native pathans were expected to fold up their umbrellas
if they were open when they met an Englishman on the street. If
not, it was considered a sign of disrespect. Many incidents over
this rule were reported and I remember one which caused much
hilarity. It happened in the Gallis, a small hill station in NWFP
where most Englishmen posted in the Province went to escape
the summer heat of the plains. A British officer met a pathan on
a lonely road and as it was raining, the pathan had his umbrella
open. As the two men crossed each other, the pathan failed
to close his umbrella and was immediately pulled up by the
Englishman and asked to explain his conduct. Hot words were
exchanged and when the Englishman abused him, the pathan,
a high-spirited young man, beat him up, tied him to a tree and
went on his way, his umbrella still open. It was a lonely road so
the Englishman remained in this state for a considerable time! It
was a silly enough incident but the publicity it received and the
obvious delight with which it was recounted spoke of the strong
feelings of resentment between Europeans and the natives.

CHAPTER 4

When Father was carrying out his contract work in other parts of the country, at times he had to live for considerable periods near the site of the project. He would then arrange for his family to come and stay with him. He was once involved in a three-year project in the construction of the railroad from a place called Kosi to Mathura in the United Provinces which was to form part of the main Mathura–Agra railroad. And so he made Mathura his headquarters. He travelled between Mathura and Kosi on horseback and I often accompanied him, riding a beautiful gray horse. I was only about ten years old but was always at his side when he went out on inspection.

In those days the countryside was rich with wild life and a huge variety of birds. During those rides we would often come across large herds of deer, flocks of peacocks, ducks, cormorants and several other birds. It was a wonderful experience for a boy my age. Between Mathura and Kosi we rode along a canal, occasionally through villages. I noticed how the rural folk and their cattle and crops differed from those in our part of the country. The women's costumes big, colourful swirling skirts were particularly eye-catching, in contrast to women's attire in the Punjab.

Mathura city was an exciting change from Rawalpindi with its multitude of temples on the banks of the Jamuna, and the pandas, the priests, well known for their enormous bellies, and for the amazing quantity of laddoos they could put away. They were greedy and corrupt, unashamedly hungry for money. Father employed one of them as a guide and servant, and we became quite fond of him, even though we knew he was a rogue and was not to be trusted. However, he was an entertaining rogue and showed us all around Mathura and the neighbouring town, Brindaban, with its plethora of temples, the scenes of which depicted Holi and Janamasthami. While Mathura was the centre of pilgrimage for thousands of people, Brindaban occupied a special place in Hindu hearts. It was considered to be the playground of Krishna and his gopis.

Mathura was famous for its mischievous monkeys. They invaded houses, carried off food and clothes; sometimes even attacked people, especially children. But as they were considered sacred by Hindus, no one could take any action against them. Our house was well protected against these pests, all doors and windows fitted with iron bars. But when we ate in the open courtyard in the evening, a guard armed with a long stick stood by to keep off the monkeys.

I had an air rifle with which I used to fire at birds and one day, foolishly, without realizing the consequences I shot a pellet into the stomach of a large monkey sitting on the wall. He let out a cry in pain and came at me in anger. I ran for shelter into the house, but in seconds the house was surrounded by shrieking monkeys. Soon people started gathering around the house accusing me of having shot a monkey! I was quite frightened at the commotion, but Father came to my rescue. Our panda was summoned and asked to deal with the situation which he somehow managed to do, and we were left in peace. One welcome outcome of this unfortunate incident was that from then on I had only to point my air gun at any monkey to have him beat a hasty retreat.

In those times Indian children, regardless of their family's status, seldom came into contact with Europeans. I played cricket and other games with Indian friends. The only time I met Europeans was either when my father went to call on the

Deputy Commissioner and, on rare occasions, took me along; or when the cricket club, of which I was a very young member, played against the European Gymkhana Club in Rawalpindi. One of those games is a vivid memory. The Europeans had a fast 'demon' bowler named Lancaster. I was a good batsman but was only about 12 years old and quite short. So when I went in to bat Lancaster must have felt he should take it easy on this youngster and not bowl too fast. He sent down a couple of medium paced balls which I shot to square leg boundaries. After this he let fly at me with all his strength. I scored quite a respectable number of runs and my performance earned me a reputation in the local cricketing circles.

On another occasion, very different but memorable, during the early years of the All India Home Rule League,* I found myself close to a European officer. In 1906 or so there was very little activity regarding this movement in Rawalpindi but I remember great excitement when the great nationalist leader, Lala Lajpat Rai, came to our city from Lahore. A local committee was formed to welcome him at a public meeting to be held in the mandi, the main market place. Mr. Agnew, the District Magistrate, immediately issued orders prohibiting such a meeting, but the local committee defiantly went ahead with their plans. An angry Agnew went to the police headquarters in person and summoned the organizers; among them were three of the city's most prominent lawyers. I was with my father at our house in the cantonment when he received word of what was happening, so we drove immediately to police headquarters. Agnew was talking to the three lawyers. Very excited to be there, sitting with Father, listening in, I watched wide eyed when Agnew warned

* The All India Home Rule League was a national political organization founded in 1916 to lead the national demand for self-government, termed Home Rule, and to obtain the status of a dominion within the British Empire as enjoyed by Australia, Canada, South Africa, New Zealand and Newfoundland at the time.

them sternly against holding the meeting and they responded calmly stating that they would consider the matter. A furious Agnew told them that if they persisted in holding the meeting, he would order the police to break it up. They again insisted that they would consider the matter. In those early days the British rulers were held very much in awe and this open act of defiance of the District Magistrate made a deep impression on me. In my eyes the lawyers were great heroes even though, in the end, the meeting did not take place.

At about the same time another event took place which reduced the general feeling of awe in which Indians held the Europeans. Prisoners of the British from the Boer War in South Africa were sent to India. They were held in POW camps but were allowed to circulate in the cantonment during the day, and for us it was quite a thrill to have these white men, mostly well built and good looking amongst us, offering little objects they had carved out of from soft stone for sale. They were trying to supplement their small POW allowance. Looking back on this one feels these incidents were the precursor to Mahatma Gandhi's Civil Disobedience Movement many years later, which destroyed the belief in the white man's superiority.

Other early, vivid and happy memories were the annual summer visits to Murree, our nearest hill station. We made the 40-mile journey in a special kind of tonga, a sturdy two-wheeled vehicle drawn by two horses. The first 17 miles were over flat country, with the horses changed every eight to ten miles. But as the road to Murree, which lies at 7000 feet, grew steep the horses were changed every four miles. The drivers were generally excellent coachmen, many of them rascals but a sporting lot who took great pride in their vocation. The horses were well fed and looked after and as Father at one time ran the service between Rawalpindi and Murree, he and the family were well known to the coachmen. Therefore we always had the best tongas, horses and drivers. We looked forward to these journeys with anticipation, excitement growing as the tonga moved faster into a gallop. We held on for dear life because the back seats were always at an angle, sloping backwards. And at that speed you were always scared of being thrown out.

Once we travelled all the way to Kashmir at a comfortable pace, a 200-mile journey, in our landau drawn by our own horses. It took several days. I was too young to remember any details but several years later, after I joined the I.C.S., we went to Kashmir by the same road, but by car, covering 200 miles in one day, and I could hardly believe that I had once done that journey in a two-horse carriage!

CHAPTER 5

At the beginning of the 20th century young Indian boys were often sent abroad for their education. From an early age I was keen to go to England for no real reason other than the glamour of going to wilayat! Also, when I was old enough to think about my future, my ambition was to get into the Indian Civil Service which at that time was extremely prestigious.

Father encouraged my enthusiasm and it was reinforced when my brother, eight years older than me, and one of my cousins, left for England. I kept on pressing Father about letting me join them as well. I was sure that with a little persistence I could win him over. However, my mother was strongly against it. She felt I was much too young to go alone and several friends of my father agreed with her. I overheard one of them, who was a practising lawyer, say, 'But Malikji, the boy is much too young! You know what terrible temptations youngsters are exposed to in those foreign lands.' Father replied, 'Babuji, my son has been well brought up. He has my blood in his veins. I know he will never do anything that is unworthy or dishonourable. If he does, he will no longer be my son. I will forget that he ever was.'

I wonder if Father realized the tremendous impact his words had on me. They were embedded in my memory. Father's faith and confidence in me was a great source of comfort throughout my life. My mother's objections and those of our friends were understandable. In those days youngsters went abroad for studies after they had graduated from Indian universities. It was almost unheard of for a young boy to go for schooling in England.

Eventually Father agreed to my going but he imposed one condition: I was to make all the arrangements myself, only then would he be convinced that I could look after myself. In those days going abroad was much simpler than it is today. Passports were not required, they came in only after the First World War, and there were no foreign exchange problems. All one had to do was to buy a ticket for a steamer voyage to England. This I did, my father paid for it, of course, and in April 1908 I left for England on one of the Peninsular and Oriental (P&O) ships that sailed regularly between Bombay and Marseilles.

There were many goodbyes to be said, and I still recall an old barrister friend of Father's telling me, 'My boy, be very careful when travelling by train in England. Never let yourself be alone with a young girl in the same compartment!' Forty-five years later, as India's Ambassador to France, I was invited to be the chief guest and speaker at a banquet given in the City of London by one of the great livery companies. The distinguished guests included the Lord Mayor of London and Cabinet Ministers along with leaders of industry. I was given a free choice of subject and I decided to speak on Indo-British relations, rather a sensitive subject before such a gathering even then, and I was a little nervous. At the last moment I had a flash of inspiration and started my speech by relating the advice I had received at the age of fourteen. I began my speech by saying, 'I spent many years at school and college in England, but in spite of all my efforts, I never succeeded in finding myself alone with a young lady in a railway compartment!' There were roars of laughter. And so in that relaxed atmosphere I was able to speak frankly about the relations between our two countries.

I had never been at sea, and when we reached Bombay, I was thrilled at my first glimpse of the ocean and the harbour. In those days Bombay had no docks to take in the large steamers going out to sea, so they were anchored out in the open sea and we had to go out by launch from where the Gateway of India now stands. I can still remember that awful emptiness in the pit of my stomach as I stepped into the launch after I had touched my father's and mother's feet and embraced my brothers in farewell. I felt small, miserable, but somehow managed to hold back tears.

Once aboard, however, the excitement of the upcoming voyage and the novelty of everything overcame my homesickness. I cannot remember details of travels on board the P&O *S.S Morea*, only a few general impressions and incidents. I had been warned that officers of the Company were generally rude to passengers and unfriendly to the few Indians aboard the ship. It was also believed that the British ignored Indians up to Port Said—the north-eastern Egyptian city near the Suez Canal—but thereafter their attitude, though still far from warm, improved slightly. This I found to be true. Generally speaking, the English kept to themselves. In the dining saloon there was no mixing of the two communities, nor was there intermingling in the bar, or in the deck games which were very popular as the weather remained fine throughout the voyage. The only exception was deck cricket in which a couple of us who were keen cricketers were invited to participate.

One vivid memory of the journey was the fancy dress ball. I had never seen ballroom dancing before as Indians were not allowed in British clubs where most of this took place, and there were no restaurants with a dance floor. So, at the age of fourteen, I found my first fancy dress ball quite fascinating! Everything was exciting, the music, mostly waltzes in those days, or two steps and, of course 'the Lancers'—couples swaying to the music, the women in beautiful dresses. I can still remember a lovely girl that evening in a tight-fitting white satin dress which showed her curvaceous figure to full advantage.

Among the passengers were a couple of Indian princes. One of them, the Thakore Sahib of Limbdi, who was taking his son to

England to put him in school, was extremely charming. Seeing that I was travelling alone, he took me under his wing and was most kind to me. His friendliness, along with that of another Indian passenger helped me overcome my homesickness. I thoroughly enjoyed the voyage.

The other Indian prince on board came from a well-known family that had acquired an unenviable reputation for drinking and debauchery. When we saw him he was often inebriated and in the company of women. He never mixed with the other Indian passengers. At Port Said I saw him leaning over the deck rail, fascinated by a singing girl who was accompanied by a musician sitting in a small boat alongside the ship. I was greatly impressed when he threw down a couple of gold sovereigns to her.

We made the usual stop at Suez followed by the passage through the Suez Canal to Port Said where our ship stopped for a few hours. While fresh coal was taken aboard for the engines the passengers went ashore. Port Said had the reputation of being a den of iniquity, of pimps and prostitutes and pickpockets, but I saw nothing of this for the whole of my time ashore was taken up playing a cricket match between the local club and a team of players from our ship! We played on an asphalt pitch covered with matting and the local demon bowler took great delight in bumping balls. However, they bounced so high that balls flew over one's head avoiding any great danger of injury.

CHAPTER 6

The journey through France from Marseilles—where I disembarked—by the De Luxe Express with its sleeping car was a sheer delight. Everything was a new experience for me: the scenery, the speed of the train which was incredibly fast compared to the trains in India. However, I was miserably seasick while crossing the Channel from Calais to Dover, but mercifully it was over quickly, and I set foot in England. It was something I had been looking forward to for so long. I was particularly looking forward to being reunited with my brother, Teja Singh, after a whole year. He was waiting for me at Charing Cross Station at the end of the two-hour train ride from Dover to London. Once the train pulled in in the evening, we hugged one another and then drove in a hansom to his boarding house in West Kensington. Taxis had yet to appear on the London streets and the few cars, belonging to the wealthy, were electrically driven. Carriages were the private transport and most busses were still pulled by horses, the motor bus was just making its first appearance. The famous London underground railway was the other available public transport.

My brother's boarding house was in Upper Addison Road, in what was then one of the better parts of the city. It was run by Mrs. French, a typical London landlady. She was still handsome at fifty, and one could imagine her having been quite a beauty in her youth. She had a beautiful twenty-year-old daughter. Mrs. French had five or six boarders half of whom were Indian students. We had for company a young, pleasant Muslim student from an area not very far from Rawalpindi. Always elegantly dressed, he quite liked the ladies and certainly pursued our landlady's daughter. But this young lady, a keen student of music, had no time for him or indeed for any of the boarders and did not mix with us. Some years later, she married her music master, a man old enough to be her father.

I think Mrs. French felt sorry for me as I was so young and far away from home, so she was particularly nice to me. But, in spite of that, I was utterly disgusted at my first meal in England the night I arrived—boiled mutton with caper sauce, boiled potatoes and Brussels sprouts! I ate nothing, longing for some of our delicious Indian food.

London, so strange and different from home, was exciting and full of interest. In early summer, the parks were lush, so carefully protected and looked after; the trees, plants and flowers were all a joy to see. On holidays when my brother was not attending University College, where he was studying Civil Engineering, we went for long walks together, and also on bus rides to Kew Gardens, Hampton Court and other places.

My brother graduated in 1910. He returned to India that year to join the Public Works Department in Delhi where he had a very distinguished career. He became Chief Engineer, Delhi, and was responsible for the construction of the great government buildings that were the main feature of India's new capital, including the Viceroy's House, now Rashtrapati Bhawan, designed by Sir Edward Lutyens and the two Secretariat Buildings designed by Sir Herbert Baker. He eventually retired with a knighthood.

Soon I joined a preparatory school—normal for a boy my age—before going on to public school. I had a peaceful, uneventful year at Linton House, in Notting Hill Gate, the same area which much later became notorious as the scene of ugly rioting between West Indian and Asian immigrants and the local 'toughs'. The Headmaster, Mr. Hardie, was a typical British headmaster, a strict disciplinarian, but kind and understanding. It was my first experience of a school of any kind and I was lucky to find one like Linton House.

In August, my brother and I went to Scotland travelling by train to Glasgow. On one sightseeing trip we drove on a coach, a 'four in hand' sitting next to the coachman, through the famous Trossachs, known as the 'Highlands in Miniature'. Although it was August, it started to rain and grew bitterly cold. As we were completely exposed to the elements, I thought we would freeze! Fortunately, the rain stopped, the sun came out and we got a wonderful view of the two beautiful lakes, Loch Katrina, and Loch Lomond of the 'bonny, bonny banks'. This was Sir Walter Scott and Rob Roy country, so I was particularly excited, being a great admirer of Scott's vigorous poetry. I kept on repeating to myself: *Come one, come all/This rock shall fly from its firm base as soon as I!*, visualizing that redoubtable warrior Roderick Dhu facing his Saxon enemy. In spite of all that romance and beauty I was frozen and greatly relieved to reach Callander—a small town near Stirling—and warm up with hot tea at the local inn.

Headmaster Hardie had arranged for me to enter Clifton College, one of the well known English public schools. I passed the essential preliminary entrance examination, and arrived at Clifton one day before term was to start as advised by Mr. Rintoul, my future House Master. Mr. and Mrs. Rintoul were pleasant and friendly and we dined quietly *en famille* that first night as the other boys were expected to arrive the next day. During dinner someone mentioned going to chapel and I gathered that all the boys were expected to attend. I asked if as a Sikh I would also have to attend, and Mr. Rintoul told me that it was compulsory. This annoyed me very much and I told him that I would not attend chapel as I did not think it was right to force me, as a non-Christian, to attend a Christian religious service. Mr. Rintoul explained patiently that this was the rule and I would have to conform. I decided that in that case Clifton was not for me! The next day I returned, bag and baggage, to London, much to my brother's consternation.

Later, I joined Eastbourne College, a good public school, though not as famous as Clifton. I was admitted to Blackwater House where the House Master was a clergyman, Mr. Atkinson. I got to know him well much later when he became my guardian in England as I stayed with him and his charming family during the holidays.

At Blackwater House, every evening before the boys retired for the night, there was a short service in the dining hall where a hymn or two were sung followed by the Lord's Prayer: *Give us this day our daily bread*. I did not attend this service and no one asked me to do so. When I got to know the boys and was beginning to feel more at home, I decided one day to take part. I enjoyed it so much that thereafter I joined in every night and began attending the daily service in the school chapel as well, which I also came to enjoy. The idea of something being compulsory does not always work as well as freedom of choice.

My three years at Eastbourne College were happy ones. Blackwater was a good house, well run by Mr. Atkinson, a strict disciplinarian, and his wife, a sweet woman, gentle and charming, and a most efficient housekeeper. They had two equally charming daughters, both quite young, and the Atkinson family gave Blackwater a wholesome, homely atmosphere. I made it to the College Cricket XI in my very first year, so I escaped the nagging and bullying to which most new boys in English public schools were subjected to. For the same reason I only had a very short spell of 'fagging', which involved serving the senior boys by looking after their rooms, which new boys had to do during their first year.

The only bit of bullying I experienced was the very first night at school. After supper in the House, a group of five or six boys led by an Irish boy called Dennys—whose father was a very good friend of my father's and had been Cantonment Magistrate in Rawalpindi—surrounded me and asked me to take off my turban as they wanted to see what was underneath it! I told them I was a Sikh and would not take off my turban. They advanced towards me saying that they would take it off for me. I was furious but I said very calmly that while I was outnumbered, I wouldn't be able to stop them but the first one who touched my turban I would kill, sometime, somehow. Word had gone around that Sikhs carried knives, kirpans, and the boys realized that while they were just teasing, it was something I took very seriously. So they backed off, unsure of what this native might do. I was left in peace. This incident must have made the rounds, for during the years at school, while playing hockey or football if a boy collided with me displacing my turban he would immediately apologize.

The students and the staff took great pride in the school's tradition even though it was relatively not as well known as Eton and Harrow. The Headmaster, Mr. Williams, was able and conscientious but did not dominate the scene as was the case in some public schools. The strongest personality among our Masters was Mr. Arnold, known as O.G. He was dedicated to the school, a stern disciplinarian and the boys in his class, the VI Form, in their last school year, were all terrified of him; all except Schrager, a German-Jewish boy, older than most of us at school. Unlike the rest of us he was much travelled and a bit of a maverick. He strongly objected to the rule of having to wear black socks with our dark blue or black school uniform. So, one day he turned up wearing purple socks. Old O.G. spotted him at once, summoned him to his desk and reprimanded him. Schrager appeared completely unmoved which exasperated O.G further. Finally, he said, 'Schrager, you're an absolute disgrace! You will write out a thousand times, "I am an unmitigated idiot" and produce those lines before me at tomorrow's class!'

Next day Schrader dutifully produced the thousand lines but instead the line read: *You are an unmitigated idiot.* O.G.'s face turned purple, and we boys who were watching eagerly—with some glee, I must confess—thought he would have a fit. He looked at Schrager, speechless. Finally, in a voice suppressed with anger, he said, 'Get out!' Schrager, who had already decided to leave the school, quietly picked up his books and walked out in pin drop silence, and was never seen at school again.

Perhaps I am unduly hard on O.G. because he was one of those Englishman who could not tolerate any foreigners leave alone Indians. He tended to ignore me along with two other boys from Jodhpur, Rajasthan, who were also at Eastbourne. If O.G. had had his way none of us would have been there. I found this attitude rather unusual as from my own personal experience the British were often racist in their colonies but in Britain they were known for their sense of fair play, sportsmanship, and humanitarianism. I made very good friends during my schooling in Britain and later over the years.

At school, thanks to the excellent grounding in English and maths given to me by professors Ponsonby and Mukherjee, I was immediately placed in the fifth, the next to highest form. However, in Latin and Greek, both new subjects for me, I was placed in a lower form. Mr. Matheson, my Master in these two subjects, was a crusty old man, very gruff but with a kind heart and I made good progress. Later, I grew to love reading the great Latin and Greek classics. Mr. Matheson was particularly nice to me and for years I held on to my first Greek book in which he had written on the first page: *Tout vient a point a qui sait attendre.* All comes eventually to the one who knows how to wait.

I took an active part in other school activities. In the Officers' Training Corps (OTC) I enjoyed the drill and physical training as well as the rifle shooting which was part of the OTC curriculum. I played all the games—cricket in summer, hockey in winter.

Rugger was the school winter game and we always had a good rugger team but much as I wanted to play rugger, I could not do so because of my turban.*

I was a good all rounder at cricket, efficient with both bat and ball, and loved it. We played during the summer term and always had a good list of opponents. We played against other schools, the local club and against touring teams such as the Sussex Martlets and the Blue Mantles. The big match of the year was the one against the M.C.C.—the Marylbone Cricket Club, the highest authority for cricket in Great Britain, whose home club is Lord's in London—which made a point of playing against most of the public schools. They sent a couple of professionals along with a mixture of amateurs and some older cricketers, and generally at least one celebrity. One year, we had George Robey, the famous comedian, who kept us all in gales of laughter at lunch. On another occasion, the guest artist was Sir Arthur Conan Doyle, the creator of Sherlock Holmes.

The two boys from Jodhpur were cousins, the elder one, Narpat Singh, was an excellent shot and the younger, Dalpat Singh, a fine cricketer. He led the Jodhpur Lancers in a charge in Palestine in World War One and was fatally wounded. Narpat rose to important administrative positions in Jodhpur, and we met occasionally in India when I returned home to serve in the Government. He died in 1971.

---

* Rugger, known today as rugby: a kind of football played with an oval ball. The small pagri Sikh sportsmen now wear called the 'patka' would have been the answer but in those days no one thought of it.

CHAPTER 7

Two events during those early years stand out in my memory. The first was the famous Houndsditch case in the East End of London where some desperate criminals armed with pistols and guns took shelter in a house defying the police for several days. The police surrounded the house until they smoked them out and the Houndsditch Siege became sensational news. Such prolonged open gunfire was unheard of in England in those times. Winston Churchill was the Home Secretary in charge of Law and Order, and, true to his type, personally organized the siege, exposing himself to the bullets.

The second incident, of a totally different nature, was the path-breaking invention of wireless communication by the Italian, Guglielmo Marconi, which for the first time allowed transmission of messages through the air without cables or wires. Marconi's invention played a crucial role in helping the police apprehend Hawley Harvey Crippen, an American physician who was later hanged for the murder of his wife. Crippen was wanted by the London police for the brutal murder of his wife and some other women. Before he could be caught Crippen boarded a transatlantic liner and sailed for America with his secretary. Through the new invention of wireless the London police informed the ship's captain of his presence. Media reports informed the public all over the world that Crippen was under surveillance. But this fact was kept hidden from the people aboard the ship, Crippen included. He was arrested in New York immediately on arrival. And so Crippen went down in history as the first criminal to be captured with the aid of wireless communication.

After my brother returned to India I spent part of my school holidays in London. I stayed along with my brother's older student friends at the same boarding houses. Our life consisted mostly of going for walks together and occasional visits to a theatre or music hall.

One of these boarding houses on Grover Street was run by a family called Spriggs who had a lovely daughter, Cicely, who we used to call Cissie. We were all fascinated by her and some of us, whom she favoured, were also allowed to mildly flirt with her. She was older than me, but I was very young and really enamoured. I remember carrying around her photograph and, in a weak moment, showing it to my guardian, Mr. Atkinson. He asked me who she was and when I expressed my fond feelings he and his sweet wife very gently explained to me that this attachment should go no further as I could easily make a fool of myself. So that was the end of my first romance.

In those years the All India Home Rule Movement was gathering momentum among Indian students in London. Bipin Chandra Pal and Surendranath Banerjee were amongst the Nationalist leaders to visit England from time to time, addressing meetings in Caxton Hall and other places under the auspices of the Labour and Socialist Parties, both comparatively small and unimportant but supportive of Home Rule. Amongst the students one of the most active was Veer Savarkar, who later became the famous Hindu Mahasabha leader.

The greatest stir, however, was created by the assassination of Sir Curzon Wyllie at the hands of a quiet young student, Madan Lal Dhingra, an Indian freedom fighter, political activist, a revolutionary studying in England. The assassination was hailed as one of the first acts of the revolution in the Indian independence movement. Political assassinations were a rare occurrence in England, so this was truly sensational. Most of Dhingra's friends among Indian students promptly disowned him. Veer Savarkar was the one honourable exception and openly acclaimed Dhingra as a hero and a martyr to the cause of Indian independence. Savarkar was promptly arrested and I well remember how excited and thrilled we were on hearing that he had escaped while being taken to India under police custody. When his ship touched Marseilles he slipped through the porthole of the cabin in which he was locked up. How furious and indignant we were when the news came that the French had captured him and turned him over, illegally, to the British!

CHAPTER 8

I finished school at the end of the summer term in 1912. I was fortunate in having passed the college entrance examination and was admitted to Balliol College in Oxford. The three-month holiday between school and university was spent at the Atkinsons', playing a great deal of cricket and tennis, and golf for the first time. I was having a good time. There was no question of returning to India during the holidays with the long sea voyage involved, so I was not able to go home between 1908—when I first arrived in England—and 1919. When I eventually returned to India after World War One, it was after a long stretch of eleven years!

Oxford was a huge change from school life. In those days undergraduates lived in college for the first two years. I was fortunate enough to get a very nice set of rooms: a bedroom and sitting room, in that part of the college with baths in the basement. This was a huge convenience for us, unlike other under-graduates whose rooms were in other parts of the college, and who had to go a long distance for their baths.

A manservant known as a 'scout' looked after a number of undergraduates. He cleaned the rooms, and made the beds along with performing other tasks. Many scouts were old timers, and were unique characters. My scout was called Bliss! He was a distinguished personality at 60, with wide side-burns. There was never any question of treating him but in the most courteous manner, nor was there ever any hope of getting him to hurry over anything. He had his own pace, and if treated with courtesy and allowed to do things his way, he was most cooperative and made an excellent gentleman's gentleman. We became good friends and though at times I found Bliss too talkative, I enjoyed his reminisces and encouraged him to talk. He reminded me of Shiv Ram, my servant in Rawalpindi.

Balliol College, under the famous Master, Jowett, was home to a number of undergraduates who later became public figures and held high office in the British Government and public life. Among them was Lord Curzon, at one time Viceroy of India. Bliss had been Curzon's scout. When I asked him what Curzon was like as an undergraduate, Bliss said he was arrogant and unbearably rude. This was interesting because for all his brilliance, Curzon was always considered aloof, proud, vain and unfriendly. When I joined the College, the Master was Strachan Davidson, a scholarly, introverted man, quite the opposite of the famed Jowett. As freshmen, we were invited to tea in batches to meet the Master. When my turn came I was somewhat nervous although those who had already been through the ordeal told me that he was a very kind, simple person. I was warned, however, to be nice to the Master's cat because she was his great favourite. This really terrified me as I have always had a great antipathy towards cats. The day grew close and the Master invited my batch to tea. He sat down with us and the usual conversation ensued. The cat was very much there, moving around and to my horror, jumped into my lap! My first instinct was to throw the creature off but I had been warned that the Master judged the undergraduates' character by the way they behaved with his feline, so I controlled myself and, actually stroked the creature. She was a beautiful Persian, and purred contentedly. To my great relief she slipped away after a while, and I hoped that I had passed the test.

One did not see very much of the Master and I remember only two other occasions when we met. Once he called me to say that they had never had anyone with a beard and turban before, and he asked whether it would be easier for me to get

along with the other undergraduates if I looked like them. I
explained that I was a Sikh and that my beard and turban were
not just a matter of personal idiosyncrasy but what my religion
required. At this Strachan Davidson, the gentlest and kindest of
men, became most embarrassed and said, 'Oh please forgive me.
I did not know and I quite understand.'

The other instance was during the first year of the war when
life at Oxford had undergone tremendous changes. There was a
small patch of garden next to the chapel and the Senior Common
Room known as the Fellows' Garden, a particularly hallowed
spot where undergraduates seldom intruded. I remember vaguely
that somehow one evening an old friend of mine, Hickey, and I
found ourselves in the Fellows' Garden playing a game of French
cricket. It was played with a tennis racket and tennis ball. To our
horror the Master suddenly appeared out of nowhere. This was
the only time I saw him really angry but he just said curtly, 'The
Fellows' Garden is not meant for games!' We apologized and
slunk away, feeling thoroughly ashamed of ourselves for having
upset the dear old man.

We were fifty freshers. Amongst our group of freshers was Harold
Macmillan who was to be an outstanding Prime Minister of
Britain. I came across him only a day or two after entering
Balliol. I happened to be sitting next to him at dinner, which
we had every day in the College Hall. Macmillan was from Eton
and a typical snob, coming as he did from one of the aristocratic
English families. He was related to the Duke of Devonshire.
We exchanged the usual pleasantries. Then he asked me which
school I came from and when I said Eastbourne, he raised his
eyebrows in surprise, and said with a superior air, 'Eastbourne...
Eastbourne? Where is that?' Irritated, I asked him from which
school he came knowing very well that he was an Etonian. When
he said he was from Eton, I pretended I had never heard of the
place. No close relationship followed!

'Brocas' Burrows was a useful fast bowler in the Balliol Cricket XI. His father, Sir Montague Burrows was Advisor to the Indian students in Oxford, appointed by the Secretary of State for India, and Indian students believed, perhaps unfairly, that he was placed there to spy on us! Brocas joined up in the Cavalry soon after the war began, and was captured early on by the Germans. He spent the rest of the war as a prisoner. In the long years of captivity he learned Russian and German so well that he later became one of General Edmund Ironsides' staff officers in the Archangel Expedition. Our wicket keeper was Walter Monckton, later to be one of the most distinguished lawyers in England, who became the friend and advisor to King Edward VIII at the time of his abdication. He was a charming man who became a good friend, and I saw a good deal of him when he came to India as Advisor to the Nizam of Hyderabad. He played an important role at the time when the Nizam was flirting with the Razakars which finally led to the takeover of Hyderabad by the Indian Army in 1948.*

Con Benson was another close friend from a famous banking family. He was friendly and warm hearted, with a good sense of humour; he was responsible for what was a unique event in Balliol life. About twenty of Con's friends, including myself, dressed up in authentic Japanese kimonos, each holding a parasol—the whole costume presented to us by Con—held a tea party in the main college quadrangle! The Japanese tea party with the

* The liberation of Hyderabad in September 1948 was the operation by the Indian armed forces that ended the rule of the Nizam of Hyderabad and led to the integration of the Princely State of Hyderabad into the Indian Union.The operation was necessitated as the Princely State of Hyderabad under Nizam Osman Ali Khan, Asif Jah VII, decided to not join either India or Pakistan after the partition of India. The Nisam's defiance was backed by Qasim Razvi's armed militias, known as Razakars and had the moral support of Pakistan. When all attempts to persuade the Nizam to act friendly towards India failed, and wary of a hostile independent state right in the middle of India, Deputy Prime Minister Sardar Patel decided to annex the state of Hyderabad. He sent the Indian army and the Hyderabad State Forces were defeated within five days.

undergraduates in these fancy costumes was an unusual enough spectacle but, when, after tea, all the 'Japanese' played a shadow rugger match on that beautifully kept but sacrosanct strip of lawn, and in their flowing kimonos, it was sensational! The incident occurred in summer when many sightseers visit Oxford, and we heard that those who came to look at Balliol that afternoon were astounded at this eccentric undergraduate frivolity! But to the young much is forgiven and those of us who participated in the kimono escapade got away with it without suffering any disciplinary action. Photographs of us in our kimonos, holding our parasols so elegantly, either reclining on the lawn or standing in groups, provided much amusement to my family later, for I looked quite unique with my beard and turban!

Herbert Close was unlike any other of my English friends at Balliol. He wrote poetry under the name of Meredith Star. He was a genuine 'conscientious objector' to the war. The son of a former ambassador, he stayed with his widowed mother, a typical society woman. Meredith's interests in religion and poetry were alien to her way of life. Meredith persuaded me to visit a clairvoyant friend of his, who, after going into a trance, said she saw 'us two boys as children playing on the banks of the Nile as brothers'. Meredith believed it all but I was skeptical. After the war we lost touch but in 1928, while I was posted in Rohtak, I received a long letter from him to say that he had become a disciple of the famous Mehar Baba, the 'silent saint' of Ahmednagar. Meredith was to succeed him and passionately urged me to give up service and join him. When I declined I never heard from him again. But years later in a book on Subud, an international spiritual movement founded in Indonesia in 1929, Meredith Star was described as a British psychiatrist and occultist and a follower of Subud.

Among the foreign students at Balliol was Hassanein, a Turk from Egypt, a man of great charm and culture, who later became young

King Farouk's Chamberlain. Hassanein's coffee parties at the
college, serving thick sugary Turkish coffee were famous for the
get togethers of an interesting cosmopolitan group of students. I
met Hassenein again only in 1938 when as Trade Commissioner
of India to America my wife and I with our children stopped
in Egypt on the first leg of the journey from India to England
by the P&O flagship, the *Viceroy of India*. I wrote to Hassanein
that I was passing through Egypt and would very much like to
take the opportunity of renewing our old friendship. When our
ship arrived at the entry to the Suez Canal, the Governor of Suez
came aboard with a message from Hassanein Pasha saying that
I was to come to Cairo with the Governor and have lunch with
Hassanein. He would ensure that I got to Port Said at the other
end of the canal in time to catch the ship. So, off I went to Cairo
by car with the Governor and two fellow passengers with whom
I had become friendly. My family was not invited.

Before we left the ship the Captain warned that they were
sailing from Port Said at 8.p.m., and to make absolutely sure
that I was in Port Said in time, for the ship was not going to wait
for me. The *Viceroy of India* was the flagship of the P&O, and
what is more we had on board Lady Lintlithgow, the wife of the
Viceroy of India, and her two daughters, the most important of
all VIPs. This, of course, made the Captain even more officious.

Hassanein welcomed me most cordially at Cairo at the
Mohamad Ali Club for drinks and lunch. I had told our host that
we must be back in time to board the ship, and he assured me
that he would see to it. I had no idea at that time what he meant
by that. We were still in the middle of an excellent lunch when I
realized that our train from Cairo to Port Said must have already
left. Somewhat concerned, I mentioned this to Hassanein who
sent for his secretary and told him to send a message to Port Said
for the ship not to get port clearance until his guest was aboard.
I could hardly believe my ears. In those days of the Raj, for the
P&O flagship to be held up by order of an Egyptian official, with

the Viceroy's family on board, was inconceivable. We continued with our lunch. However, over coffee and liqueurs I pointed out to Hassanein that we were in danger of missing the last train out of Cairo. He immediately issued instructions that the train was to wait for us as well! So we caught the train and arrived at Port Said, having held the ship up for three hours. The Captain was fuming, humiliated at being held up by the 'Gyppos', as the British disparagingly referred to the Egyptians. But there was nothing he could do about it. My poor wife, not knowing what had happened, was worried to death when I failed to turn up at the appointed hour, as she thought the ship would sail without me. But she was pacified when I told her the whole story.

The incident, small in itself, was significant of the waning influence of the British Empire in that part of the world. A few years earlier, after the First World War, Great Britain which had control of Egypt gradually was being forced by growing nationalist feelings to withdraw their Army of Occupation, and relinquish control.

CHAPTER 9

M y tutor at Oxford was Francis F. Urquhart, better known as Sligger, a history don and a very well known figure in Oxford life. At school my preferred subjects were Greek and Latin. I would have decided to study the Greats, ancient philosophy and literature, were it not for Sliggger who persuaded me to take up modern European history with the period 1720 to 1820 as a special subject. He was not only a marvelous teacher but a true guide, philosopher and friend.

The tutorial system of those days involved a group of us meeting at least three times a week in the tutor's room over coffee or tea to discuss papers read out by members of the group, with the tutor guiding us. The papers were prepared after the tutor had given us a subject for our essay, along with a list of books which he recommended for our reading. At the same time, at the beginning of each term, the tutor would go through the list of university lectures ticking off those he thought would be of individual interest for each of us. There was no compulsion, and we were free to attend any lectures we liked or none at all.

As a method of education it was excellent, ensuring the greatest freedom of choice on what one should read. The tutor was easily accessible, usually not only extremely well read and an excellent teacher but also a friend who watched over your progress. Under this system it is true that much was left to the whims of the undergraduates, and there were some who spent their time at Oxford just having a good time, not concerned at all with the university exams. But they were a minority and most students received an excellent liberal education. At Balliol everyone had to work for the Honours degree and anyone who just wanted a good time soon found himself to be persona non grata and was asked to leave the college.

Those taking history had to study Logic for what was our first public examination which we had to pass before we could appear for our finals. Our Logic professor was Neville Talbot, a loveable giant of a man, 6 feet 8 inches tall and proportionately broad. He had a head like that of the Greek hero Achilles whose bust he kept in his study on a pedestal against which he leaned during his lectures. We all loved Neville, but he had to dispense discipline from time to time for he was the junior dean. He did so with such goodwill and justice that no one ever resented the punishment. He played cricket with us and who can forget the sight of Neville covering the 20 yards of his run in about seven or eight gigantic strides, his arms waving, his floppy hair flying in the wind with the ball. He put the fear of God into the batsman, but the ball, when actually delivered, was comparatively slow with no venom. I don't believe that Neville had the heart to bowl fast as he felt he might hurt the batsman! He was a clergyman and joined up as an army chaplain immediately after the war broke out. He survived and went to South Africa as Bishop of Pretoria.

We had the usual group of Rhodes scholars, those from Australia, Canada, New Zealand, America, Germany, France and Ireland. One came into contact with them in college life. An American I became friends with was Howell; his mother and sisters had come to live in Oxford. They were generous, well liked, and most hospitable. Howell and I were both enthusiastic lawn tennis players, although my chief preoccupation was cricket and golf. Something I feel very typical of the American attitude towards sport came out in our tennis encounters. Howell was a better player than I was but I almost inevitably beat him during the first year, because he lost a lot of points by trying out difficult shots and taking risks instead of playing safe. When I told him about this one day he laughed and said, 'I know. I don't mind losing now but you'll see when I have mastered those shots, you won't have a chance!' And that is exactly what happened. He kept on losing but never gave up trying those shots until finally he did master them and completely outplayed me.

Another American, William Yandall Eliot, became a lasting friend. A typical, tall, lanky American from the South, with an unmistakable drawl, he had a big heart and great sense of humour. He later became Professor of History at Harvard University, and when we were in America we renewed our friendship, and I spent a delightful weekend with him and his large family in their home in Cambridge, Massachusetts. He still had the same old enthusiasm of the Oxford days.

A friendship from Oxford that lasted many decades was with Grey-Edwardes, a Welshman, who came up to Balliol from Winchester. He could always be trusted to do the unusual. One evening in Oxford as we were going into the theatre, a hansom cab with a very thin, obviously starved horse pulled up. Grey went up to the horse and very loudly and conspicuously started counting its ribs, 'One, two three...' The cabby's reaction was immediate and vitriolic, and we quickly retreated. I asked Grey why on earth he had done that and he said with a twinkle in his eye that he had just wanted to see the cabby's reaction!

He commanded a Fighter Squadron of the Royal Flying Corps (R.F.C.) during the war. Later, when I was in the R.F.C. and stationed not far from where he was, I visited him and saw the respect and affection in which he was held by his squadron. After being severely wounded in France, he'd had no choice but to take leave. His attempt to join the I.C.S. after the end of the war was stillborn. At the interview with the Civil Service Commissioners he was so irritated at what he considered their stupid questions, that he picked up his hat and walked out.

Another good friend from University days, although he was not in my college, was Paramasiva Subbarayan from Madras. He was later prominent in Indian politics and became Chief Minister of Madras, and then a Cabinet Minister in the Central Cabinet in New Delhi. The common bond between Subbarayan and myself was cricket, and we first met when we were both selected to play in the Freshmen's Match at the Parks, the university cricket ground.

Subbarayan's wife, a charming, extremely well educated woman, was with her husband in Oxford. Many years later, in India, she made her own name in politics before Independence as an elected member of the Central Legislative Assembly, which in those days consisted of elected and nominated members.

CHAPTER 10

The First World War marked the end of an era of comparative peace and stability in the world. It was to be the beginning of a new phase in history, an era of great transformation in national and international relations, in ideologies as well as in racial and social relations, along with startling advances in technology, often related to the requirements of war. The war broke out in 1914 towards the end of my second year at Oxford in the middle of the long summer vacation which I was spending in England playing cricket. I had been playing a good deal of club cricket in Sussex, and making a lot of runs. The Sussex County Cricket Committee heard about this and I was invited to play for the County, something that all young cricketers dream of. Naturally, I was thrilled. I was to play for Sussex against Kent in Canterbury during the famous Canterbury Week. The opening day of the match was 3rd August 1914 and on the evening of the following day, when both teams were dining with the Dean of Canterbury, the news broke that Britain was at war with Germany.

For days the tension had been building up and there was almost a feeling of relief when war actually broke out. There was even much light-hearted banter. Almost immediately we saw troops marching through the town, people cheering them on, singing popular songs, many from the crowd shouting, 'Bring us back some German sausage, lads!' It was almost like a carnival. Little did we imagine the grim struggle that lay ahead, the destruction and the terrible carnage, the agony and the trials the warring nations were to undergo during the long years before the Armistice.

County cricket, and much else came to an end immediately and normal life was soon replaced by the various activities war entails: among them mobilization of troops, arrangements for future rationing, precautions against possible air raids, planning for war-related industries. In Britain itself, of course, there was no fighting—the air raids came much later—but the refugees who fled to Britain from Belgium in the face of the German invasion, and the growing casualty lists of the British Expeditionary Force as the wounded started to trickle in, made the war a reality all too soon. The uniformed convalescents, soldiers who had recovered from their wounds and were allowed out of the hospital into the cities and countryside, became a familiar sight in London and other cities, bringing the war home in grim reality.

When war broke out one of my closest friends, Clairette Preiss from Alsace, who had been in Eastbourne, was desperate to get back to France. Clairette and I had both lived in Eastbourne with Mademoiselle Specht, whose home had become a second home to me in my years in England, and we had become the best of friends. In fact, my children used to tease me claiming that I had been in love with 'Baby' as we used to call Clairette! Her father, Jacques Preiss, a lawyer, was one of the most distinguished leaders in Alsace, fiercely resentful of the surrender of Alsace-Lorraine by France to Germany after the Franco-Prussian War of 1870.

Fearlessly patriotic in working for the freedom of France, he was an elected member of the German Reichstag in 1914 and was immediately thrown into prison. Clairette was extremely worried about his fate and was determined to get to Alsace but, technically, she was a German subject, and should have been interned in England. Under the special circumstances, however, she was permitted to return. She had to travel through Holland—a neutral country at that time—where her mother was to meet her. But she was nervous about travelling alone. I told her I would escort her but before leaving England I had to get a passport! This was the first time I saw a passport as they were not necessary for travel before the First World War. I wrote to the Master of Balliol, telling him of my plans and asking for his approval. However, sensing that he would disapprove, I did not wait for his reply but escorted Clairette to Flushing in Belgium.

It was terrible crossing the Channel for the both of us. We were miserably seasick, although Clairette looked immaculate and beautiful throughout the journey. I suppose I was very much in love with her, but I had made up my mind even then that I would not marry outside my own country.

After spending a day with Clairette and her mother I returned to England. In those days Flushing was full of spies because of the war, and when we sat down to dinner in the hotel, I had the feeling that someone was behind the screen next to our table, so I got up and pushed the screen aside and, sure enough, there was a man hiding there who ran for his life when he saw me. The Germans must have been watching mother and daughter. When I got back to Balliol, I found the Master's reply telling me it was a foolhardy thing to do, and forbidding me to go. But since no harm was done, I never heard anything more from him.

The Belgian refugees flooded Britain immediately after the occupation of Belgium, and there was great sympathy for them. In Eastbourne I attended a concert organized to raise funds for their relief by the world-famed Belgian violinist, Eugène Ysaÿe, who had lost his wonderful collection of old violins during the invasion but had managed to escape with his family. When he played, following the recital of a poem on the 'Rape of Belgium', written by the famous Belgian poet, Emile Verhaeren, the entire audience burst into tears—most unusual for a British audience.

At Oxford there was a Flag Day for the Belgian Relief Fund, and one morning as I came out of college, I was accosted by a very attractive Belgian girl to buy a flag. I agreed readily but when I dipped into my pocket for a shilling or half-crown, I found that I had no change. I pulled out a one pound note from my wallet and asked her if she had any change. She put the note into her box, stepped up and pinned a flag on my lapel, saying with a smile, 'Sorry, no change!' I immediately put my arms around her and kissed her soundly, saying, 'I have my change!' She took it very sportingly but my friends could hardly believe their eyes at such boldness from quiet Malik!

After the war broke out, regular university cricket stopped but in the summer term of 1915 we still had some players, young men who, for one reason or another, were not considered physically fit for entry into the armed forces, along with a few foreigners. So some cricket was organized. The Royal Naval College at Osborne invited us to bring a team over to play them and I collected quite a good team, including Donald Knight, a very fine batsman, who later made his name in first class cricket. We left Oxford by train for Southampton where a destroyer was waiting to take us to Osborn on the Isle of Wight. We had reserved a saloon for the entire team and when we got to Reading, where we stopped for five minutes, my team all rushed off to the refreshment room for a beer.

As the train started to pull out there was no sign of them and I was in a state of complete panic at the thought of arriving at Southampton without my team. We were steaming out of the station when I saw the players running on the platform trying to catch up, without any hope whatsoever as the train had already gathered speed. In desperation I pulled the alarm chain, the train slowed down and my team climbed aboard. The guard was furious and wanted to know who had pulled the chain. The penalty for pulling the chain without cause was five pounds. I explained my predicament and offered to pay the penalty. When I told him I had done so as it would have been impossible to arrive to play a match against the Royal Naval College without my team the guard, being a true sportsman, beamed, telling me he quite understood, and that was the end of the matter.

These were the days of the White Feather when enthusiastic, but misguided middle-aged ladies went around looking for young men who were not in uniform, and presented them with a white feather as a sign of cowardice. Many amusing stories were told about this. One of them I can vouch for personally as I knew the man concerned. An infantry officer who had been wounded in action in Northern France and been awarded the Victoria Cross was sitting under the sun in a London park dressed in civilian clothes. He had just been discharged from hospital and was on leave before rejoining his regiment at the Front.

As he was relaxing one of these busybodies tripped up to him and handed him a white feather, saying, 'Young man, you should be serving your King and Country!'

Amused, rather than annoyed, he turned to her, 'Madam, are you married?'

'No,' she replied.

He went on, 'Have you any children?' Scandalized, she retorted, 'Of course not!'

'Well, go and get some at once, and do your duty to your King and Country!' he said.

She ran!

The other incident involved my friend Grey-Edwardes who had joined the R.F.C. early in the war, and was shot down and badly wounded. After several months in hospital, he was on convalescent leave in London and happened to walk into the Lord Mayor's Show in 1915. He joined a group of spectators and some people in the crowd got after him making objectionable remarks, asking him why he wasn't in uniform. Being very independent and rather cantankerous, he shot back, 'What the hell has that got to do with you! Mind your own bloody business!' He wasn't inclined to explain that he was a R.F.C. pilot recovering from battle wounds. It could have turned into an ugly incident when he spotted a damaged plane carried on a truck as part of the show and recognized it as his own plane. He slipped away quietly.

* * *

At Oxford I found it very difficult to carry on as usual. I felt strongly that every young, able-bodied man should play his part in the war effort. In a way we young Indians, studying in England, were in an anomalous position. We were told that this was a war for freedom and it was natural for the English to join whole heartedly in the struggle. But as Indians we ourselves were under foreign rule, so how were we supposed to join in this war for 'freedom'? We knew that whatever the outcome, it would make little difference to our Indian condition. In spite of this I had a strong urge to join up. Practically all my British friends at Oxford had volunteered and were absent when I returned to college in October, and I found Oxford a very different place. While studying for my degree, therefore, I continued to make enquiries about getting a commission like most of my friends.

The official British attitude towards Indian students was not helpful. It was as if most of us were looked on as potential revolutionaries and terrorists not to be trusted in the fighting services. I was told that I had no hope of getting a commission. In fact, it was suggested to me in all seriousness that the only way in which I could fulfill my wish to take part in the war was to accept the job of an orderly in the hospital at Brighton where some of the early casualties among the Indian troops who had been fighting in Flanders were being looked after. That was hardly my idea of war service.

I took my degree in 1915 and soon after, I got my chance to take part in the war. With the help of my good friend and tutor, Sligger Urquhart, I received an offer from the wife of the French Military Attaché in London, Madame de la Panouse, to join the Croix Rouge Française as an officer ambulance driver. She ran the London Committee of the Croix Rouge Française, and was in some way related to Sligger.

When I joined up I was told I was to take to France an ambulance, which Lady Cunard of the famous shipping family, had presented to the French Red Cross, and which was then being properly equipped for duty at the Front. I immediately started taking driving lessons for until then I had never driven anything on four wheels, only a motor cycle. I had already taken French lessons from Mademoiselle Specht, my friend in Eastbourne. Fortunately, I found I had an aptitude for the language, and by the time I took over Lady Cunard's ambulance my French was adequate.

The ambulance was actually the chassis of an old Wolseley on which was fixed the body of an ambulance. One fine day I set off from London and drove to Southampton to board a ship for Le Havre. From there I was to drive through Normandy to Cognac, in central France, and report for duty there at Hôpital Auxilaire No. 3 of the Croix Rouge Française. Being a complete novice at driving a motor car, I started my journey with some trepidation as the ambulance was a large vehicle and did not feel at all confident. My knowledge of the engine and chassis was limited to the little I had picked up during the short period in which I was learning to drive. What I did practise a good deal of was changing tyres and repairing tubes, important in 1916 as with prevailing road conditions and the quality of tyres punctures and tyre bursts were common.

It was a beautiful summer morning and all went well in the beginning. My boat did not leave until evening, so I had the whole day to reach Southampton and drove at an easy 30 miles per hour, stopping for lunch at what looked like a nice little inn. After lunch, I tried to start the ambulance by cranking the handle, for in those days there were no self-starters, but as hard as I tried, the engine would not fire. Soon a crowd gathered, naturally curious about my beard, turban and uniform. They were friendly and helpful. Several people had a go at the handle but with no luck.

As always on such occasions several volunteer mechanics were around. We opened up the bonnet and I tried to manipulate the wiring magnets etc. I was purely trying to save face as I hadn't a clue about such intricacies. But there was still no spark of life. I was beginning to be alarmed at the prospect of missing the boat at Southampton when someone spotted that the tap which controlled the flow of petrol from the tank to the carberator had not been opened! I had closed it before going in for lunch to avoid any waste of petrol, just as I had been instructed, but had completely forgotten to turn it on again. The crowd found this highly amusing and burst out laughing. As for me, I was just relieved at being able to get off to Southampton and make the boat.

I crossed the Channel, along with the ambulance, during the night to Le Havre and after getting off the ship I set off for Cognac. The route lay through a very beautiful part of Normandy with its peaceful rivers, green valleys and lush fields, then through the picturesque Chateaux country of the Loire, and finally through the rolling landscape of the Charente, to my destination. I had no time to linger but the entire drive was sheer delight because of the novelty of the scenery—I had been in France before, but only to Paris—and the French countryside, which was so different from the English landscape, was new to me. The people en route were friendly and the food in the small inns and cafés everywhere was excellent. I spent one night in a small town called Corneville, which was familiar to me because I knew the famous song 'Les Cloches de Cornewille'. I remember sitting up in bed in the inn listening to those church bells.

CHAPTER 11

On arriving at Cognac I reported at Hôpital Auxilaire No. 5. They were astonished to see an Indian ambulance driver, especially a young Sikh complete with turban and beard, and in uniform. Moreover, despite my protests, they thought that I was an Indian prince thanks to my turban. Being an Oxford graduate also added to my prestige. The eight months in Cognac were a rich, fascinating experience for me. I worked with people of a kind I had never met before—the hospital administrative staff, the doctors and nurses, the patients, both officers and men, wounded in the fighting, from different parts of France and the French colonial empire. Many of them became friends, others mere acquaintances.

The tempo of life varied a great deal. My duty every morning was to drive the *infirmières*, voluntary women workers—some of them qualified nurses, others who were given odd jobs to do in the wards—to the hospital. At the end of the day I drove them back to their homes. The *infirmières* were of varied ages, from young girls of eighteen to elderly ladies still able to help out. They came from all kinds of backgrounds—the wealthy ones came in their own cars, but the majority, from middle class families, were transported in my ambulance. After the initial shyness on both sides, most of them were friendly and kind, and I thoroughly enjoyed driving them.

My routine changed only when there was a rush of casualties arriving on trains from the Front, and I had to carry the wounded to the hospital. I also had spells of duty at the Front, very different kind of work to normal life in Cognac. I spent some time with the troops during the terrible Battle of Verdun, with its ghastly human carnage and destruction, and witnessed the unbelievable endurance and valour of those who took part in it. It was monumental stupidity and callousness of those responsible for strategy which threw wave after wave against steel and concrete defenses manned by troops armed with every kind of lethal weapon. A criminal waste of precious lives without achieving any decisive effect, it was a human disaster from which France never really recovered.

The Chairman of the Hospital Committee was the head of Hennessy, one of the great French brandy firms, Monsieur Castillon du Perron. A very sweet, kind old gentleman, he was about 80 years old, while the active Director of the hospital was Monsieur Pataa, the head of one of the rival brandy firms, Martell. They were two very different personalities. M. du Perron was a friendly, benevolent aristocrat, while M. Pataa, was a self-made man who had risen to his high position in the industry through his own hard work and initiative. He was what the French call a *parvenu*, whom we now describe as *nouveau riche*. M. du Perron was universally respected and loved while M. Pataa, an extremely efficient executive, was feared. However, the two made an excellent team and ran the hospital very efficiently.

In time I began to be invited to some French homes. The French are normally very conservative about inviting strangers into their homes, particularly foreigners, but I found them friendly and hospitable. I was a frequent visitor to the du Perron home. The family consisted of M. du Perron, his wife, his married daughter and two sons. Madame du Perron was very nervous and highly strung as was the daughter. Both sons, one about 30 years, the other about 20, were mentally handicapped.

M. du Perron once took us all on a big shoot near La Rochelle, and we shot many pheasant, hares and some woodcock. I was somewhat nervous at finding myself alongside the two sons carrying shot-guns. But they had been trained with firearms from an early childhood and there were no accidents. The old man himself was a magnificent shot. When I complimented him on his shooting he told me he was considered as good a shot as Britain's King Edward VII with whom he had sometimes hunted in Scotland. He was reputed to be one of the finest shots in Europe. Our 'bag' was distributed to the hospital in Cognac.

Cognac was then, and remains today, the centre of brandy production in France. In those days the banks of the beautiful river Charente, which runs through the town, were lined on both sides with great casks of brandy, the size of small rooms, connected with each other through large pipelines. The brandy was matured in these casks and, at specific times of the year, passed from one cask to another. In Cognac I learned that brandy has to be matured in wood and, unlike wine, once it is bottled its character does not change. The legend went that in the famous Cognac-producing families there were always some children who were mentally unbalanced or at least feeble minded. I was told that apart from the du Perrons, this was true of several other families. It was a popular belief that this was a kind of curse on those who made their fortune out of liquor. But perhaps the cause was inbreeding, which I was told was common among the wealthier families in the region.

My own introduction to alcohol was in Cognac, at the first dinner I had with the du Perrons in their beautiful chateau about a dozen miles from town. I was fascinated by their castle home and impressed by their standard of living. They had seven cars. In those days that was the real height of luxury. After a sumptuous dinner M. du Perron offered me brandy with my coffee. I declined and told him I did not drink alcohol, to which he retorted, 'But this is not alcohol, my boy, this is ambrosia! It is brandy a hundred years old from my own cellar.' I realized that in his eyes it would amount to sacrilege if I refused, so I

took a sip. I found it most mellow and must confess that ever
since I have had a taste for fine brandy! Later, after I left Cognac
and joined the R.F.C. and visited France from time to time a
whole case of Hennessy Cognac would arrive addressed to me,
wherever I was posted, with the compliments of M. Castillon du
Perron. This most welcome gift made me very popular with my
fellow officers in the squadron.

I frequently met the doctors and surgeons at the hospital
premises where I lived, and was a member of the Officers' Mess
where all officers working in the hospital ate, along with the
soldiers who were convalescing. It was simple but excellent food,
our *cuisinière* being a countrywoman whose soufflés were out of
this world. In the Mess I learned the French custom of eating the
meat separately from the vegetables for in this way you get the
real flavour of both.

The wounded officers came from all parts of France as well as
from the French colonies in Africa. A young Corsican, excitable
and loyal, who stayed only a short time, became a good friend of
mine. For the locals my turban and beard were always a source
of curiosity. I knew it to be innocent so I never took objection
to it but my Corsican friend, nicknamed Sang Bouillant, boiling
blood, took this as bad manners. One day when we were together
in a box at the cinema, the door opened and some town youths
looked in and kept staring at me. Sang Bouillant angrily jumped
up from his seat and sprang towards them, shouting 'Vous
voulez quelque chose?' 'You want something?' A fight seemed
imminent but to my great relief they retreated.

Another friend was the Major from Algeria, a full-blooded,
darkest of dark Africans. Powerfully built, extremely dignified
and well educated, he was a person who made his presence felt
in any company. When the two of us and some of the white
French officers met in the Mess, we discussed everything under
the sun—the weather, philosophy, religion, racialism.

An interesting incident concerning my Algerian friend vividly demonstrated the difference between the British and the French colonial racial attitudes. He and I were on leave together in Paris walking down one of the famous boulevards. A young white French Lieutenant passed us without saluting my Algerian friend who was a Major. He immediately pulled up the young officer, saying, 'Monsieur, vous faites partie de l'armée Francaise?' 'Sir, do you belong to the French army?' The young officer immediately realized he was in the wrong saluted the African major and went on his way.

I noticed the great contrast between the French attitude and that of the British soldiers in India towards the Indian commissioned officers when I came home after the war whilst still serving in the Royal Air Force. I deliberately avoided wearing my uniform during this visit because I didn't want to put myself in a position where I'd be insulted by the British soldiers' neglecting to salute me simply because I was an Indian. I would have been able to do nothing about this because it was the accepted British practice.

In Cognac I was highly amused to hear what the French officers—many of whom were professional soldiers—thought of the British, and compared this to what I had so often heard my British friends say of the French! The French thought of the British: 'Oh les Anglais, they know nothing of soldiering. Their artillery is ludicrous; they cannot hit a haystack at a hundred yards! They have to have their comforts, their good food etc. They hold only a few miles of the fighting line in Flanders while we French hold four hundred miles, and yet they talk and behave as if they are bearing the heaviest burden.' The French, of course, looked on themselves as the real soldiers with a long military tradition and hundreds of years of experience fighting in Europe. The British, on their part, called the French 'Froggies' who were no real fighters, with no stamina when things were going badly. If it were not for the British Expeditionary Force, said the British, the Germans would have overrun France. These greatly exaggerated views on both sides were nowhere near the truth but still commonly accepted belief except for a few who knew the truth. Deep-rooted national prejudices built up over the years die hard, as we all know and the French and British had a long history of hostility and rivalry.

The officer with whom I became the friendliest at Cognac was Captain Jacques Senat, an artillery officer hailing from the Hautes Pyrennées. Over six feet tall, he was a powerfully built man with a great sense of humour, and a very deep voice, most impressive in company. He was generally popular because of his friendly disposition. We maintained our friendship and kept a rather irregular correspondence after the war. When I was posted as Ambassador to France in 1949, he was one of my French friends whom I most looked forward to meeting again. It was not to be, however, for he died just before I got to France. It was Senat's uncle, Monsieur Lespieu whom my wife and I met when we passed through Paris in 1919 after our marriage.

Senat was very keen to take me to Bordeaux to a restaurant where we could eat the most delicious lobster in the world, he said, *L'Homard Américaine*. So one day we set out from Cognac. A vivid recollection of this trip is the dramatic crossing of the River Loire in a small ferry at Royan where the river enters the Atlantic Ocean. It was extremely rough and we literally hung on to the ship's railing for dear life to save ourselves from being swept overboard by the waves which came crashing over the deck! But it was worth it for at the restaurant, one of the most fashionable in Bordeaux, the *Homard Américaine* was all that Jacques had promised it would be.

My other memorable experience of Bordeaux was my astonishment when a young French mother carrying her baby, opened up her blouse and fed the baby in the restaurant, in front of everyone. Only I was surprised for it would never happen in a big London restaurant! Senat told me that this was quite normal in France where people had no inhibitions about certain acts of nature.

CHAPTER 12

Thanks to the French Red Cross I was able to participate in the war. In many ways I greatly enjoyed my time in Cognac, but from the very beginning I had wanted to be at the Front and felt frustrated at being just an ambulance driver. I kept constantly enquiring from my French friends in Cognac if I could possibly be taken into the French forces preferably the Air Force. In those times, flying seemed extremely romantic. Today supersonic jets and high technology have made civil and military aviation so complex, requiring long, intensive training, together with increasing automation that to associate flying with romance is difficult. But in 1916, with our fragile planes, constructed mostly from wood and fibre held together by winding wires, and given the short, intense life span of most pilots flying to many of us symbolized the very spirit of romance. Finally, I got a hint that I might be taken into the French Air Force as a pilot. I immediately wrote to my old tutor, Sligger, about this. He replied without delay that on receipt of my letter he had gone to see General Henderson, then Head of the Royal Flying Corps, and told him how scandalous it was that although I was a British subject, the British Armed Forces had no use for me, while the French were willing to enlist me. This outspoken protest had immediate effect. Soon I received communication from the War Office telling me that on my next leave in London I was to call on the General.

I arranged for a short leave, and upon reaching London, secured an appointment with the General. At the end of a pleasant interview he told me, to my great delight, that he would be glad to take me into the Royal Flying Corps, as soon as I was able to secure my release from the French Red Cross, if I was found medically fit. General de La Panouse, who had originally arranged for me to join the French Red Cross, was still at the French Embassy in London and secured my immediate release. I returned to Cognac to bid a sentimental farewell to my many friends, and we were genuinely sorry to part company. In wartime one was not afraid of showing unabashed sentiment, and even today, after so many years, I look back on my days in Cognac with nostalgia.

Around that time I wrote a letter to my brother Teja Singh, on joining the R.F.C. hoping that the family would approve of my decision, explaining: *For I do believe that a man is all the better for having been tested in the forge of modern warfare and having been brought face to face with the elemental problems is fitter to live like a man, when all this war and the talk of war is over.*

There is of course the risk, but then the risk is not to be magnified. There are millions of human beings running the same risks today and surely one is not fit to live if one is not ready to face death and smile. Besides, we Sikhs have a great fighting tradition and we should not make too much fuss about death. I am not so foolish as to think of nothing. Naturally, one takes one's precautions—all possible precautions—against death for the sake of those who are left behind, but you, being a religious man, will I think, agree with me when I say that one should utterly despise death and scorn it.

Life in the Royal Flying Corps started under rather trying conditions for me. I enlisted as a cadet in early 1917 and was posted to Aldershot, Hampshire, along with other cadets. We were sent to a camp which was extremely badly equipped because of overcrowding. In the bitter cold, with sleet, snow and rain, we didn't even have adequate bedding. We were often soaked to the skin, and were unable to dry our clothes as there were no heating facilities. Arrangements for washing and other essential facilities were primitive, and we had to use taps located outside the barracks. As a result of these deplorable conditions many cadets developed pneumonia, and in those pre-Penicillin days, some actually died. It was a shocking state of affairs. Mercifully, I kept fit through this period, which luckily lasted for a short time, and soon we were sent off to Reading.

Before I left Aldershot, however, an incident occurred which could have ended my career in the R.F.C. there and then, but for the tact and understanding of our Commanding Officer. I naturally wore a turban, dyed a khaki colour, instead of a hat with my uniform, and the very first day I appeared on parade, the Sergeant Major in charge spotted my turban. He was the very stereotype of a Sergeant Major in the British Army of those days—a strongly built man with a red face and big moustache, a commanding voice and a neck like a bull.

'Why aren't you in uniform?' he roared. I replied that I was and that I didn't understand what he meant. He pointed to my turban, 'Where is your hat?' I tried to explain that as a Sikh I must wear a turban which had to be accepted as part of my uniform. But he would have none of it, and might even have tried to force me to put on a hat. Fortunately, the Adjutant, who was watching the parade, noticed the ensuing argument and immediately came to my rescue. He defused the situation by telling me that the case would have to be referred to the Commanding Officer; meanwhile I could wear my turban. I heard no more about it officially, but I learnt later that the question had been referred to the War Office and a special dispensation was given in my case authorizing the turban as part of my uniform. This could be called the first round of the 'battle of the turban' which in later years figured conspicuously in the British Press in connection with the refusal of certain local bodies in England to allow Sikh bus drivers and conductors to wear a turban! Even today the issue continues to come up from time to time.

At Reading cadets wanting to be pilots were initiated into the mysteries of the flying machine, with lectures on the theory of flight and instruction on 'rigging'. Rigging was a vital skill in those days when the aeroplane had a wooden body with wings made of wood and fabric, the wings being held in position by bracing wires which had to be kept at the correct tension to ensure balance and safety. This constituted 'rigging'. Later, when I was flying, I realized how rigging made all the difference in the feel of flying a plane. One recognized how a pilot's life could literally depend on the skill of the squadron's riggers as there was a vast difference flying expertly rigged Bristol Fighters as opposed to flying the same planes with the same engines in another squadron where the riggers were not so good.

Lectures on the internal combustion engines, both rotary and stationary, with which the planes of the R.F.C. were fitted, were equally important and, of course, along with this, we had plenty of the regular military drill and physical training. It was a busy and full life, learning a great deal in a comparatively short time. In Reading, I was billeted with a working class family who was greatly intrigued at having me living with them, and after the first very natural doubts and uncertainties, treated me as one of their own. Several months later, when I was shot down and wounded in France and my picture appeared in the *Daily Mirror*, I received a very sweet note from this family, saying how proud they were of their 'wounded hero'.

At Reading I witnessed an unforgettably moving event, that of an officer being cashiered.* Our Commanding Officer, Col. Bonham Carter, was a member of a distinguished family, very dignified, with a slight limp, who always looked both severe and sad although he was reputedly a very kind man. Rumour had it that having been shot in the war, he was in constant pain from

---

* Cashiering: referred to as a degradation ceremony, is a ritual dismissal of an individual from some position of responsibility. It is especially associated with the dismissal of military officers of high rank.

his wounds. Because of this his commanding the Cashiering Parade* lent the already highly dramatic occasion an even greater solemnity and sense of tragedy. The parade was held at dawn. All staff officers, and those under training, had to be present. The officer found guilty of misconduct, a young 2nd Lieutenant, was brought forward and the sentence of the Court Martial was read out. He had been found guilty of cheating and other dishonourable acts, of 'conduct unworthy of an officer and a gentleman'. The sentence of the court was that he be cashiered. An officer then stepped up to him, and tore off the badges of his rank from his tunic, and then, one by one the buttons of the tunic were torn off. It was deeply moving and painful to watch. The young officer, with no expression on his face, went deathly pale and those who witnessed this grim display would never forget it. The man was then marched off and out of the Royal Flying Corps.

At Reading I first met Harold Boston who was to become one of my dearest and lifelong friends. It was here that I was also able to continue playing golf because the Sonning Golf Club was just outside the city, and I got away from work, probably more often than I should have, to play there with the Secretary, the famous Harold Hilton who was in his day the greatest golfer in the United Kingdom, having won both the Amateur and the Open Championships. He was extremely good to me, encouraging me in every way, and I thoroughly enjoyed playing with him. After the game, over a glass of chilled beer, I learned much about golf for he was most knowledgeable about the game and those who played it.

We were all very impatient to move on to training squadrons to learn actual flying, and after a month or so of our ground

* The Cashiering Parade was held when an officer found guilty of conduct demanding the severest penalty was officially stripped of his officer's badges and other signs of his rank in a public parade.

training we were all posted out to various training schools. I was fortunate enough to be sent to a flying school in France at Vendôme, in the Loire Valley, run by the Royal Naval Air Force. This was before the R.F.C. and the R.N.A.C. were merged to form the Royal Air Force. Vendôme in the summertime, in the heart of the picturesque chateaux country was extremely pleasant. The flying school was commanded by a Naval Captain named Briggs whom we never saw, unless we were in trouble—I was indeed to see him later!—who maintained iron discipline, running his school as if it was a battleship of His Majesty's Navy! My flying instructor, Captain Carr, was a particularly pleasant person, and under his guidance, I learned to fly quickly and with confidence. We started with dual instruction on a French aircraft known as the Cauldron, which was very heavy on the controls. Under Carr's instruction, I made rapid progress and after only three hours 'dual', when one flew with the instructor with dual controls, I was allowed to go up solo in a Curtiss, an American plane to which pilots graduated after grappling with the Cauldron.

I shall never forget the thrill and excitement of my first solo flight! I was quite nervous and while gathering speed at take-off, I pushed my control wheel down a bit too much, almost hitting the ground with the propeller! Fortunately, I didn't actually hit it and soon found myself in the air, exhilarated to be actually flying my plane! In my exuberance I circled the airfield several times but, at the thought of bringing the plane down to land, my confidence vanished. I had seen so many of my colleagues mess up their first landing, breaking up their aircraft, sometimes being injured themselves. The first solo landing was always tricky. If a pilot crashed, the invariable drill was for him to go up immediately again in another plane, unless he was injured. The reason was that after a crash, under these conditions, it was essential to restore the learner's morale with a successful landing. I saw some boys who crashed on their first landing, and unable to try again immediately, break into a cold sweat when they approached a plane the next time they were to fly. In some cases, trainees could never get over their nerves and had to be declared unfit for flying. Fortunately for me, in spite of my fears, my first landing was a success.

The month at Vendôme passed quickly. As we had good weather most of the time, I was able to put in all the required flying hours. I was also lucky to have a natural aptitude for flying, and I thoroughly enjoyed it. At Vendôme we did only the preliminary training of learning to pilot a plane; advanced flying came later. The tests were simple and under Carr's able guidance I passed all of them in good time, and was ready to leave Vendôme for more advanced flying training in England.

We had a pleasant lot of officers under training at Vendôme, and I was one of the lucky ones in the congenial group sharing the same Nissan hut. We got to know each other well, going out on jaunts in the countryside, and also to Vendôme itself where we dined from time to time at the Hotel du Commerce. It was small and pleasant, with excellent cuisine and rather attractive waitresses with whom we all flirted outrageously. Four members of our group, Harold Boston, Stewart—an Englishman from the Midlands who was killed in a crash subsequently in England while still training—Jock Munro, a quiet, agreeable New Zealander and myself were often together, with others joining us at times. Among these were a Canadian named Bradford, and a really wild little Irishman named Dalrymple Willes. His name sticks in my memory for some unknown reason when many others are forgotten. I never saw him again after Vendôme. Perhaps it is because he gave me a photo of his taken in a flying kit by the side of his plane, signed, *Yours till my engine seizes, Dalbloody Rymple Willes.* Typical of his flamboyant personality.

The day of my departure from Vendôme arrived and having passed all my tests, I graduated from the Vendôme Flying School. I was given permission to return to London and report to R.F.C. Headquarters in Duke Street. I had been granted two days leave and decided to spend them in Paris with my friend from Cognac Jacques Senat, who had been invalided out of the Army because of his wounds. After saying goodbye to Captain Carr, I was just about to leave for the railway station to catch the Paris train when an orderly arrived with the message that our Commanding Officer, Captain Briggs, wished to see me.

I was surprised, not being aware of having done anything to provoke a summons from the Great Man. I went immediately to his office. I knocked, went in and saluted him, standing at attention while the C.O. remained seated with his back to me. After a little while, which seemed very long to me, Briggs, whom I had never met at close quarters, swung his chair around and said, 'Second Lt. Malik, you have not done your altitude test.' And he reeled off a whole lot of other tests as well. 'You have broken all the rules that I have made for this aerodrome. You shall not leave the station until you have done all these tests. Your leave is hereby cancelled.' I was taken aback as I had done all the tests, and had not, to my knowledge, broken any rules. I tried to explain but before I could utter a word, Briggs barked at me, 'That will do!'

I realized that I could do nothing about it so I saluted and walked out. I never discovered what or who was responsible for Briggs' strange behaviour. I was fuming and went straight to Carr who was as puzzled as I was. He said obviously there had been some misunderstanding, but no one could argue with the old man, so he said he would put me through all the tests again straight away, and I would still be able to leave Vendôme that evening. But, he added, 'Of course, your leave has been cancelled and you had better not stop over in Paris. Go straight to London.' I didn't tell him but I was so furious over the unfairness of it all that I decided, discipline be damned, I would take not two but four days leave in Paris! I did just that, and reported at Duke Street in London at the end of it, a little apprehensive of what action might result from my unauthorized leave. The young officer-in-charge was much too busy to look through my papers closely, and of course, knew nothing of my somewhat foolish escapade. All he saw was the fact that I was coming from France. He said, 'You have come from overseas and are entitled to a fortnight's leave. Would you like to take it?' 'Certainly, Sir,' I said without a flicker of doubt, quietly chuckling to myself.

CHAPTER 13

After my leave I was posted to Filton near Bristol where I learned to fly other aircrafts like the BE2C—very stable and dependable. Pilots were weeded out for more advanced training according to their potential. Those with good hands, and I was one, were to be scouts or fighter pilots. They were to fly the small, fast but unstable Scouts or fighters like the Camel, Bristol, SE-5 and similar aircrafts. Others became artillery observation and reconnaissance pilots, flying heavier planes like the RE-8.

Berkeley Castle, the home of my friend Lord Berkeley, was not far from Filton, and as soon as I felt I could handle my plane confidently, I flew over Berkeley surveying the area for a possible landing. I could use a large meadow near the castle to land and take off again. So, on a fine day, I flew over and landed, successfully, in the meadow. Airplanes were a comparative novelty at that time and, apart from the Berkeley family, who soon arrived on the scene, almost the entire population of Berkeley village, including the local Mayor, complete in his top hat, arrived to see my plane! Although a little anxious about the comparatively short run for the take-off on the way back, I was able to do so. My last glimpse of the crowd, surprised by the gust of wind raised by my propeller slipstream, was of the Mayor chasing his top hat! No one at Filton knew about my escapade, but when I returned, having taken a good deal longer than the normal practice flight, some straws on my tail skid gave me away. My instructor, Captain Chadwick, asked me where I had been, and I had to confess the truth. He pretended to be angry but we had become friends, and when I persuaded him to come and have a cup of tea with Lord Berkeley and his daughter, Sybil Jackson, he was pacified.

Lord Berkeley was a tremendous personality—a scientist, a Fellow of the Royal Society and a fine sportsman. Coming from one of the oldest families in England, he had inherited Berkeley Castle with its spacious grounds including a nine-hole golf course in Gloucestershire. The castle had witnessed several historic events. It had been the place for intrigues and murders, including I recall the murder of King Edward IV. The modern part dated back to the Tudors, and Queen Elizabeth I had slept in the castle. I had the honour of sleeping in the bed in which she is said to have occupied. Sir Francis Drake had also stayed at Berkeley Castle and some of its furniture was his loot from Spain. Lord Berkeley had also owned Berkeley Square in London where as legend goes the nightingale sang, but he had to sell it off to pay off high death duties.

At Filton I flew several aircrafts, including the Avro, Sopwith Pup, Bristol Scout and others , and thanks to my good instructor, Chadwick, I was given the coveted emblem, my Wings,* after only two and a half hours duel flying and 24 hours of solo. The Wings were worn on the tunic, the Maternity Jacket, as we called it affectionately, to show that one was a fully qualified pilot. I was then posted to Yatesbury in Wiltshire where a fighter squadron, No.28 Squadron, was being formed for service in France.

Two R.F.C. squadrons were under training in Yatesbury, a bleak spot on the Wiltshire Downs where an aerodrome had been established. There was nothing there, only hangars for the planes, the Nissan huts in which we lived and, of course, the landing ground which was just grass. In 28 Squadron we flew mainly Avros, wonderful planes for learning acrobatics which

* When a pilot qualified he was awarded his 'Wings', the emblem that was sewn on his uniform and also worn as a small brooch.

was vital for a fighter pilot. As a Scout Squadron we were expected to be familiar with these skills—'looping the loop', 'spinning', 'rolling' and 'Immelman turns'—apart from marksmanship. The life of a fighter pilot in France, depended on his ability to outmaneuvre the enemy by handling his aircraft with skill and confidence, making it do any trick the occasion demanded. Before the squadron was finally fitted up with 'Sopwith Camels'* to take our place with the R.F.C. in France, we flew different types of Scouts, the Nieuport, Bristol Scout, the Sopwith Pup and a new plane made by the De Havilland Company, the DH 6. This plane had excellent visibility for the pilot as its upper wing was behind him instead of in front of him, but that was about its only merit. It was clumsy, heavy on the controls, and incapable of rapid maneuvring and was therefore discarded.

I shall always remember one flight on that plane because it was very nearly my last. I had taken the DH-6 up to do some stunting and started to spin it at a height of 8000 feet above the airfield. I spun for about 4000 feet and then pressed hard on the right-hand rudder bar. When one did that with the Avro or any of the Scouts, the machine gradually pulled out of the spin into a dive and then straightened out into a normal flying position. This wretched plane, however, continued to spin in spite of my pressing the rudder bar. It looked as if I was going to spin into the ground and be crushed to death! Suddenly there flashed through my mind a casual remark I had heard one of our pilots make over a drink in the mess: *To get these bloody machines out of a spin you have to stand on the bloody rudder!* And that is just what I did—literally stood on the rudder, with the whole weight of my body. To my huge relief the plane began to straighten out when I was only just about a thousand feet above the ground. I landed safely, scared to death, just happy to be alive. Pilots

---

* The Sopwith Camel was a British World War I single-seat fighter biplane introduced on the Western Front in 1917.

on the ground had watched the whole thing, and much to my amusement, were very impressed by what they thought was my daredevil spirit in spinning so near the ground. I did not disappoint them!

The Sopwith Camels were considered the best fighting machines in the R.F.C. at that time because of their high maneuvrability. But the Americans considered it a highly dangerous machine. And years later in Canada, a friend of mine Lt. Col. Bennet told me the doggerel the Americans quoted before going up in a Sopwith Camel, 'Mother, put out your candle tonight, your son's gone up in a "Sop"!' Our armament was two fixed Vickers machine guns* placed directly in front of the pilot with a telescopic sight between them. They could not be moved around so you had to fly your plane literally on to your target and then open fire, controlling the firing by push button switches located on the joy stick placed between the pilot's legs with which he controlled the fore and aft as well as the lateral movement of the plane.

In the Camel's cockpit the pilot, who wore his flying helmet, was totally exposed with no protection from rain, hail, sleet, snow or bullets, only a small windshield protected him from the headwind created by his plane's flight. He had no parachute or wireless telephone, although the latter was introduced at the end of the war. The Camels initially had Gnome** rotary engines of 80.h.p. so the machines were comparatively slow and could not operate much above 12000 feet. Later, the aircraft was fitted with

---

* The Vickers machine gun or Vickers gun is a name primarily used to refer to the water-cooled .303 inch (7.7 mm) machine gun produced by Vickers Limited, originally for the British Army.

** The Gnome rotary engine was an early type of internal-combustion engine, usually designed with an odd number of cylinders per row in a radial configuration, in which the crankshaft remained stationary and the entire cylinder block rotated around it. The design was used mostly in the years shortly before and during World War I to power aircraft.

the more powerful Le Rhone and still later the Clarget engines, which greatly improved the plane's performance.

At Yatesbury, the squadron had a number of good pilots and excellent officers. The most outstanding was a youngster named White, not more than 20, who seemed to be completely fearless, taking every kind of risk in the air, a real dare-devil whose great courage and spirit of adventure, combined with a natural modesty and gentle sense of humour, was a real inspiration to the whole squadron. Sadly he crashed and died just before we left for France. Had he lived, he would certainly have commanded the squadron and perhaps done great deeds.

Before going to France we were all sent to Gunnery School in Turnberry on the west coast of Scotland. This was a pleasant interlude for apart from learning to shoot from the air, I was able to play golf on the delightful course attached to the luxury hotel where we stayed. I got a chance to play with the famous professional, Tom Fernie, who had been badly wounded and invalided out of the army. He returned to Turnberry where he had been a professional before the war. He was a first class golfer and a very charming man and I thoroughly enjoyed our games. The school was commanded by a Canadian, Colonel Bell-Irving, belonging to a prominent family in Vancouver, British Columbia. He and his two brothers were fine pilots in the R.F.C. and R.N.A.S. He was extremely kind to me and many years later, in 1947, it was a great pleasure to meet him and his wife when I went to Vancouver as Indian High Commissioner in Canada.

CHAPTER 14

O ur squadron flew over to France, ready and equipped for service overseas. En route we were to land at Lympne, a town near Kent for refuelling and a final check-up. To my disgust, I found my plane was the only one which had developed a minor defect which held me back while the rest of the squadron flew on to St. Omer in France. I followed as soon as my plane was ready. Naturally excited at the thought of soon being in action at the Western Front, I must have been in a kind of trance. When I came down to land at St. Omer—the rest of the squadron was already assembled on the airfield—I found that my speed was much too fast to land so I pulled the throttle to keep going airborne. I only managed to get down at the third attempt, but the machine kept on running. Only then did I realize that I had landed downwind instead of against the wind—a basic rule that every pilot knows almost by instinct! An aerodrome officer came running up, yelling, 'Next time remember to land against the wind!' I felt like a complete ass and, of course, had my leg pulled mercilessly by my fellow pilots. I recovered sufficiently to retort, 'Any fool can land up wind. It takes a real pilot to be able to land down wind!'

From St. Omer we moved on to a small village called Droglandt in Flanders at Number 8 Naval Squadron with Sopwith Triplanes.* One of two squadrons posted there were moving on and we were to replace them.

* The Sopwith Triplane was a British single-seat fighter aircraft designed and manufactured by the Sopwith Aviation Company during the First World War.

A pilot named Little, of No. 8 Naval Squadron was a legend
of his time. Of the many stories told about him my favourite
was when he flew over to Baron Von Richthofen's* squadron
which was just a few miles away. Richtofen, had already become
a legend in his lifetime and he and his squadron were known
as formidable enemies, much admired and feared for their skill
and daring, and respected for their chivalrous behaviour. The
Red Baron became one of the most famous names in military
aviation. Soon after this, he was killed, almost by accident in
an aerial combat which should have been child's play for him
compared to his tremendous triumphs in the air.

   When Little was over their airfield he dropped down a pair
of fleece-lined boots we used for flying which came up to the
thighs worn by us for the bitterly cold winter flights. He placed
a note inside the boots which read: *You will find these very good
for cold feet.* He had been unable to spot a German plane for
some days so he hoped that pulling the Boche's leg would do
the trick. And it did, for when the boots were picked up, swarms
of German planes took off and Little and his fellow pilots had
plenty of sport!

The landing ground at Droglandt was a small orchard which had
been cleared for our practice sessions. In the winter, however, it
was almost a marsh, typical of the weather in Flanders where it
rains all the time, or so it seemed to us. Cinder tracks had been
laid down in this marsh on which we had to land. When the wind
was in one direction it was impossible to take a long straight
glide on the small field. One had to slide-slip in in order to lose
height before touching down, which made every landing tricky.
For a Camel with its great maneuvrability it was no problem,
but for other less sensitive planes, it was very risky. And when a

   * Manfred Albrecht Freiherr von Richthofen was a German fighter pilot
known as the Red Baron. He was the most successful flying ace during World
War One, being officially credited with 80 confirmed air combat victories.

squadron of DH-4s posted in Droglandt came in to land six of their planes crashed by over-running the field hitting trees and bushes after landing. Following this incident the squadron was posted to another airfield.

We lived in wooden Nissan huts, four officers in a hut, and our mess was a larger thatched enclosure. It was rough going compared to the luxury we had enjoyed in England while training, but it was great luxury compared to what life in the trenches meant for the wretched ground troops, especially in bad, wet weather. Our squadron of 18 planes was divided into three flights, each under a Flight Commander. I was posted to Flight C, commanded by a Canadian, Billy Barker, who later became one of the most famous pilots in the various Air Forces. By the end of the war he was awarded the Victoria Cross, the Distinguished Service Cross, the Military Cross (M.C.) and three bars: the Distinguished Flying Cross, the Legion of Honour and the Italian Flying Cross—known to us in the R.F.C. as the Spaghetti Medal! This was lucky for me as Barker was not only a skilful fighter, but took great trouble over training us young, inexperienced pilots.

When I knew Billy Barker his only decoration was the M.C. He had been honoured while still in the Canadian infantry before transferring to the R.F.C. Quiet and unassuming, he had only one thought at that time, to become a first class pilot and marksman in order to shoot down as many Germans as he could without being killed himself. And so he worked day and night towards this goal, familiarizing himself with the various types of enemy aircraft, their fighting tactics, their blind spots, the safest and surest methods of attack. Above all, he would take every opportunity to practise shooting until he became a first-rate marksman. He imparted much of the knowledge he gained to his flight pilots, but of course he could not inject into us, much as he would have liked to, his tremendous dedication and application. There were many pilots in the force who were more skilled than Barker and could perform tricks with their planes which he would never have attempted considering them unnecessary and foolhardy. But he was a fine pilot. He had complete control over his plane, making it perform all the aerobatics required during combat. It was his expert marksmanship and his great fighting spirit that brought him astonishing success.

Although he joined the squadron only after we reached France, I soon got to know him well and came to admire him, though in many ways he was a tough nut. Our squadron was commanded by Granville, an old regular, quiet, colourless, and quite ineffective as a Squadron Leader. Barker soon established himself as the real leader, both with the pilots and with those higher up in the hierarchy. He would take up two pilots at a time over the lines and initiate them into the intricacies of fighting in the air. He himself practised a great deal, flying whenever he could to acquaint himself with the whole area. This was of vital importance when many pilots were shot down before they had become accustomed to the light. Enemy often came out of the sun, or maneuvered themselves into the blind spot under the enemy pilot's tail therefore being difficult to spot.

I learned this dramatically on my first flight over enemy lines. I was flying alongside Barker in what looked like an empty sky, keeping a sharp lookout for planes, both our own and the Germans. Suddenly Barker signalled to me, pointing backwards and above us. Almost immediately I saw the German diving in on us. If he had gone for me, he would probably have shot me down before I even saw him. But, luckily for me, he came towards Barker who had already spotted him. Before the German could get close enough to shoot, Barker did a climbing turn, evading the Hun who continued his dive. Barker, who had gained height while the Hun was losing his, then dived on the enemy and shot him down. The whole episode was over in a few seconds. It was a perfect object lesson for us novices from our Flight Commander.

It being winter, with generally cloudy and wet weather, flying was severely restricted as we had no wireless or radar communication with the ground. When visibility was bad, we had to fly just with the help of the compass. As a result pilots often lost their bearings, landing on other airfields on our own side, or found themselves on the wrong side of the lines, which of course could be disastrous. We flew as much as we could. Often when the weather was not good enough for patrols, we flew in our own area during fine intervals, practising our tactics by having mock battles among ourselves. When the weather grew even worse and we were completely grounded, we studied the shapes and tactics of enemy aircraft, and mess discussions centred on talk about such matters. We also practised firing at targets to improve our marksmanship, but this being comparatively dull, we did not follow our Fight Commander's example and never paid it the attention it deserved.

Weather permitting we flew regular daily patrols, generally in flights of six, looking for Germans. As we were posted directly opposite the crack German squadron of Baron Von Richtofen, we frequently ran into German planes, sometimes in groups, sometimes just a lone plane. From time to time there were scraps, we downed a few Germans, they got some of us, but on the whole losses were not heavy unless, of course, there was a 'push' when the R.F.C. came in for its share of the fighting and our casualties grew. As fighter pilots, our job was to engage any German planes we saw, particularly their Fighters, to prevent them from interfering with the work done by our reconnaissance planes—the slow and clumsy RE-8s engaged generally in artillery observation, directing our gunners on the ground to find their targets. These planes, as well as the artillery observation balloons, were frequently attacked by German fighters and it was our job to protect them.

Sometimes two or three squadrons were assembled together to fly in a group. This was always a tricky business as formation flying had not been well developed at that time, and there was always the danger of collision, especially with inexperienced pilots of which there were many. I remember one such flight when three squadrons got together, and after some rehearsals, we flew across to engage the enemy. It was a tremendous thrill to be part of such a large formation, over 50 planes, all looking for Germans! We ran into a smaller group of Germans, taking them by surprise. Shooting started and there was considerable confusion. Our planes and those of the German got hopelessly mixed up. There were bullets flying in all directions! We had been instructed that each pilot was to pick out one particular target, and I soon found myself diving on the tail of an enemy who, instead of turning back to attack me, kept on diving. He must have been as frightened as I was! I must have started shooting from too great a distance, for at first nothing seemed to happen. But suddenly I hit him and his plane started first to smoke, and then went down spinning in flames. Since there were no parachutes a pilot's greatest fear was to go down as a flaming torch. I started looking around for other planes but could see none. Then I looked up and saw the battle was raging about five to six thousand feet above me. I saw some of the planes, both ours and German, hurtle down past me. While fighting the German I had inadvertently lost about six thousand feet in height, a very foolish thing to do, for it left me completely isolated and a sitting duck for the enemy who might have spotted me. Fortunately, Barker saw me and brought his group down to collect me. After the scrap, regarded as a great success, we all flew back and there was much celebration as all the fellows from our squadron were unhurt. However, some planes were hit, but we had registered several kills—including my first German.

Anti-aircraft guns had not been developed much at that time, and although occasionally a plane was lost by a direct hit this was exceptionally unlucky. On almost every patrol though we were shot at and it was always unpleasant to hear the sound of anti-aircraft—'Archie' as it was called; but on the whole an Archie was not taken too seriously. On some beats the Germans had concentrated more guns but these were known and avoided by us. The element of chance was always there, and on one occasion, returning from a patrol during which we had been shot at by an Archie, I was landing my Camel when I found to my horror that when I tried to straighten out from the mild dive while approaching the airfield, there was no response when I pulled the joy stick back to flatten out. So, I dived straight into the ground and my plane broke into three pieces. I found myself still strapped in my seat with that section of the plane upside down, the petrol from the gravity tank pouring down my face! Fortunately, the plane did not catch fire, and I was pulled out by our mechanics who had rushed out to the crash. The gods were certainly with me because I did not even have a scratch! When we examined the wrecked plane we found that one of the wires from the control stick to the elevator had been badly damaged. It had been hit either by a bullet or by an Archie, and the one strand that was holding it together must have snapped when I tried to pull out of the dive.

CHAPTER 15

We had a happy time on the whole in spite of the mostly miserable weather. Comparatively our squadron did not have too many casualties, though our lives were saddened now and then by one of our newer pilots crashing while practising mock fights, or not returning home from patrol, being shot down, killed or captured. Still, as we were all young, it was a good time to be alive. This comparatively smooth existence, in spite of the realities of war, was rudely shattered one evening. We were at dinner when we heard shouts that the hut was on fire! We all rushed out to see, and sure enough, it was our hut, and my three colleagues and I lost everything we owned except for the clothes in which we stood. Nothing could be done when once these wooden structures caught fire. We were quite devastated for although no one had much there were things of sentimental value—much-prized photos, souvenirs, books, letters—now lost for ever. For a few days we carried on with borrowed clothes but we rehabilitated ourselves on our next leave and with more important things on our minds, our losses were soon forgotten.

In November, during the Battle of Passchendaele, our armies attempted to push forward in order to gain control of a small village by the name of Passchendaele, the same criminally stupid strategy employed on the Western Front resulting in some temporary gains but, once again, at the cost of heavy loss of human life. We also lost a large number of our pilots during this battle. I was lucky enough to get through all my encounters without a scratch. My plane was hit several times, and I managed to bring down a couple of Huns.

My exit from the squadron came soon after in a curious, most unexpected, way. Barker, who was always looking for action, was quite impatient whenever we were grounded for several days due to bad weather. So, on one such day of very low clouds and rain, he conceived a plan of flying by compass to the German airfields almost immediately opposite our part of the lines, about 25 miles away, to shoot up the Germans on the ground and return by compass. It was a foolhardy plan and our C.O., Major Granville, turned it down. In his usual way, Barker persisted, and Granville finally agreed to let Barker go if he could persuade the Wing Commander who was responsible for our squadron and several others under him, to give him permission. Barker obtained this without difficulty. He called for volunteers and three of us, Fenton, Cooper and I, offered to accompany him on what promised to be an exciting adventure.

The four of us took off and were immediately lost in the clouds. I managed to keep very close to Barker but the other two were soon out of sight. After about fifteen minutes we flew into a gap in the clouds at about 4000 feet where the sky was quite clear. Some Germans also made for this clearing and soon we were surrounded by a dozen German fighters and a dog fight ensued. A German dived on me and hit me almost immediately but only in the right leg. He was obviously as scared as I was, for instead of flying off, he continued past and below me, still diving, and I simply pressed the triggers of both my Vickers guns straight at his tail as he flew past, and had the satisfaction of seeing him burst into flames. I saw Barker also in a struggle surrounded by German fighters, and with the odds, I felt both of us were done for.

I had been hit in the right leg and immediately smelled petrol so I feared that the plane would explode into flames. However, inexplicably, the plane didn't catch fire. The bullet that had hit me pierced the main pressure petrol tank which, in the Camel, was located immediately below the pilot's seat. Fortunately for me, the bullet, which must have been red hot, came through the lower part of the tank which was still full of petrol. Had it hit the tank a little higher where the petrol vapour was collected, the plane would have immediately exploded. It was a fantastic, almost miraculous bit of luck!

I was still being attacked by German planes and returning their fire as best I could, but it was impossible for me to climb above them as the supply from the pressure petrol tank failed, and I had to rely on the emergency tank in the wing which fed the engine by gravity. As soon as I put the nose of my plane up to climb the engine started to splutter. Realizing my predicament I immediately headed straight west. I had no idea where I was but I knew it was in enemy territory and to get home safely I had to fly due west as fast as possible. I was being chased by four German fighters, each of them taking turns to fire at me. I was easy target practice! They hit my plane again and again—I was told afterwards that there were over four hundred bullet marks on my machine! But, miraculously one might say, they didn't hit me again, and they never got a vital part of the plane. The only thing I could do was to keep my head well down in the cockpit and hope for the best. I remember bullets hitting the wooden part of the plane immediately behind my head and ricocheting off over my head. After a while the four planes turned back. The only explanation seems to be that they ran out of ammunition. I was almost like a winged partridge running along the ground unable to fly, with four guns blazing away. The strange thing was that while in the first few moments I felt sure I would be killed or at least shot down and captured, when that did not happen, I felt quite calm and confident, believing that I was under divine protection, and would escape. My pursuers just did not have the bullet with my name on it.

I had been flying for about twenty minutes, barely above the tree tops, being fired at from the ground too with everything imaginable, including small inflammatory grenades known as the Flying Onions. I was emptying my Vickers guns at every target that came on my route westwards, until every bullet was fired, when I spotted a triangular piece of water known as Zillebeke Lake—a famous landmark known to all pilots in that area. This was on our side of the lines and I knew then, at last, that I was safe. I had made it! Just about then I ran out of petrol and crash landed in the shell-torn area which had suffered the severest fighting for nearly three years, leaving the earth like a sponge pocked with shell holes every ten yards.

After the crash I must have fainted through loss of blood as I had been bleeding from my leg wound for over half an hour. I came to to find myself on a stretcher being carried into a casualty clearing station just behind the lines. I found out later that I had two bullets in my leg but for some reason the surgeons decided not to take them out telling me that I would have no problem but at times might have a little pain. I seem to recall that the theory was that since the bullets had passed through the petrol in the tank they had been sterilized so there was no infection! I did, however, have some pain in damp weather when the injury was still fresh but after that I never had a problem.

After a couple of months in hospital in December 1917, first in France, later in London, I was able to rejoin my squadron after convalescent leave. By then the squadron had moved to Italy as part of the British forces sent there to rally the Italians on the run from the Austrian army.

My miraculous escape had a profound effect on my life. It convinced me that one dies only when one's time comes, a conviction which led to a kind of fearlessness which has given me strength throughout my life in facing several crises in the years to come. When I rejoined the squadron, I read Barker's report after the incident. It had been made on his return after spending a day or two further south where he had landed, unhurt. His report and the one I sent back from hospital were almost identical, word for word, although we were about 500 miles apart when we wrote them.

The journey to Italy by boat and then by train had its amusing moments. We were four young pilots, three Britishers and myself, and as we embarked at Folkstone, the officer on duty, who had served in India, said to my British colleagues, 'Look after this Indian officer'. As it turned out, it was I who had to look after them! We stopped a night in Paris on the journey, all staying together at the same hotel. My colleagues, very naturally, wanted a taste of the famous Paris night life and went out telling me that they would see me in the morning in time to catch our train to Italy. In the morning I noticed that they all had red eyes. I said, laughing, 'I see you had a pretty good time!' 'Anything but!' was their reply, for they had picked up some women who took them home, and in the morning threw pepper into their eyes, temporarily blinding them, robbed them of their money and told them to go! They just made the train.

Flying in northern Italy was a comparatively easy time for us compared to the days in France. Soon after I joined the squadron, we were celebrating Christmas with another R.A.F. squadron that shared the same airfield. It was a fun evening with plenty of Italian champagne—far too sweet for me, making me very sick—when we suddenly heard planes overhead. Shots were fired at us, and we rushed to our planes and took to the air. They were Austrians and we were able to shoot down some of them and capture some. We found that members of the Austrian crew who survived were completely drunk! When they sobered up they told us that they too had been celebrating Christmas when someone suggested they get into the air and shoot at the British airfield. By then most of them were too drunk but they went up all the same and, sadly, for several of them, it was their last Christmas.

While in Italy I developed an allergy to Castor Oil used for lubricating our engines. Some of the oil often splattered on to our faces and kit while we were flying and I would get violently air sick every time I went up. Our Commanding Officer decided to send me back to England with the recommendation that I should be assigned to planes with stationary, as against rotary, engines, for stationary engines did not use Castor Oil. I found myself posted to Squadron 141, equipped with Bristol Fighters at Biggin Hill, near London. This squadron had won fame, while at Biggin Hill, by winning the competition held among the various squadrons posted near London for Home Defense duty, for formation flying and fighting in the air. Biggin Hill became a very famous airfield during World War Two, and someone wrote its history in which I figure in an amusing episode, as 'the Flying Sikh: the Hobgoblin of Biggin Hill.' It reads: ...*a few days later an additional pilot arrived, Lieutenant Hardit Singh Malik, a Sikh from Rawalpindi. He turned up late one night, long after the orderlies had gone off-duty, and was given an empty room in the requisitioned cottage. In the morning the other officers were woken by piercing yells, and dashed out of their rooms to see what was happening. A batman, entering the new arrival's home with shaving water, had been startled out of his wits by the turbaned and black-bearded head on the pillow and fled before streams of Hindustani invective from the indignant Malik. A keen cricketer and golfer, Malik was one of the most popular officers at Biggin Hill. He staunchly refused to part with his turban and somehow managed to fit over it an outsize flying-helmet earning the affectionate nickname of 'flying hobgoblin' from the ground crew.*

During this posting I was operated on for a broken nose, the result of an earlier crash, at one of the posh hospitals in London's Eaton Square. It was the London mansion of a wealthy family converted into a hospital for the R.A.F. One lived in real luxury which included wine from the well-equipped cellars which was at the patients' disposal. As mine was to be rather a lengthy operation, I was given a generous dose of anesthetic which in those days was some form of chloroform. It made me very sick and also rather violent in the semi-conscious state. Apparently my turban threatened to come off several times. Later, I was told that my young and attractive nurse from South Africa was most upset about this and took a great deal of trouble to make sure that it did not come off. My three fellow officers who shared the ward with me had told her that if the turban came off while I was under her care, she would have to marry me! She took their joke rather seriously. Later, when I had got to know her quite well during my convalescence, I took her out to dinner and while we were dancing I told her that I had heard the whole story and how disappointed I was to know that she was so scared at the thought of marrying me. Most embarrassed she could only say, 'Well, H.S., I didn't know you then!'

During active service in France I was able to go on leave from time to time and also had two convalescent leaves, one after being shot down in France, and again after the surgery. These pleasant, relaxed interludes in wartime, spent with good friends like the Tookers, the American family who had become my good friends in my Oxford days, and Berkeley and Sybil, were all the more enjoyable, as in times of war one had no idea what one's span of life would be.

A delightful memory of those days was a visit to the famed Cavendish Hotel in Jermyn Street which was run by the notorious Mrs. Lewis, known in history as the mistress of Lord Ribblesdale, one of the well known figures in London's high society in the days of King Edward VII known for his pleasure-loving ways. I was dining there one day with my friend Grey Edwards, who was staying at the Cavendish, and he took me to Mrs. Lewis for a drink before dinner. She was an old lady then but still a tremendous personality. We got along very well and she asked Grey, who she knew well, why I wasn't staying at the Cavendish!

In 1917 the Cavendish was the favourite rendezvous of the elite of London's society, the period when the famous beauties, Lady Diana Manners, later Diana Duff Cooper, and her equally beautiful sister, were the toast of London. I was too much of a realist to have any ideas of getting involved in that circle, nor could I afford to stay at the Cavendish, although Grey told me that when Mrs. Lewis liked anyone, she charged very little, making it up on the bills of other clients! That memorable evening ended by my walking out of the hotel in the early hours of the morning to make my way to the R.F.C. Club nearby. One of the men dining at the Cavendish was Lord Gough,* who had lost an arm in the war, and whom I met for the first time that evening. Slightly inebriated, he insisted on walking with me to my club saying, 'My dear fellow, I wouldn't dream of letting you go alone. There are a lot of loose women around who will take you home with them and god knows what you may pick up!' So, we walked the streets together, Lord Gough and I, until we reached 17 Bruton Street where we bade each other an affectionate farewell, never to meet again.

---

* Somerset Arthur Gough-Calthorpe was a senior British admiral during the First World War, who served with the Grand Fleet, as second sea lord and as Commander-in-Chief in the Mediterranean.

CHAPTER 16

While at Biggin Hill I was detailed to fly to France with three pilots and hand over four planes which were required urgently to replace planes lost in severe fighting to the base at St. Omer. Major Baker was commanding our squadron. He later became Air Marshal Sir Brian Baker. He was an extraordinary man, most efficient, with a tremendous sense of humour, a strict and just disciplinarian, yet with a sweet disposition. He put me in charge of our party and told us that after handing over our planes to the C.O. at St. Omer, we were to fly back to England in a large Handley Page* used to ferry pilots between England and France. We watched this aircraft land at St. Omer after we had handed over the planes. The Handley Page did not have a good reputation and I did not like the way the pilot, with whom we were supposed to return, handled the plane. As the officer in charge of our party, I took the responsibility of telling the C.O. at St. Omer that we could not fly back with that pilot as I did not consider it safe. The C.O. was furious but couldn't do much about it. So we returned to England by boat. At Biggin Hill that evening Baker informed me that he had received orders from the General to put me under arrest for disobeying the C.O.'s orders at St. Omer. I explained my reason for refusing the orders and Baker told me I had done well for he had just heard that

---

* Handley Page Limited was founded by Frederick Handley Page in 1909 as the United Kingdom's first publicly traded aircraft manufacturing company noted for producing heavy bombers and large airliners.

the same Handley Page had crashed on landing at Lympne and everyone in it had been killed. In spite of this I was to consider myself under arrest until the General countermanded his orders. But Baker indicated that this was a mere formality and I was free to go where I liked which gave me a chance for pleasure flying, including a visit to my old golf club at Eastbourne. The old members were excited when I landed on my old school football field alongside the golf course.

Soon I was back in France, this time with No. 11 Squadron with Bristol Fighters stationed at Bapaume. It was the midsummer of 1918 when the Allies had started pushing the Germans back, the action which culminated about four months later in the defeat of Germany followed by the Armistice in November. So rapid was the allied advance that at times we found our aerodrome had been moved forward while we were still out on patrol! These were tremendously exciting days for us when for the first time we had aerial superiority over the enemy, both in numbers and in the performance of our planes. In many combats we scored well over the Germans, but it is only fair to add that by now the Germans, suffering from the shortage of petrol, could stay in the air only for limited periods. No. 11 Squadron, with a number of experienced pilots, was fortunate in having a first-class team of fitters and mechanics who serviced and tuned our planes to perfection. So each flight was a joy.

Major Heath, our fine C.O., was Australian. He had been a great tennis player in his day, and was liked and respected by all of us. The Bristol Fighter was a two-seater plane unlike the single-seater Sopwith Camel I had flown. Each pilot, who was armed as in the Camel with two fixed Vickers guns firing through the propellers, had an observer, usually a trained gunner, who sat behind the pilot, armed with a Lewis machine gun, which could be swung around allowing the observer to fire in all directions, unlike the pilot who could fire only in front. The lives of both pilot and observer depended on the skill and courage of each of them. Therefore, a perfect understanding between the two was essential, and generally they became good friends.

I was lucky to have a fine fighting Scot, Jock Crichton, as my observer. He had served in the famous Scottish infantry regiment, the Royal Scots. Jock and I became great friends and we had a perfect rapport when at last we gained real superiority over the enemy in the air. This happy state was all too short as the Armistice came soon after I had joined the squadron. We moved up from Bapaume to a small place called Aulnoye and it was there that we celebrated the Armistice on November 11th 1918. And what a celebration that was! From Aulnoye we moved on to Namur, and finally to Nivelle, near Brussels, for my last days with 11 Squadron.

When the Armistice was announced there was a tremendous sense of relief. Most of us had come to feel that the war could never end. One of my most moving memories of the Armistice is watching an infantry battalion returning from the trenches marching past our airfield at Aulnoye, totally exhausted, covered with mud, some of them still bloody with slight wounds, half asleep as they walked on. They showed no reaction to the Armistice, too fed up and weary to care—a great contrast to the boisterous spirit of the R.A.F. personnel that day. We had a really rough night of it with much shouting, singing, shooting off Very lights,* coloured flares, one of which landed in an officer's eye! We were joined in our celebrations by some pilots of a French squadron who landed at our airfield. They shared our dinner and spent the night with us. The next day some of us flew over to their airfield to lunch with them and later they presented us with bits of the white flags flown by their plane which they had flown finally marking the end of the war brought the German representative in the Armistice talks.

* A coloured flare fired from a special pistol for signalling at night, especially from sea.

At Nivelle a South African officer was very unpleasant to me when I joined the squadron because of my race and colour. Quarrrelsome and mean, he was thoroughly disliked by other officers. I treated him with the contempt he deserved. But at dinner in the mess one night he made an insulting remark about 'natives' being in the R.A.F. Jock Crichton immediately leapt across the table and seized him by the neck saying he must aplogize or he would kill him! Thoroughly frightened, he apologized but the Major saw to it that he was transferred.

In the post-Armistice days life at Nivelle became very boring with absolutely nothing to do. I decided to try to see my dear friend Clairette Preiss in Coemar in Alsace. Her father had died and she had been imprisoned by the Germans during the war. Major Heath could not give me permission to fly to Colmar, and since going by train was impossible at that time, I decided to fly anyway. Pretending to test the engine, I took off for Colmar, hoping to return to the squadron.

Half an hour away from Colmar, however, the oil pressure failed and I had to find a place to land in hilly and wooded country. I managed to do so, and the moment I landed, I was surrounded by both coloured and white American troops. When I emerged from the cockpit and took off my flying helmet which I wore over my turban, they were amazed to see a turbaned pilot flying a R.A.F. plane!

I explained who I was when an officer arrived, and they were then most friendly. The C.O., a Colonel from the deep South, took me to the Officers' Mess and scouts were sent around the town of Commercy to find me a billet for the night. In spite of the Prohibition supposedly imposed in the American Army we drank mulled Claret over an excellent dinner. Under the influence of this warm hospitality, I became garrulous and, stupidly, remarked on how the Americans treated the Blacks, something I really knew little about. Under the influence of the excellent wine, the lively argument that followed was most amicable. Meanwhile, the scouts reported that no bed was available.

The Colonel offered to share his room and I accepted. However, there was only one bed and my host insisted I take it and he would take the sofa. I refused his offer and since neither of us would give in, we ended up by both sleeping in the same bed. Unbelievable perhaps as this was at the height of racial discrimination in the States and I was a man of colour and so was he. And we had never set eyes on one another before.

My American friends had my plane patched up, and after a couple of days I took off for Nancy, which was nearby, I was lucky to hand my plane over to the Independent Wing of the R.A.F. I got a lift in a military car to Paris and hoped that from there I would be able to return to my squadron at Nivelle. If I had been responsible for the loss of the plane as well as being absent without leave (AWOL) the consequences could have been really serious.

As it was in Paris I went to the Chatham Hotel for lunch and immediately ran into Major Heath. He knew about my escapade and asked me what I was doing in Paris. After he had heard my story he was sporting enough to laugh it off and take me back to the squadron with him. He must have straightened out what could have resulted in a Court Martial. I was pardoned as the common sentiment was 'that the war was over, the chap has done his bit, so forget about it'!

Soon after I rejoined the squadron, General Brancker, who had served in India and took a special interest in me, happened to visit our squadron and asked me what I would like to do now that the war was over. I told him that I would like leave to go home. After that I hoped to continue in the R.A.F. in India. As I had originally intended to get into the I.C.S. General Brankner was kind enough to arrange for eight months leave for me, and I left my squadron for England, and soon after, sailed for India. I was going home after eleven years!

CHAPTER 17

I had to spend a couple of weeks in camp in Marseilles awaiting a military transport to India which, by a strange coincidence, turned out to be the same P&O ship in which I had travelled from Bombay to Marseilles in 1908 eleven years earlier. During the war it had done excellent service as a troopship. We stopped at Suez for a week, finally reaching Bombay in March 1919 after a pleasant voyage. A good many Indian officers were aboard, along with a few British officers of the Indian Army returning to India. Among these was Captain Keen of the 28th Punjabis, a pleasant friendly person, and we got along well. One evening, we started talking about the Indian Army over some drinks and he asked me what my plans were. I told him that after my leave I intended to stay on in the R.A.F. in India. At that time, of course, we had no Indian Air Force, only some squadrons of the R.A.F. After a good many drinks he said, 'Malik, don't do that!' This surprised and rather annoyed me, and I was more annoyed when, on asking him why he thought it wasn't a good idea, he replied, 'You know, we don't want Indians in the R.A.F. You will find one day you will go up and your plane will break up in the air!' I was quite angry and told him he was talking nonsense, but he persisted to make his point. This made me even more determined to stay on in the R.A.F. However, soon after returning home, I fell in love and got married and both families made me promise I would give up flying.

* * *

My homecoming was quite dramatic. As the first Indian pilot to fly with the R.A.F. I had received a good deal of publicity in the Indian press. So, when I arrived at my hometown, Rawalpindi, I received a real hero's welcome. Not only was my own family at the railway station to meet me, but a large crowd was present as well. And I was paid the compliment, rare in those Raj days, of having the Commissioner of the Rawalpindi Division, Sir Frank Popham Young, come to receive me. This was considered a great honour for in those days the Commissioner of a Division, always an Englishman, was a very big man in the official hierarchy and for him to come to receive an Indian, who was only a Flying Officer in rank, was most unusual. I was taken in a procession to the city where I was welcomed at a big public meeting at the gurudwara before going home. I was extremely moved by all this, but at the same time very embarrassed as I truly felt that I had done nothing to deserve all the fuss. Being only human, however, I must also confess that it made me very happy. And, of course, my family was thrilled.

Inevitably, the question of my marriage came up. I was going to be 25 and I was an eligible bachelor. In the true Indian fashion, messages came from several families, among them from one of the prominent Sikh families offering a dowry of one lakh rupees—a considerable sum in those days. My elder brother's wife, who was very fond of me, was told to suggest the names of some suitable young ladies.

Meanwhile, soon after my return, my mother had a tea party so that I could meet some relations and family friends. She told me to pass around a plate of shakarparas, small white sugary sweets, to the ladies. I was doing my duty and as I was somewhat embarrassed I was avoiding eye contact, when one of them kept dropping the sweets back into the plate. So I looked up and saw a very beautiful young lady. I was told later that she was my sister-in-law's younger sister. Up to that time I had not seriously considered marriage but at that moment it occurred to me that it might be a good idea. So when my sister-in-law was going through her list I asked her jokingly why she didn't mention her own sister, Prakash. She was very young, just fifteen, my sister-in-law said. And there was no way in which she could recommend the name of her own sister she said. But, by then, I had fallen for the young lady and had made up my mind that she was the only girl for me. Later, Prakash told me that when she had seen me at the railway station she had decided then and there that I was the only man for her, and that when I had passed her the sweets, she had been so nervous that she kept dropping them! I used to tease her later on saying that she had done all that on purpose so that I would notice her.

We were engaged and as I was due to leave for England soon the families decided that we should get married before I left. April 13th, Baisakhi, was the date fixed for the ceremony, as that is an important festival for the Sikhs. Three hundred years earlier on the same day, Guru Gobind Singh, the 10th Guru and great saint, poet, scholar, and warrior, created the Khalsa. Therefore, it is always considered an auspicious day for a wedding. Little did we know then that this day would go down in history as one of the most tragic, bloodiest days in Indian history. It was on 13 April 1919 that General Reginald Dyer perpetrated the massacre of hundreds of innocent men, women and children at Jallianwala Bagh in Amritsar, an act of criminal folly which gave a tremendous impetus to the whole freedom movement, ultimately to culminate in the freedom of India in 1947. Martial law had been declared throughout the Punjab and it was in this highly tense atmosphere that our wedding took place.

Father had planned a grand wedding. I was to ride in procession, dressed in a white brocade achkan and churidar on a gray charger escorted by a number of friends on horseback, accompanied by the band of one of the cavalry regiments stationed at Rawalpindi. Due to martial law the band was left out, but the bridal procession went as planned. However, there was some problem over the actual wedding ceremony. My father-in-law, Bhagat Ishwar Das, a prominent lawyer in Lahore, a brilliant man, known in his day as one of the first men in the Punjab to acquire the M.A. degree, was active in the somewhat aggressive Hindu Reform Movement, the Arya Samaj. He was a very keen student and admirer of the Vedanta, and he wanted our wedding ceremony to be according to the Vedic rites. My mother-in-law was a Sikh and therefore both religions, Hindu and Sikh, were followed in my wife's family. My father was acknowledged as a leading figure in the Sikh community. As far as my family was concerned, the wedding had to be according to Sikh practices—the Anand Karaj ceremony. Controversy over this question arose. I found all this very distressing as instead of the atmosphere being one of rejoicing it grew embittered with feelings running high. I, therefore, suggested a compromise: we would have both the ceremonies. Happily this was accepted and peace was restored.

According to our custom my wedding procession, the baraat, ended at the bride's house where I was to spend the night. At 4.a.m. the following morning the Hindu wedding ceremony, the hawan, was performed by Brahmin priests according to the Vedic rites. At about 9.a.m. the Sikh ceremony, the Anand Karaj, was held in the house of a relative who lived near the bride's house. Everything was going along very smoothly. I was seated with my bride before the Guru Granth Sahib and the ceremony started in the usual way by the singing of shabads from the Guru Granth Sahib. Then, according to custom, the Sikh 'bhai', the priest conducting the ceremony, began his oration. But instead of the ritual explanation of the meaning of grahasthi, or the married state, he began chastising our family for agreeing to a Hindu wedding ceremony, calling it a great disgrace.

Listening to this most untimely attack, I became angry. I felt like stopping his outburst, but my elder brother, who was sitting by me, restrained me, quite rightly, as any such interruption on my part would have been most unseemly on such a solemn occasion. I was most upset, however, and am told I got red in the face—a condition which the congregation felt was an eloquent testimony of the emotional state of love that I was in.

I was blissfully unaware of the problems my bride had been facing. Because of martial law it had not been possible to prepare her trousseau which was such an essential part of weddings. Apparently it was suggested to her that the wedding be postponed so that all these preparations could be done but she said that she just wanted to get married. So she was married in her elder sister, Lilaji's, new clothes which were rather large for her diminutive figure, and her only jewels, the dawani she wore on her forehead, belonged to her mother. I was to give her her first piece of jewellery in London some months later.

We left for Kashmir for our honeymoon, with Lilaji whose husband was the Private Secretary to the State's Prime Minister, Raja Daljit Singh. In those days, newly married couples did not go off on their honeymoon alone, so it was quite natural for us to travel to Kashmir in Father's Overland accompanied by my sister-in-law and her two little sons. We were lucky to cover the rather rough journey of 200 miles, largely mountain road, to Srinagar, after just one night's halt, without any incident. Often this journey could take several days because of landslides or car breakdowns. En route at a place called Kohala where the road crossed the Jhelum River, we had to stop to pay the toll—this was the frontier between British India and the State of Kashmir—and my bride and I strolled over to the bridge. Below was the river Jhelum, a torrent running through a gorge, and my bride, very shy and very much in love, said, 'What would you do if I fell into the river?' And when I replied that I couldn't swim so could do nothing, she pretended to be very upset. But she often told our children that she wasn't pretending because she really wondered what kind of man she had married.

Kashmir, ruled by Maharajah Pratap Singh, a Dogra, a Hindu, had a predominantly Muslim population, most of them having been converted to Islam during the reign of the Mughal Emperor, Aurangzeb. The power in the state, however, was in the hands of Kashmiri Pandits, Brahmins, distinguishable from the Kashmiri Muslims by their fair skins, and known for their intelligence and their capacity for intrigue. There is no doubt that in those days the Kashmiri Muslims, in spite of their great skill in carpet weaving, embroidery, woodcarving, metal work and other handicrafts famous all over the world, were looked down on by the Kashmiri Pandits, and even by the visiting Punjabis, many of whom settled in the Valley. They were often treated as inferiors. These unfortunate attitudes almost certainly laid the foundation for the Kashmiri Muslim's resentment after Independence which still exist today.

The Maharajah had been ruling for many years, and although he was generally regarded as a benign ruler, he was extremely orthodox, resisting all attempts at modernization. He also discouraged the acquisition of land by non-Kashmiris and in a quiet, shrewd way, resisted any attempt by the British to exert their influence in state matters. He was addicted to opium, and was often in a semi-conscious state, but curiously, this did not appear to affect his good sense in his periods of lucidity. My father-in-law, who knew him, took me to pay my respects. He received me with kindness, the meeting lasting about half an hour. He knew about my war record and asked me several questions about flying and air combat. But after each question he would doze off for a couple of minutes and then resume exactly where we had left off! It was a fascinating encounter.

Kashmir itself was incredibly beautiful—the valley rich with wild spring flowers, cherry blossom and peach trees in bloom, the surrounding Himalayas rising to majestic heights with its snow-capped peaks. To me the great mountain ranges of Europe and America cannot match the beauty of this great valley, in places as much as fifty miles wide, ringed with its mountains rising to over 20,000 feet.

After some glorious weeks, and a very tearful goodbye from my wife, I left her to go to Calcutta to take the ship for England. However, the ship, once Kaiser Wilhelm's personal yatch, broke its steering gear, and after a day's sailing down the Hooghly, we were towed back to Calcutta. Perhaps in answer to my wife's secret prayers for it turned out that when I finally did leave for England it was along with her. When I found out that the ship was to be held up indefinitely for repairs, I sent a telegram to Headquarters in Delhi and was given leave until they could find another transport.

It was June. I returned to Kashmir to rejoin Prakash and we stayed there until July when I got my orders to take the ship from Bombay. I got permission for my wife to accompany me to England. So we retuned to Rawalpindi to board the train for Bombay

Our train, which had come in from Peshawer, was crowded with British Army officers returning from one of those frequent 'wars' with the tribal Pathans on the border of the North West Frontier Province. I was in uniform, and after settling my wife in a first class ladies compartment I was looking for a berth for myself. The only one I could spot was in a coupé, a two-seater compartment, which seemed to be occupied by a single British officer, obviously a senior officer, judging by his appearance. I could not tell his rank as he was in his shirtsleeves, and in those days officers did not wear badges of rank on their shirts. He was standing at the door and I asked him politely if he could kindly move to one side so that I could get in. He replied very rudely, 'There is no room for you in here. Go and look somewhere else!' I kept my temper and told him that I had looked up and down the train twice and could find no other seat. Without moving from the door he barked, 'Go and look a third time!' This was too much. 'I am getting in here!' I said and pushed him back rather violently. He was a little man and, taken by surprise, he fell down. Picking himself up, furious, he said, 'What is your name and your regiment?' Equally furious, and not giving a damn who he was, I told him, 'My regiment you can see!' And I pointed to my uniform, 'As for my name I will tell you mine after you have told me yours.' He did not reply but picked up his pipe and papers from the seat and I sat down. When I had calmed down I looked up to the peg where his tunic was hanging to discover that he was a Brigadier General. It was just as well he was not wearing his uniform when I pushed him. I would of course have been in serious trouble—a Flight Lieutenant knocking down a Brigadier General! And an Indian Flight Lieutenant to a British Brigadier General at that!

CHAPTER 18

In Bombay we were booked on the *Dufferin* a military transport—a small steamship of about 5000 tonnes. It later served as a training ship for the Indian Navy for many years. The ship was overcrowded with Britons on their way home. Men and women were segregated on the ship. My poor young wife, only 15 and very shy, had never been to sea before. She was appalled at the idea of being separated from me and having to share a cabin with three British women. I told her that she could still change her mind and not come, but she bravely decided to ride it out.

Conditions at sea were dreadful as we were in full monsoon with huge waves washing right over the deck. Our small ship was flung about violently and everyone was very sick. It was too dangerous to be on deck, so we were all confined to our cabins or in the lounges. In 1919, with no air conditioning it was like being in a Turkish bath! To make matters worse, one of the occupants of Prakash's cabin, a common English woman from the Channel Islands, was a frightful creature and she and her daughter were very nasty to my wife. One day upon seeing Prakash using the washbasin, the daughter shouted across to her mother, 'Look, Mum, there is that *dirty* girl washing in *our* basin!' The only saving grace was that the third occupant of the cabin was a very sweet, young English girl who was horrified at the behaviour of these women. She was too young and timid to say anything to them but apologized to my wife for her compatriots' behaviour.

Up to Aden the journey was a nightmare. After that we had a smooth voyage and spent as much time as possible on deck. We docked at Southampton and I was struck all over again by the greenery of the countryside. My wife, to whom all this was so new, found it very beautiful. We stayed in London at the Coburg Hotel, later known as the Connaught, one of London's best hotels, since I had saved up a considerable amount of my leave pay.

I was still on leave but I soon managed to get my demobilization through and was out of the Royal Air Force. I had applied for the Indian Civil Service, hoping to be recruited under one of the temporary recruitment schemes set up to allow officers to fill up the vacancies in the Service caused by the war. This meant sitting for a special examination for those who had served in the war. In those days the I.C.S. could really be called a premier service with a large number of very able people joining it. It was described by an eminent British statesman as the Steel Frame of the British administration in India. Initially it was exclusively British, but in 1922 when I joined, there were already several Indians in the Service, some of them occupying senior positions. Entry was through extremely tough competition. Only a small number who scored the highest marks were selected out of the very large number of applicants.

We enjoyed visiting friends during my remaining leave. Until I got my appointment we had nothing much to do so we joined my old friend, Ethel Whitehorn and her mother in the South of France in a beautiful villa belonging to the famous 'Steel King of Luxembourg', Monsieur Mayrisch. En route, in Paris, we met the uncle of my old friend Jacques Senat from Cognac; M. Laspiau, a handsome bachelor of about 40, looked after us for a wonderful week in Paris. Like my friends in England he was charmed by Prakash, although she could speak very little English at that time. When we first met he told me, 'Mon ami, *ce n'est pas une femme que vous avez mariez, c'est une morceau de porcelaine.'* 'My friend, you have not married a woman but a piece of porcelain.'

Paris had already changed from the Paris I knew in 1910. Then, with practically no motor cars, one could enjoy one's aperitif in a pavement café with no roar of traffic. The Champs Élysées was lined only with private homes with trees along the centre of the avenue. Mr. Lespiau, the Peugeot Company lawyer, arranged a second hand car and a Parisian chauffeur to drive us south. The chauffeur was invaluable for in those post-war days petrol was scarce but he was able to use his charm on the petrol dealers, the women in particular, to allow us to reach our destination, the little village of Bormes les Mimosas.

We spent three happy months in the beautiful villa situated high on a hillside, surrounded by a beautiful terraced garden. In those days many Britishers spent the winter months on the Côte d'Azur to escape the British winter—the French would never think of going there in winter—and the Côte was quiet and peaceful, very different from the commercial Riviera of today. In Bormes, Ethel's Belgian friend, Monsieur Van Ryselberg, a well known artist, insisted on painting my portrait in my colourful 'Erratics' blazer, and it is a prized possession which has accompanied us on all my postings.

Years later, when we were living in Paris we revisited Bormes les Mimosas during a family holiday on the Riviera and my children insisted we try and find the villa. We found it and met an old caretaker who seemed to remember something of our visit. The garden looked unchanged and there was much reminiscing with Prakash telling the children how our favourite post-dinner pastime was to throw walnuts on the floor, then scramble to pick up the kernels—a very un-British activity!

CHAPTER 19

In 1920, having passed the prescribed examination, I was appointed to the Indian Civil Service. Under the rules new entrants had to spend a year at Oxford or Cambridge during which they studied criminal law and other subjects considered relevant to the Service before being posted in India. Having already spent three years at Oxford and with my degree in History Honors, I suggested to the authorities that I might be exempted from this probationary period and be posted immediately to India. Sir Samuel Montague, then Secretary State for India—later to be involved with the Montague Chelmsford Reforms—granted me a personal interview to discuss the matter, and although he was most courteous, he ultimately wrote to say that no exception could be made.

Prakash and I wanted to return home as early as possible but the prospect of another year at Oxford was by no means unpleasant. And it turned out to be a very pleasant year. The work was light, so I was able to play a great deal of golf and cricket, and soon found myself back in the Oxford Golf team led that year by Roger Weathered, who with Cyril Tolley, also a member of the team, were the two star amateur golfers at that time. I had the honour of being number 3 on the side in what was probably the strongest team Oxford has ever had in its history. We also made history by inflicting the heaviest defeat on Cambridge at Hoylake in 1921. Our players won every match except one. The solitary Cambridge winner was Jim Douglass from Chicago, an American Rhodes scholar, who was to become one of my dearest friends and later served as Eisenhower's Secretary for Air.

My wife patiently watched some of the important matches in which I played, but at other times had to keep herself busy. Determined not to be a 'golf widow', she took up the game with me as coach. She created quite a sensation by playing in her flowing sari, improvising a variation of the sari with a doublefold to prevent it from blowing up in strong winds

I was also able to introduce my wife to old friends, amongst them Mademoiselle Specht, a lady from Alsace, who had settled in Eastbourne as a young woman. I had spent many holidays with her as a paying guest while at Oxford, along with other young boys and girls, mostly French, who were at Oxford to learn English. It was here that I met Charlotte Preiss. Mademoiselle Specht was about fifty years old when I met her, a strong character, deeply religious—she belonged to an old Huguenot family. She was like a mother to us youngsters and being so far from home, I was fortunate to find a home away from home with her. The very soul of virtue, truth and humour, she exerted a tremendous influence on us all, and on my young wife who she treated as a daughter.

I passed my exams at the end of one year and was posted to India. My examiner for the Viva Voce, a distinguished judge, asked me the difference between 'culpable homicide and murder', but when he realized that I really didn't know the answer, he said with a twinkle in his eye, 'Never mind. How are Sussex doing this year?' He obviously knew I had been playing county cricket for Sussex and I passed!

This was the end of my long association with Balliol and Oxford. I owe much to both. Apart from the education, the experience and knowledge I gained from daily contact and frequent discussions with my tutor, with other dons, with fellow undergraduates, has enriched my life, and equipped me for the

many years of work and service that lay ahead. In the truest sense
of the word it was a liberal education. The knowledge I gained
also inculcated in me tolerance an ability to appreciate points of
view which differed from my own. To me this is one of the most
important things in life—to realize that other people have their
beliefs which they value as much as I value mine. I believe this
to be the very basis of civilized living.

One of my contemporaries, who later became a Don at Balliol,
Roy Ridley, wrote a letter to me in 1946, which is one of my most
treasured possessions. He was referring to Englishmen interacting
with Indians: *What I do always expect is to find a difference, and
probably more differences than with a foreign European, which makes
inter-communication of ideas difficult. But I always felt that you years
ago contributed to and have contributed since, more to the Anglo-
Indian understanding than any man I've known, not in the least by
being 'de-Indianized' which would have wrecked everything as much
as the de-Americanized and stupid Anglophile Rhodes scholar does,
but by simply being yourself, Indian, through and through and yet not
only understanding, but being understandable, by the English.*

CHAPTER 20

We arrived in India at the end of 1921, and I started my I.C.S. career as Assistant Commissioner to Sheikhapura, now in Pakistan, near Lahore. At that time Sheikhapura was one of the strongest centres of the Akali agitation for the liberation of Sikh gurudwaras from the mahants, or priests, who controlled most of them. The gurudwara reform movement, the Akali Movement, played an important role in the history of the Punjab during the early 1920s.

Some gurudwaras, particularly sacred with valuable land and considerable income had for several generations been controlled by the mahants. Many mahants had over the years misused the gurudwaras' income and become not only increasingly corrupt but notorious for drinking and debauchery.

Increasingly resentful at this state of affairs, the Sikh community had asked the Government to intervene and safeguard gurudwaras through a law. Government inaction led the Sikhs to take forcible possession of the gurudwaras which, in turn, invited action against them. Matters came to a head with the Nankana Sahib Massacre when a large number of Sikh women and children assembled at the birthplace of Guru Nanak at Nankana Sahib Gurudwara were butchered by the mahant's armed retainers. Following this thousands of Sikh volunteers joined in peaceful demonstrations all over the Punjab and the jathas, the groups of volunteers, offering themselves up for arrest in a remarkable demonstration of non-violent passive resistance, were mercilessly beaten. When the Government still took no action against the mahants, the Babbars or Lion Akalis, the warriors, threatened to take over the peaceful movement. With law and order in the state under threat, the Government finally passed the Gurudwara Act, as demanded by the Sikh in 1931, regulating the management of the gurudwaras. The agitation ended and the Akalis emerged as a political force for the first time.

It was in these troubled times that I reported to the Deputy Commissioner at Sheikhapura, Charles Barry, an Englishman, on 6 January 1922. He was a man of integrity—conscientious, hardworking, and loyal. At the same time he was devoted to the people among whom he served, full of sympathy and understanding for them. To my mind he was the best type of British I.C.S. officer, free from the eccentricities, foibles and prejudices from which, as I later got to know, many of them suffered. He was a just and firm administrator, and a good judge of character. When I reported to him he was in camp at Sheikhapura as the new District Headquarters had yet to be built. An enthusiastic horseman, Barry did all his touring of the district on horseback, and as soon as he knew that I was being posted there, he got in touch with my father and asked him to provide me with two horses. Father presented me with a beautiful Waziri Gelding which served me well for many years.

When I learned of my posting to Sheikhapura I realized that as a Sikh whose sympathies were naturally with my people seeking gurudwara reform, it could have been embarrassing for me to carry out the Government policy which regarded the whole Akali Movement as an illegal agitation against which it was taking strong action. When I got to know Barry better I voiced my fears to him but he reassured me that while he would act as required by law as he was bound to do he sympathized with the Gurudwara Reform Movement and would do his best to have the situation settled peacefully.

My first test came just a few days after I had started service. Prakash had not come with me so I was staying in the local Dak Bungalow along with Barry. One morning while we were at breakfast a large number of Akalis came by the house in procession shouting slogans and singing shabads from the Granth Sahib. Barry and I came out to see what was going on and were told that the Akalis had come to take forcible possession of the gurudwara which was in the hands of the mahant. Quickly sizing up the matter, Barry realized that the local police were inadequate to handle the situation and decided to gain time by negotiations. He asked to see the leader of the group, Kartar Singh Jhabbar, a prominent Akali, hailing from a village near Sheikhapura. Kartar Singh came forward and shook hands with Barry and me. He explained that they had come to take the gurudwara from the control of the mahant who, he said, was a drunkard, unfit to be in charge of the holy place. After they had taken possession of the gurudwara their plan was to blacken the mahant's face, put him on a donkey and parade him through the town.

Barry persuaded him to come into the garden and sing there. Kartar Singh accepted the invitation, the Akalis all came in and we all sat down as they sang. Tea was served while Barry and I discussed the situation with the Jathedar.*

It was thanks to Barry's diplomatic negotiating capacities that a settlement acceptable both to the Akalis and the mahant was reached, without any violence, with the Akalis taking peaceful possession of the gurudwara.

For me this was an early, dramatic demonstration of what a cool head combined with sympathy, patience and understanding of a situation can achieve. With a different District Officer this situation could have developed into a major provincial agitation.

* Jathedar was the leader of a jatha, although later it also referred to a position in the Akali political structure.

The unhappy events at Guru ka Bagh, and Jaito* in 1923 which led to so much suffering and bitterness were examples of similar situations being mishandled until they got out of hand.

It was typical of Charles Barry to make a thorough job of my training. He visited personally every village in his district at least once during his tenure, so he knew not only the conditions in the villages but could listen to people's problems himself. He also knew the personalities of the local officials who exercised direct authority over the villages. These rounds of inspection meant riding cross-country, avoiding village roads. When I became District Commissioner I followed the same practice. In those days the Deputy Commissioner had a great deal of authority and prestige, enjoying almost complete freedom from political pressures and an active, alert Deputy Commissioner who kept in direct touch with the people, encouraging direct access to him, could do much for the people in his district.

Apart from our inspection of the villages and official duties, we spent a lot of time together in camp as well as at Headquarters when we often messed together when Prakash was not with me, and I learned a great deal from his experience. Ironically, some years later, while doing settlement work in Campbellpur District, Barry fell while riding through rough country, broke his spine and died. His death was a real loss to the Service.

After I had put in only 18 months service Barry recommended that I should officiate in his place as Deputy Commissioner during the period of eight months while he was on leave. This was unprecedented as the normal practice in those days was to wait until an officer had put in seven or eight years service before giving him charge of a district. Some of the senior officials raised their eyebrows at this proposal. Barry, however,

* Jaito Morcha was the name given to the Akali agitation for the restoration of Maharaja Ripudaman Singh of Nabha, a Sikh princely state in the Punjab, to his throne.

assured the Governor, Sir Edward Macglagan, that I was capable of shouldering the responsibility. And in 1923, when Barry went on leave, I took over as Deputy Commissioner. I was, of course, delighted and excited at the prospect, little realizing what I would be up against.

CHAPTER 21

S oon after I had taken charge as Deputy Commissioner a
situation arose which could easily have ended my I.C.S.
career. A mahant was murdered at Nankana Sahib Gurudwara
which lay in my district. Great tension still prevailed between
the Akalis and the mahants, and I knew that this incident could
have extremely serious repercussions throughout the Punjab.
I immediately deputed a senior Muslim magistrate to enquire
personally into the case instead of permitting the police to carry
out the investigation as was the usual procedure. The magistrate
reported to me within a few days that the Akalis were not involved
in the murder which was the result of a family quarrel.

At this time the Punjab Government was facing great trouble
with the Akali leaders and was seriously concerned about
the situation. The Inspector General of the Punjab Police, an
Englisman who had the reputation of being a strong but an
unscrupulous officer he saw in this murder an opportunity
to discredit the entire Akali leadership by turning a simple
murder case into a conspiracy. He felt that in this way he
could at one swoop solve the entire problem by putting all
the important Akali leaders out of the way. He won over some
senior Government officials to his line of thought. His first
step was to arrest a prominent Akali, Sardar Buta Singh, while
he was actually sitting in the ante-room of the Chief Secretary
of the Punjab waiting to see him. Buta Singh was Manager of
the Janam Asthan Gurudwara, Guru Nanak Dev's birthplace.
He was charged with complicity in the mahant's murder and

was arrested and brought to me in handcuffs by the police at Sheikhapura. The police wanted an order from me to keep him in police custody until the murder investigation was completed, and the case be sent up for trial. I asked Neville, our Superintendent of Police, who headed the police party, to produce the evidence that Buta Singh was involved in the murder. He stated that they had no evidence but expected to get it. Neville then told me that Buta Singh had been arrested by the orders of the Punjab Government. I ordered him to remove Buta Singh's handcuffs and let him go free. Neville was horrified and protested. I told Neville that I did not care as the murder had taken place under my jurisdiction. Since there was no evidence against him, he could not be detained by the police. I ordered that he be released immediately. Of course my orders were carried out and Buta Singh was released.

Subsequently, the police concocted a false case against him and some other Akalis and they did go up for trial. However, they were all acquitted and the case failed miserably because I had taken the precaution of having a magisterial enquiry made at the earliest possible time to establish the facts. Very angry over the whole matter, I felt my action was completely justified. My superior officers did not agree and I was summoned to Lahore where I had to face a Commissioner and Chief Secretary, both angry at what they called was my defiance of the Government. Langley, the Commissioner, a good enough chap but somewhat limited, was furious. I tried to explain my action but he was in no mood to listen. The Chief Secretary was equally furious with me for having released a man whose arrest he had ordered and refused to accept my explanation. He also said that he would have me transferred.

I waited in suspense for some days, expecting the order of transfer, and fuming at the injustice that I thought was being done to me. The orders never came. Instead, I was called to Lahore again, to see the Lieutenant Governor, Sir Edward

Maclagan, the very example of the best British-Indian civilian—
able, calm, and gentle, a true Christian. He told me that he had
received the Chief Secretary's report with the recommendation
that I be relieved of my charge, but before passing the orders,
he wanted to hear my explanation. I told him the facts and
expressed my resentment at being condemned for what seemed
to be the just thing to do. He listened patiently, smiling quietly
now and then, and finally dismissed me by saying that I had no
cause to worry. After that there was no word of my transfer. A
few weeks later, however, orders came through for the transfer
of the Muslim magistrate whom I had deputed to hold the
enquiry. I was extremely upset and went immediately to Lahore
to see the Chief Secretary. I told him of the injustice at my
subordinate being punished for following my orders. The Chief
Secretary assured me that this was a routine transfer and no
punishment was involved. I explained to him that whatever the
reasons the transfer would be taken by the people of my district
as a punishment, and would therefore be most unfair and
unfortunate. I pressed for the transfer orders to be cancelled
which was agreed to, so the whole incident which could have
taken an ugly turn for me, ended happily.

Soon after this I received a message from Lahore that Sir
Edward Maclagan and General Birdwood, the Commander-in-
Chief, were driving out to Sheikhapura that same afternoon
to have a look at the Haran Minar, an ancient tank outside the
town, which, at one time, was the favourite hunting spot of the
Mughal Emperors when they visited Lahore. This was unusual
because in those days visits of the Lt. Governor or Commander-
in-Chief were extremely formal affairs. However, it turned out to
be a very pleasant occasion. Prakash prepared tea for our guests
and then we drove out to the Haran Minar. My old jamadar, the
senior chaprasi, an ex-soldier, a veteran Sikh with a handsome
beard, looked very impressive in his uniform. He wore all his
medals and was thrilled when Birdwood made straight for him,

recognizing him as a soldier who had served under him, and greeted him warmly.

Sheikhapura was a typical District Headquarters and being newly established the population was even smaller than in older headquarters. It was really just a village with the dominating fort of the Rajah of Sheikhapura, a landowner, not a ruling prince. New houses were constructed for all the officials—the Deputy Commissioner, the Assistant Commissioner, the Superintendent of Police, Extra-Assistant Commissioners, Revenue Officers, and the Civil Surgeon who was the Chief Medical Officer responsible for the medical services in the whole district, and his assistants. Plots of land were sold to non-officials—lawyers, businessmen and others who wished to settle in the new town—and to those rural landowners who wanted to build a home in the town, or build houses to rent out.

We had no electricity and no water supply. We used oil lamps for lighting, and water from wells for drinking. It was a new kind of existence for my young wife.

Sheikhapura was a virgin town with very few trees and practically no vegetation except in the nearby canal irrigated areas. In summer, with no electricity, the only protection against the stifling heat were the punkhas, large rectangular cloth screens attached to a frame, suspended from the ceiling, pulled by a boy sitting in the verandah outside the room. He pulled at a rope strung through a hole over the door on a pulley. It was generally very hot in the verandah, and often the boy would doze off, and the punkha would stop until he was shaken awake. We acclimatized ourselves to these conditions but escaped to the hills, usually to Kashmir, at least twice a year during my two fifteen-day spots of casual leave. I was thrilled as in Gulmarg I was able to play some competitive golf in tournaments. In those days Prithipal Singh, a Sikh from Lahore, and I, were the only two Indians competing in golf in Gulmarg.

CHAPTER 22

While I was still in Sheikhapura the Prince of Wales, later the Duke of Windsor, visited India and I was able to renew my contact with him which was first established at Oxford in 1912. At Oxford he was popularly known as 'the Pragger Wagger'! Naturally shy and comparatively immature at eighteen, he naturally attracted a great deal of attention but he avoided publicity. We attended some of the same lectures but the Prince's tutor, known to be a very strict man, would never have approved of the heir to the British throne befriending a native. But even at that time the Prince was known for breaking protocol. Our meeting in Lahore was typical of his informality and somewhat unorthodox behaviour. In the winter of 1922, the Prince was visiting Lahore which was very close to Sheikhapura. I wrote to his Private Secretary mentioning that I would very much like to have the honour of meeting him when he came to Lahore as I had known him at Oxford, and also during the war. To my disappointment I received the usual stereotyped reply regretting that the Prince's full programme did not permit for such a meeting.

However, I decided to be in Lahore when the Prince was there as I had always liked him and hoped to get a glimpse of him during one of the public functions to be held in his honour. I had no luck but on the last night of his stay I had gone to bed early when at about 10.p.m. the Senior Superintendent of Police arrived at my father-in-law's house and announced that His Royal Highness, the Prince of Wales, wished to see Mr. Malik. I dressed hastily and went along with the Police Officer to Government House where a ball in the Prince's honour was being held.

The moment the Prince saw me he came up to me and greeted me most warmly. Later, I was told by the Governor that at dinner someone had casually mentioned H.S. Malik and the Prince overhearing immediately asked if I was there and when he found I wasn't, he sent for me. We had a very pleasant talk about old times and he also asked me questions about the Akalis as gurudwara agitation was then at its peak. Finally, Lady Maclagan, the hostess, came up to me saying, 'Mr. Malik, you are the most unpopular man in the room at this moment! All the young ladies are longing to dance with the Prince and you are keeping him away from them.' The Prince smiled rather helplessly and we said goodbye. He was known for his unorthodox behaviour. In Bombay, one evening finding that he was again seated next to the Governor's wife, he slipped in to the dining room before dinner and changed her place card with someone younger and more attractive.

Barry never came back to Sheikhapura after his leave, and in time a man called Bradford was posted as the permanent Deputy Commissioner. I went off for a couple of weeks to undergo my training which was long overdue.

In 1924 I was posted to Gujrat, now, like Sheikhapura, also in Pakistan. Though not very far away from Sheikhapura, Gujrat was quite different with its predominantly Muslim population as against the mixed Muslim-Sikh population of Sheikhapura. It turned out to be a most difficult posting for me—a tough test in many ways. For several years the district had been administered by an Indian officer who came from the princely Kapurthala family of the Punjab, known for its intelligence and its progressive views. A senior member of the Indian Administrative Service, he was an able and charming man. But he was incurably lazy. For days on end he wouldn't move out of the house even to go to his office, leave alone tour the district. As a result, the administration was extremely loose, corruption was rife and in general the district was in a bad state. All this was explained to me by my immediate senior officer, Alan Stow, the Commissioner of the division in which Gujrat lay. Stow told me that I had a tough job ahead of me promising me his fullest support. He himself was an admirable man—intelligent and understanding, kind but firm and with an excellent sense of humour. But for his help and support I would not have been able to handle Gujrat.

As a predominantly Muslim district, Gujrat had a powerful Muslim peasant population with influential landowners with whom the Deputy Commissioner was expected to be on good terms. In Gujrat city itself, were many Hindu and Sikh families, but there was only one Hindu family of any standing, while there was a sizeable population of Kashmiri Muslims. They had the reputation of being mischief makers or sharartis; among them were a couple of lawyers with unsavory reputations. As a Sikh officer with a reputation for being strong, I knew I would be put to the test here. And very soon I was. The first indication of the demoralized state of the district administration, thanks to my easy-going predecessor, came to light very soon after I took charge. The Superintendent of my office was a Muslim, a well-built young man. One day he was absent without leave. When he repeated this several times I demanded an explanation. He had none. On making enquiries I found that he was a notorious character, known to have beaten up people and even committed a couple of murders. But everyone was so frightened of him that no action had ever been taken against him.

I realized that his absenting himself from duty was deliberate. His intention was to let me know that even though he was my official subordinate, in reality, he intended to remain the real boss. I took up his challenge, charged him with being consistently absent without leave and suspended him, pending the result of a departmental enquiry. The moment I suspended him there was consternation in the city. I was warned by several well wishers that this man was a most dangerous gangster who would stop at nothing, that my life would be in danger, and I was advised to let him off with a warning. I also received anonymous letters threatening my wife and me. I was warned that this man and his gang would waylay me on my daily horseback ride from my house to the office and back, and publicly shoe-beat me. This threat was particularly ominous as it was looked upon as the ultimate in humiliation and disgrace. With the authority and prestige that the Deputy Commissioner enjoyed in those days such an attack would have a tremendous psychological effect on the whole population. I ignored these threats and went about my work as usual without even bothering to have a rider or a police officer accompany me on my daily ride.

After recording the explanation he gave in his defense I dismissed him. This shook everyone, and was undoubtedly the first and most vital step in setting the administrative system straight. He appealed to the Commissioner against my order of dismissal and the Commissioner rejected his appeal in such a way that I had no further trouble in running the district.

After this I had very little trouble in Gujrat. A couple of other incidents, which seemed very crucial at the time, have their amusing side as well. The first was the perennial question of jhatka and halal meat which used to crop up so often in pre-Independence days in cities with mixed populations. Jhatka is the method of slaughtering poultry or sheep and goats, whereby the animal's throat is slashed with just one stroke of the knife. The Sikhs and Hindus follow this. Muslims, on the other hand, are bound by their religious laws to eat only halal meat. The orthodox halal method requires a slow cutting of the animal's throat while some verses from the Quran are recited. I have always found it extraordinary that such strong feelings can be aroused over this, often leading to violent riots, resulting in huge loss of life and property.

A small town in the district called Pindi Bahanddin, had a predominantly Muslim population, but with some Hindus and Sikhs. The Hindus are not so particular about this issue unlike the Sikhs. They applied, therefore, for a license to open a shop to sell jhatka meat. The Muslims objected, stating that there had never been a jhatka shop in the town and there never would be! The cry was taken up by professional agitators in other parts of the district. As District Magistrate I could either sanction or refuse the license. My sense of fair play compelled me to agree to the Sikh request which I considered reasonable, but I knew that as a Sikh my action would be considered by my Muslim detractors as a further example of my anti-Muslim sentiments. The whole problem caused me a great deal of worry but I was determined to do what I considered just. Fortunately, Agha Saradat Ali Khan, the Superintendent of Police in Gujrat, was a fine Pathan officer and a good friend. Being a Muslim, he could not be accused of anti-Muslim bias, and I was able to convince him of the justice of the Sikh claim. He was sporting enough to agree to my request and announce to the Muslims in Pindi Bahanddin that the jhatka shop had been sanctioned and there should be no trouble. After this there was some agitation but nothing serious.

British district officers, unlike Indians, never faced the charge of communalism. I had made up my mind from the very beginning of my service to be scrupulously fair in my actions irrespective of whoever I was dealing with—Hindu, Muslim or Sikh. I have always believed that each community should preserve, honour and build on its own traditions with malice towards no one. Only action by any community directed at harming any other, or threatening it in any way shoud be labelled 'communal' and suppressed immediately.

It was during our time in Gujrat that Harji, our first child, was born. Prakash was in Delhi, staying with my brother, T.S., and his wife Rajji, Prakash's sister, when the baby arrived. I was out on tour when I got the news and I rushed back to Gujrat, taking the first train to Delhi. This was in November 1924, and later Prakash brought our little girl to Gujrat.

CHAPTER 23

After leaving Gujrat I had short spells of duty in various districts. I was Deputy Commissioner of Gujranwalla District, from where I went on for a couple of months to Kaithal. This was followed by a short spell in Campbellpur District. I was assessing the compensation payable to farmers whose crops had been damaged during army maneuvres. The Campbellpur assignment had been particularly welcome as my old friend and mentor Charles Barry was Settlement Officer there, and I had a most enjoyable visit with him. The first day of our reunion was one I still remember. I arrived in Campbellpur with a very heavy cold, and after dinner with Barry and some of his friends, I went to bed feeling sick and miserable. To my surprise Barry arrived with a glassful of whiskey and hot water and a bottle of eucalyptus oil. He made me drink up the whiskey—the largest measure I have ever had!—and literally poured the bottle of oil on my pillow, and then bid me good night. I woke up late the next morning having slept soundly all night. After a bath I felt fine and my cold had totally vanished! In spite of this drastic treatment being so effective, my wife never permitted me to repeat it with the result that during all the years since I suffered for a cold for the usual number of days.

The next two years, from 1927 to 1929, as Deputy Commissioner in Rohtak District, were interesting and fruitful, full of hard work and a great deal of excitement. In total contrast to Gujrat, Rohtak was a strong Hindu Jat district with a Muslim minority, with Muslim Rajputs in the rural areas and Muslim butchers and traders in the cities. Through Municipal and District Board elections political activity had already begun to play an important part in the daily lives of the people. Election activity led at times to violence. These local elections were of course the preliminary steps in the democratic election process, ultimately leading to elections to State Legislatures and the Central Parliament.

Political activity in Rohtak naturally created local factions and rivalries based on prominent political personalities such as Chaudhuri Chottu Ram and Chaudhuri Lal Chand both of whom had served as Ministers in the Punjab Government. These in turn had their repercussions on the administration of which I was the head. Such developments were the first incursions by politicians into local administration which, after Independence, totally changed the character of district administration. I managed to steer clear of these different factions, and when I left the district to take over as Deputy Commissioner at Sialkot, I received a letter appreciating my fairness and sense of justice from Chaudhri Chottu Ram, who was practising as a lawyer during my tenure.

The most significant development in Rohtak during my posting, however, was the introduction of the Rural Uplift Movement which will always be associated with the name of F.L. Brayne, the I.C.S. officer who started this early version of rural development with tremendous zest and enthusiasm in Gurgaon, the neighbouring district to Rohtak. I first met Brayne when we were both visiting Lahore and he talked to me about the work he was doing in Gurgaon. I was greatly impressed by what he told me. He invited Prakash and myself to visit his district and showed us around. His work covered all aspects of rural life—village sanitation, crop improvement, the use of manure, better agricultural implements and techniques, including more practical irrigation methods such as the introduction of a better version of the traditional Persian wheel with which the bulk of field irrigation was done, better public health arrangements, and primary education.

Little in the life of the average farmer and his family was left untouched by Brayne's comprehensive programme. He was totally dedicated, with tremendous drive and unflagging energy coupled with an almost fanatic enthusiasm. He was devoted to the people of Gurgaon. He spoke Jatu, the local language, and was so popular and well liked that he could, with impunity, walk into the house of an ex-serviceman, a Subedar-Major, who observed strict purdah and demand that the ex-officer bring out his wife to meet him and Mrs. Brayne, something which no other officer, British or Indian, that I knew of, could have done. He can, with justification, be called the 'father of community development'.

I was completely won over by my visit to Gurgaon and decided to start a Rural Uplift programme in Rohtak. Through the combined efforts of the District Board, the village leaders, the education and health officers, we were able in due course to get the work started throughout the district. The virile and hardworking villagers took it up with much enthusiasm. The programme was carried out with the normal staff of officers, revenue officials, doctors, sanitary inspectors, school teachers, together with the village officials, the zaildars, lambardars, the headmen of rural areas and villages, mobilized for this work. Jalsas, village meetings, were held at tehsil* headquarters. At these jalsas popular songs, composed by school teachers and other locals, would be sung by the villagers themselves, advocating better methods of farming, the use of manure, improved sanitary practices and suggestions for improvements in rural life. Simple dramas, written generally again by school teachers, illustrating backward or superstitious popular habits, were staged and we were greatly heartened to see how the

---

* A tehsil was an area within a district administered under the supervision of the junior revenue officers, the tehsildars.

villagers enjoyed themselves, laughing at the jokes, many of which were aimed at them.

Our rural uplift dramas became known outside Rohtak, and we were visited by Miss Norah Richards who was making a special study of dramatic art and had settled down in India to work in this field. Many, many years later in the 1970s we met her in Andreta in the Kangra Valley where she had finally settled.

My wife and I toured throughout the district encouraging people everywhere to engage in this programme. The response was encouraging and many people were amazed at the speed and enthusiasm with which the villagers took up the work.

Prakash saw the backwardness of the villagers when she visited the women to help establish trained midwives to attend births in place of the local untrained dais. She found that the normal practice was to lay the expectant mother on a heap of ashes in a dark, airless room for the delivery by the dai. In one village she discovered the dai was blind. To persuade the villagers to change their ways was very hard, but good sense finally prevailed and trained midwives were introduced in many places.

Cattle-breeding was another important activity. Rohtak district had the Haryana breed of cows and bullocks of which the villagers were very proud. But the breed was deteriorating with old, unfit bulls allowed to roam freely instead of being put to sleep as Hindus did not believe in the killing of cattle. After discussing the problem with my local rural uplift workers, many of whom felt the matter too controversial, I placed the issue before the District Board of rural leaders from all over the district and explained the economic importance to them of preserving this fine breed of cattle. I was relieved when the Board passed a resolution approving putting down old, unfit bulls.

In Rohtak I faced the usual quota of problems for any Deputy Commissioner in the Punjab or in any part of India at that time. Some were particularly interesting. One day while I was in office news came of a critical situation developing at a spot about 20 miles away from Rohtak concerning a party of Ods. They were a nomadic gypsy Muslim tribe who spent their lives moving from place to place with their goats and sheep, earning their living as they wandered about sometimes by theft, sometimes by taking on temporary work of various kinds. They were not popular with the local peasants as they allowed their goats and other cattle to eat off the fields, even off growing crops. On this particular occasion about 200 of them were encamped out in the open, and we heard that the local Jat peasants were on the way to attack them. District Commissioners develop a subtle sense about possible unrest in their districts, and I instinctively felt that this could develop into a very serious communal problem. So, taking with me a Sub-Inspector of Police and two constables, along with two of the Rohtak Jat leaders who happened to be available, I rushed to the scene as quickly as our cars could take us. We found the Ods, men, women and children, all huddled together in their camp, in total panic, waiting to be slaughtered by the villagers who we saw marching towards the camp from all directions to the beat of drums.

I ordered my driver to drive straight towards the nearest group of advancing villagers. By a stroke of luck the ring leaders were in this group. I was well known in the district by then as in the course of the Rural Uplift work I had personally visited several villages, and they recognized me. I asked the two ring leaders what all the excitement was about. They claimed that the Ods had polluted the wells and they had come to drive them away. I knew this would result in a ghastly massacre, and I immediately ordered the Police Sub-Inspector to arrest both the men and handcuff them. The mob, armed with lathis and spears, could easily have overwhelmed our little party, but fortunately when the cry went up that the Deputy Commissioner had come, to our great relief the various groups started running back to their villages. This incident illustrated the tremendous authority and prestige enjoyed by District Officers in those days.

There was an amusing sequel to this incident. Knowing that in such cases the police had a habit of making wholesale arrests, and then released only those who were willing to pay bribes for their release, I took the precaution of immediately putting a Magistrate in charge of the investigation into the attacks on the Ods which had preceded the threatened mass attack. I had also given strict orders to confine arrests only to those who were identified by more than one person. As a result, only a handful of people were arrested. But this again raised an outcry in a section of the Muslim press which attacked me personally for being anti-Muslim, and deliberately being lenient towards the Hindus who had attacked Muslims. The worst of these scurrilous attacks came from a rabid, poisonous rag called the *Siyasat* edited by a notoriously fanatical Muslim, Syed Habib. I ignored the attacks until one day a very prominent Muslim lawyer, Chowdhury Din Mohamed, whom I had known when I was D.C. in Gujranwalla, called on me to complain about my so-called indifference to Muslim suffering which he had learned of from the *Siyasat*. This made me very angry as Din Mohamed was a much-respected man who later became the Chief Justice of Pakistan, and I was furious at his believing the utterly false propaganda carried on by this publication.

I told him the whole story, stating that my timely action had saved hundreds of Muslims from massacre. This was no more than my duty. If I had known, however, that instead of being praised for it by the Muslim community, I was to be slandered and accused of being anti-Muslim, I would have been tempted to do nothing at all. At this Din Mohamed apologized, expressed his sympathy at my indignation, and promised to let his people know the truth. I never found out if he did.

Communal trouble, particularly at the time of religious festivals of the two main communities, was frequent and a headache for most District Officers. I had my full share. One incident in particular created a lot of excitement. For the Dussehra festival the Hindus of Rohtak city applied to me for a license to take out the usual procession. The route planned went past certain mosques at prayer time. Although Rohtak had a small Muslim population, it was led by the city butchers who were very militant.

The Punjab Government had issued instructions to all District Magistrates to grant licenses without making any change, including timings of the processions. These conditions were laid down in the past as change would be objected to by one side or the other. The local Muslims came to me in deputation and asked that the timing of the procession be changed as it clashed with their prayer timing. I explained to them that under the orders of the Government this could not be done. But at the same time I told them that I would ask the organizers of the procession to refrain from doing anything which would disturb the prayers while passing the mosques. They threatened me that if the timing was not changed blood would flow in the streets of Rohtak. I told them calmly that as the District Magistrate I would see to it that blood did not flow. I also told them that I expected their full cooperation in maintaining peace. They said they wouldn't indulge in any violence but they had no control over the goondas in their community, and could not be held responsible for any trouble caused by them. I had, in fact, already taken the precaution of having the police round up the goondas to keep them under preventive arrest during the procession. The deputation left dissatisfied.

Next, arrived a deputation from the Hindu Jats of the neighbouring villages who had come to Rohtak upon hearing that the city Muslims were creating trouble. They wanted my permission to join the procession so that they could deal with the troublemakers. I told them that I would be happy to have them join the procession but only if they left their lathis behind at my house. I assured them that there would be no trouble. They were not willing to leave their lathis, so I had to keep them away from the procession. On the actual day, I sent for the members of the City Municipal Committee and told the member of each ward through which the procession was to pass that he would be on duty to help maintain peace. I said I would hold each member responsible for the peaceful passage of the procession through his ward. I warned that if there was trouble in their ward the first persons to be arrested would be them. This rather drastic warning was received under loud protests but I was determined to make the Council Members realize their responsibilities. I dread to think what would happen to a Deputy Commissioner today if he dealt in such a way with the elected representatives of the people.

I took part in the procession throughout the entire route armed with nothing but a golf club. Immediately behind me were my three peons all of whom happened to be Muslims. The tension in the city was so great that Prakash strongly advised me not to take the peons as she felt that at such a critical time one of them might lose his head and knife me in the back, but I explained to her that not trusting them in this crisis, just because they were Muslims, would be a sign of weakness that I could not afford. The procession passed off without any incident, much to everyone's relief as serious trouble had been expected. The extent of the tension was measured by my own action in moving my family to the house of a neighbour, a Sikh engineer in the Irrigation Service, with whom we had become very friendly.

On the whole, I thoroughly enjoyed the challenge of my two years in Rohtak with the Rural Uplift work. When the time came for us to leave, we genuinely felt sad as we had become fond of the people who in many ways showed their affection for us, and whom we had got to know well.

CHAPTER 24

Sialkot, where I was transferred in 1929, was a district with a mixed, Hindu, Sikh and Muslim population. Being a cantonment, it also had a large number of army officers. While in Rohtak social interaction was restricted to senior civilian officials, and most of the time was spent on tour, in Sialkot we spent a good deal of time in the town itself. It was a new experience. I was there for just a year but it was a very eventful one with events reflecting the prevailing conditions in the country.

My first problem concerned a Sikh gurudwara at a small town called Daska. The local Akalis had started a morcha, an agitation, to take possession of the gurudwara. As District Magistrate I had to enforce the law and protect those who were in legal possession of the property. The matter would probably have ended in a compromise but one of the most prominent and distinguished Sikh leaders, Baba Kharak Singh, announced that he would personally participate in the morcha which immediately complicated the situation. I had great respect for this sincere, devoted man who incidentally was also distantly related to me, and the idea of having to arrest him was abhorrent. So, I sent him a private message asking him not to take part in the morcha. An extremely stubborn man, adamant once he had made up his mind, he refused to listen to me. Fortunately, before a crisis arose the situation fizzled out in a curious way. I recognized that the agitating Sikhs who came in batches of five to take possession of the gurudwara were not ordinary criminals, and so I had, from the start, posted a Magistrate on the spot to try the trespassers immediately and sentence them till the rising of the court. This meant that they were arrested immediately and then released all within a few hours. They were thus unable to be seen as martyrs. Gradually, public interest waned and the agitation was abandoned.

While I was at Sialkot the Indian National Congress decided to step up its anti-Government demonstrations throughout the country. Sir Malcolm Hailey, probably the most able Governor of any Indian province, called all the Deputy Commissioners of the Punjab to Lahore for consultation. He made it clear to all of us that he wanted the situation in the Punjab to be handled firmly, that processions which threatened to disturb the peace were to be banned and any lawbreakers severely dealt with. Practically all the Deputy Commissioners accepted these instructions without question. I, however, pleaded with the Governor to allow the D.Cs, to handle the situation in our respective districts as we saw fit, as long as we ensured peace. I pointed out that in my district, in Sialkot city, with a fair-sized Congress presence, they would certainly take out a procession but I wanted to permit it as a good way to let the Congress supporters blow off steam. I would ensure there was no violence. If, on the other hand, I prohibited the procession and it was taken out in defiance of my orders, which was more than likely, then I would have to use force, including the use of firearms if necessary, in order to break it up and arrest those who had defied my orders. The result would be to strengthen the influence of the Congress and exacerbate the situation. Hailey agreed to my suggestion and, as it happened, the procession in Sialkot city was held with my permission and passed off peacefully. Hailey was also the man who had the perspicacity to realize that the only way to end the Akali agitation was to enact the legislation regulating the management of the shrines and brought about the Gurudwara Act.

* * *

The attitude of Indian I.C.S. officers towards the Home Rule Movement was a ticklish one particularly for those holding important administrative posts who at times were called upon to take action, including having to fire on demonstrators. A handful found this predicament impossible under such circumstances and resigned, but the majority did what was required even though their sympathies might have been with the nationalist workers. Some Indian officers did order firing on agitators. I made no secret of the fact that my sympathies were with the Nationalist Movement and that I admired the leaders, Mahatma Gandhi, Jawaharlal Nehru, Sardar Patel and others. Had I been called upon to fire on demonstrators, I would have refused to do so and resigned rather than act against the dictates of my own conscience. Fortunately, I was never faced with such a situation.

Sialkot, being a Brigade Headquarters, was my first district with a large military establishment. It had a small artillery and cavalry unit, and included both British and Indian infantry. However, the infantry was made up of mostly the Indian Army with one British Army regiment, the Norfolks. The British Cavalry Unit was the Duke of Cambridge's Own Hodson's Horse, the 9th Lancers while the Indian Army cavalry unit was the Duke of Connaught's Own Lancers, another famed regiment.

Thanks to the Army officers Sialkot had a very active social life. The club had excellent tennis courts. And, polo, very popular with the cavalry, was generally worth watching. Prakash and I got along well with several officers, all British in those days, of course, and there was a good deal of entertaining. We interacted with a number of Indian families, including Mr. C. Rai, a barrister, and the famous sports goods manufacturing family, the Uberois, and made a large number of good friends.

One of the British officers, Captain Ray Mirlees, a Scot, commanded the artillery unit. He finished up as a Major General, did well under General Wavell in the Middle East in World War Two, and was posted in India at the time of the transfer of power. He was in Delhi for the colourful final Farewell Tattoo of the British Army in 1947.* His second wife Francis, a petite and attractive American, created quite a sensation among the wives of the British officers with her sophisticated ways and her two French maids when Mirlees brought her to Sialkot as his bride. After retirement he settled down in France and Switzerland, and when we were in Paris we renewed our friendship and saw a lot of one another, both in Paris and in Le Touquet on France's Atlantic coast where the Mirlees had a charming villa.

One of the great joys of running a district was the outdoor life. I spent a great deal of time on tour. At times Prakash and I and our little Harji would be away from Headquarters for two or three weeks at a time, staying at Dak Bungalows maintained by the Irrigation Department, the Public Works Department or the District Board. Most of these bungalows had no modern amenities, and many were not well maintained or even clean. So, often, we preferred to live in tents. These were very generous in size and we made sure we had individual tents for my office, our bedroom and bath. The tents would be sent ahead of us and were pitched and ready before we arrived. On tour, we always took our own staff plus about four chaprasis.

The work was organized to cause the least disruption to my routine duties. Court cases, both revenue and criminal, were fixed for hearing as near as possible to the place where the parties came from to save them and the witnesses the inconvenience of coming to Headquarters, while the daily administrative work carried on as all papers, along with my personal mail, were sent daily from my Headquarters.

Some days were reserved for shoots. In most districts game was plentiful. We often went out on shoots, along with friends

* The Tattoo was spectacular, held in the old Irwin Stadium in New Delhi facing India Gate. It was the 'last salute' of the British Army's many years in India.

who came to stay with us. We made a point of pitching our tents in the hunting spot. And, almost every day, before and after office hours, I would just walk out with a gun and a couple of beaters to bag a few partridge, snipe, duck or sand grouse and quails for the pot. My shooting was entirely restricted to birds. Altogether it was a most enjoyable combination of work and recreation.

I have particularly happy memories of our years in Rohtak where there was plenty of wild life. Every morning Prakash and I went riding, and within a mile or two of our house we would often run into a large herd of wild deer, and it was a sheer joy to gallop along with these beautiful, graceful animals across the fields and along the canals as they raced on. The deers seemed to enjoy the race as much as we did.

Much of the wild life in the districts around Delhi, Rohtak, Karnal and Gurgaon, were decimated by the Americans stationed in Delhi during World War Two. Deer and other game were mercilessly slaughtered, often at night when the poor animals were mesmerized by the headlights of the hunters' jeeps.

CHAPTER 25

Earlier in my Punjab service I had become friends with Arthur Lothian who was serving in the political branch of the service, and he wanted me to transfer to that branch. At that time there was only one Indian officer in the 'political',* and many people regarded this branch as a superior section of the I.C.S. I consulted some colleagues and also Sir Edward Maclagan, the Governor, and he advised me against it as he said it meant nothing more than district administration in the North West Frontier Province, and I was better off in the Punjab. I followed his advice.

After some years in the district, however, I wanted a posting abroad, and mentioned this to some senior friends in the Service. In 1930, I was asked if I would like to go to London as Deputy Trade Commissioner in the Office of the High Commissioner. I accepted, so after just one short year in Sialkot, we went off to London where I served for three years under Sir Harry Lindsay, our Trade Commissioner there. This included a three-month spell in Hamburg as Trade Commissioner in Germany in 1933.

The work in London was very new to me. I found it interesting because it allowed me to see how the organizations in England dealt with the import of industrial raw materials and foodstuffs from India. It also gave me an insight into the functioning of Britain's extensive steel, textiles, leather as well as the research

* K.P.S. Menon I.C.S., later India's first envoy in China and its first Foreign Secretary.

institutes that served them. In those days, India mainly exported industrial raw materials like jute, cotton, hides, oilseeds; and foodstuffs like tea, coffee and cashew nuts. Our job in the Trade Commission was to keep in touch with the importers and do all we could both to maintain and expand trade. To India, we passed on important requirements of importers such as standardization of quality and improved packaging. We also investigated new items for export. Lindsay was pleasant to work with and the three years in London were interesting as well as enjoyable. Prakash and I renewed many old friendships and I was able to play cricket and golf again, which, of course, I loved.

We had our share of anxiety and disappointment too. Two very different events really stand out in those years. One concerned our daughter, Harji, who had a serious accident. She was knocked down by a car. There were very anxious moments as she was unconscious for several hours and had a small skull fracture. It could have been critical but happily for us she came out of it after a month of lying in bed without suffering any ill effects.

Another incident, different in nature, occurred when our Indian cricket team was to visit England in 1932. I received a telegram from my old friend, R.E. Grant Govan, then President of the Cricket Board of Control, saying that they proposed to appoint me Captain. He asked me if I would be available. I was, of course, thrilled and honoured, and approached the High Commissioner, Sir B.N. Mitra, a very gentle, kind and considerate man whom I liked and respected, to ask for permission. But he told me that he would not be able to approve my going off for the whole season to play cricket. I was deeply disappointed as it would have been a great honour and a unique experience. But I could not disobey the High Commissioner's orders, and so, with the utmost regret, I had to inform Grant Govan that I would not be available.

The team came, captained by the Maharajah of Porbander, a charming man, but not a great cricketer. I was put on the

Managing Committee of the tour along with Gowar Harrington and saw a good deal of the matches. There were some fine cricketers in this team, including C.K. Naidu, a great batsman; Amar Singh, a magnificent all rounder; and Mohamad Nissar, a very good fast bowler in his day. The team should have done well but the Captain, unfortunately, just lacked the initiative to keep the team together, and consequently the tour was not a success.

During my posting in London I was sent on duty to Hamburg, in Germany, from January to March in 1933 as Trade Commissioner. It was an eventful three months for it was just when Hitler took over the Free City of Hamburg. The Nazis were consolidating their power, and we observed how such a monstrous ideology, based on racial prejudice, involving so much cruelty and human suffering, came to be accepted by a people known for their literary culture and love of music.

A professor in Hamburg University, to whom we had been introduced though friends, invited us to dinner to meet his family. He and his wife were charming, fine examples of a good upper middle class German family, intelligent, broadminded and considerate, and most friendly. We noticed that the eldest son did not join us for dinner. When we got to know them better the parents told us that their son, who was at university, had become a full-fledged Nazi. He refused to interact with his parents because they disliked the Nazi philosophy. They complained sadly that not only was there practically no communication between them but they feared that he was quite capable of spying on them and reporting them to the Party.

The professor told us that this was the position in a great many German families in Hamburg. Germany, after its defeat in 1918, faced desperate conditions. Incredibly high inflation, overall scarcity and privation had reduced the German people to such a state of demoralization and hopelessness that they were prepared to accept any leader who promised to restore their self-respect, and release them from their humiliation and misery. Hitler was regarded as such a leader, particularly by the bitter, frustrated youth. These were the tragic consequences of the Treaty of Versailles imposed on Germany by the victorious nations after World War One, a mistake that was fortunately not repeated after World War Two when the American Marshall Plan helped to rebuild a devastated West Germany.

While we were in Hamburg Nazism had not yet taken a complete hold over the country, and at times it was even ridiculed. Once we saw a number of street urchins following and teasing a formidable looking Storm Trooper in his Nazi uniform who kept marching on, erect, ignoring his tormentors. We expected him to catch hold of a couple of them and give them a good drubbing but he took no notice of them. Even at that time, however, a sinister side of Nazism had surfaced, and my Head Clerk, a German national but a Jew, told us that there were many cases of Jews being beaten up, their houses ransacked and even burned while the authorities took no notice. He told me how each day when he left his family to come to work, he feared that his home would be ransacked and his family attacked. No redress was possible as the police just stood by and did nothing. Before we left, things had got so bad in those few weeks that the British Consul General, who was Jewish, was so afraid of being assaulted that he asked his government to transfer him from Hamburg.

I personally witnessed a scene in Hamburg that made me realize how German people feared the uniform. I was returning from a reception at the Town Hall hosted by the Burgomeister or Mayor of Hamburg. I was travelling by underground railway and there was a big crowd at the station. As the train came to a halt, everyone rushed forward towards the seats. I was standing there with one of the German officials, a civilian, but in uniform. Without any hesitation he elbowed his way through the crowd, pushing people around so that both of us could get to the front and take our seats. I thoroughly disliked doing this but he just would not let go of my arm, assuring me that it was alright and I need not worry. To me the strangest thing was that just because he was in uniform, no one in the crowd objected to his misbehaviour. I could imagine what would happen to anyone behaving like this under similar conditions in London or New York.

I had the opportunity of watching Hitler in action when he addressed a Nazi Party rally in Hamburg. It was an unforgettable experience. The way in which he deliberately worked up his audience with his hysterical shouting and gesticulation had to be seen to be believed. The man seemed to be a maniac and it was frightening to see the hold he had on the crowd.

CHAPTER 26

In 1934 we returned to India and I was posted in Delhi as Deputy Secretary in the Commerce Ministry. Prakash and Harji sailed ahead of me. My brother, Teja Singh's eldest son, Krishan, was to be married in the winter and the family wanted them to be there even if I had to follow later. This was the first time I had served in the Central Government and it was quite an experience. When I joined the Commerce Ministry, apart from the Commerce Minister, who was a member of the Viceroy's Executive Council, there were only three I.C.S. officers: a Secretary to the Government, a Joint Secretary and a Deputy Secretary. Yet this Ministry dealt not only with Commerce but also with the Mercantile Marine and Shipping, Lighthouses and Company Law.

For me the work in the Secretariat was new and extremely interesting. Even reading through old files for constant reference was actually a pleasure because of the extensive notes by past distinguished members of the Council and the Secretaries. These notes were thorough and with considerable literary merit. Apart from this, the Assistant Secretaries, men promoted because of their aptitude from the Ministry's staff of clerks, also presented cases in a similar lucid manner.

Working in the Commerce Ministry gave me the opportunity to see at close quarters the Government's general attitude towards industrial development. Colonial policy on India's economy had been structured for the benefit of Great Britain not India. It dictated that India was always to be a provider of raw materials.

Industrial development was almost ignored. By the time I joined the I.C.S., public opinion had forced the Government of India to accept that a few industries would be established initially under protection laws. But foreign firms still enjoyed a monopoly. For instance, when enterprising Indians, namely Walchand Hirachand of Bombay, ventured into shipping, initially into coastal trade, he was opposed by British vested interests such as the P&O and British India which had monopolized this field and so encountered many difficulties with little encouragement from the Government. But he continued the fight and established himself first in the coastal trade, later in international trade. It was an uphill climb all the way. However, the tremendous progress Indian shipping companies have made since Independence has been possible only because of the courage and enterprise of such pioneers.

In the Ministry I was shocked by the Government's continuing apathy towards industrialization. The trade in oilseeds for instance, India was an important exporter of oilseeds but the extraction of oil was done abroad. Obviously, the oil extracted from Indian oilseeds in India should have been exported, leading to the establishment of an important domestic industry, and also earning additional foreign exchange from the export of the oil cake, a by-product of some importance. This could only be done if oil wagons were made available on the Railways, and oil storage facilities constructed at ports, along with oil tankers to carry the oil overseas. Instead, the Government of India continued to export only oil seeds until after Independence. It is equally hard to believe that in those days, molasses, one of the by-products of the large sugar industry, now extensively used for the production of alcohol, was thrown away as waste, and sugar factories actually had to pay to have it carted away.

Much later, in 1948, as High Commissioner for India in Canada, I was involved in procuring diesel locomotives for the Indian Railways in the United States and Canada. A top

official of the Canadian company supplying us locomotives, a
man named Carson, had been head of the old North Western
Railway which before the Partition ran in the Punjab and North
West Frontier Province. We met at the little ceremony arranged
in Montreal when Prakash was asked to christen one of the
locomotives by pouring ganga jal, specially brought from the
Ganges, down its sides. I jokingly remarked to Carson, 'You know
it is ridiculous our importing these locomotives, we should be
making them in India.' Carson, a typical colonial, replied, 'My
dear High Commissioner, it will be 50 years before India will be
able to make these locomotives!' I don't know if Carson lived
long enough to see the diesel locomotives manufactured in
Chittaranjan within ten years of our conversation.

Apart from the interesting nature of the work, life in the
Secretariat could not compare with the full and exciting life
of a District Officer. It was just files, files and more files! We
all had to work hard but I found that many colleagues liked
to build their reputations as hard workers by staying late in
office every evening. I refused to do this and left punctually at
5 p.m. I was used to exercise. I had made up my mind to play
a round of golf, or tennis or even go for a run, before a shower
and a pre-dinner drink, even if my senior officers, at times the
Minister himself, were still at their desks! If necessary, I took my
files home and worked on them either in the evening or early
morning before breakfast. So I never had much of a reputation
as a Secretariatwallah!

But even Secretariat life had its exciting moments. One day, Sir
Muhammad Zafurullah Khan—whom I had known in Sialkot
in 1930 as an ordinary lawyer, but who had entered politics and
become Commerce Minister in 1937—came to my room to tell
me that I had been nominated to the Legislative Assembly to
make a speech the following day to defend the Government's
tariff policy. I told him frankly that tariffs were not my subject

that to my chagrin an Englishman named Slade had been brought in from Burma as Joint Secretary, when I should by all rights have been promoted to that post and he dealt with tariffs. Slade had cold feet, the Minister explained. He claimed he had never done any public speaking. I objected that I had not either but all the Minister said was that I was only to do my best the next day and wished me luck. I was angry but there was nothing I could do, so I was duly sworn in as a Member of the Legislative Assembly for one day to defend the tariff policy! I sat up all night reading about wheat, sugar and some other commodities, hoping fervently that these would be the items chosen by the Opposition for attack. As luck would have it, they were, and I was able to present effective counter-arguments. This was my one and only, most unwilling, excursion into politics. At least the press was good enough to make some friendly remarks about 'Mr. Malik's maiden speech'.

The Legislative Assembly of those years was a mere façade, little more than a debating club with no effective control over the Government's policies, because the Government could always carry through any motion by nominating a sufficient number of officials, even for one day, to ensure a majority. The Assembly did serve one purpose: it provided a forum for the criticism of official policies. It was also a platform for prominent personalities like Mohammad Ali Jinnah, Motilal Nehru and others to successfully bring to public attention policies that were considered anti-national by the Nationalists.

The Viceroy in the three years we were in Delhi was Lord Willingdon. He and Lady Willingdon were very active socially but he did not play any important role in the development of British policy towards India. However, both Willingdons did contribute to developing friendly relations between the British and Indians, that in itself was a valuable service. I had known them in my Eastbourne days. They lived just outside town, and their elder son, who was killed in World War One, and I had played cricket together. They were, therefore, very friendly with Prakash and me. My brother, Teja Singh, the Chief Engineer, PWD, very involved in the building of New Delhi, knew Lady Willingdon. She took a great interest in the finishing touches of the Viceroy's House. Among some amusing anecdotes about her he recounted that even the toilet paper in the Viceroy's House had to be in mauve, her favourite colour.

When he was Governor of Bombay Willingdon started the famous Willingdon Club, open to both Indians and the British. And when he came to Delhi, Willingdon started the Delhi Gymkhana Club which again was a mixed club. This was a major step at a time when most clubs were still exclusively British and closed to Indians, much to the resentment of Indians.

H.S. Malik standing beside the ambulance he drove from England to Cognac for the French Red Cross. France, 1916

Flt. Lt. H.S. Malik stands by the fighter plane presented to India by the Manchester Chamber of Commerce for the war in Waziristan. Malik was honoured by receiving the plane on behalf of the Govt. of India. Manchester, 1917

Flt. Lt. H.S. Malik and his bride, Prakash. London, 1919

*Rain doesn't deter H.S. Malik from playing golf
in Moore Park. England, 1919*

H.S. Malik's golf swing was described as one of the best in the game. England, 1938

The Malik family arrives in Ottawa. Canada, 1947
(L to R) Veena, H.S. Malik, Sardarni Malik, Harmala and Harji

The Sikh community in Vancouver welcome independent India's first envoy—Sardar and Sardarni Malik and Harji. Canada, 1947

High Commissioner Malik accompanies Admiral Lord Louis Mountbatten and Lady Mountbatten to an official function in Ottawa. Canada, 1948

Ambassador H.S. Malik arrives in Paris with Sardarni Malik, Veena and Rajah, the Collie. France, 1948

The Indian Ambassadors in Europe at a meeting called by Foreign Minister Pandit Jawaharlal Nehru at the Indian Embassy in Paris, 1951.(L to R) Standing—(unknown), Mr. R.K. Nehru, Mr. P.A. Menon, Mr. B.R. Sen, (unknown), Mr. Prem Krishan. (L to R) Seated—Dr. M.S. Mehta, Dr. S. Radhakrishnan, Pandit Nehru, Sardar H.S. Malik, Sir Girija Shankar Bajpai, Mrs. Vijaya Lakshmi Pandit, Mr.B.N. Rao

*Ambassador Malik with Mrs. Eleanor Roosevelt and
Mrs. Chandralekha Mehta at a reception at the Embassy of India.
Paris, 1951*

*An exhibition golf match was played at the St. Germain Golf Club,
Paris, 1954–55, between the great Ben Hogan and Sardar Malik as
partners against the American Army Golf Champion in Europe and
Sir Christopher Steele, British Ambassador to NATO. (L to R) Club
President, Sardar Malik, Sir Christopher Steele, Army Champion,
Ben Hogan and General Laurie Norstadt, Commander SHAPE, Paris*

Ambassador Malik briefs Pandit Nehru at the Indian Embassy.
Paris, 1951

Pandit Nehru meets the staff and officers of the Indian Embassy
in Paris informally in 1951

H.R.H. the Duke of Windsor at St. Germain watching the
Ben Hogan Exhibition Match 1954–55.
(L to R) Sir Christopher Steele, the Duke of Windsor and H.S. Malik

Dr. Radhakrishnan, Vice-President of India, is received
by Ambassador and Sardarni Malik at a reception at
the Indian Embassy. Paris, 1954–55

CHAPTER 27

A part from the few people who had made it to the I.C.S. by chance, the average Britisher in the I.C.S. was highly intelligent, with top academic qualifications and capacity for hard work. As a body of men they were of course devoted to the British Empire in India. I made many friends among them and, on the whole, found them good to work with. They were loyal, honest colleagues, and in the case of those I worked under, I found them fair and straightforward to deal with.

I made good friends such as Charles Barry, Henry Craik, Alan Stow, Maclagan and Hailey. While I was serving in Sheikhapura, the Commissioner at Lahore, Langley, was succeeded by Tollinton, or Bollinger as his friends called him because of his fondness for alcohol, particularly champagne! Where Langley was almost ascetic and a great stickler for rules, Bollinger was gregarious and hearty, generally contemptuous of rules. However, when it came to work, he was very strict, known to be quite hard on shirkers. A complete extrovert, he was outspoken, would stand no nonsense, and yet would overlook minor derelictions.

The short time I served under him was long enough to understand him and we got along famously. A lovely story about him concerned his time as Deputy Commissioner in Simla, then in the Punjab, when it was India's summer capital. Lord Chelmsford, the Viceroy, decided to have a pheasant shoot at a spot which Bollinger had already selected for a shooting party for himself and his friends. One evening when Bollinger was a

guest at one of the usual big viceregal parties, the Viceroy asked
Sir Edward Maclagan, the Punjab Governor, to bring Bollinger
up to him after the dinner. The Viceroy told him, 'Mr. Tollinton, I
understand that you have arranged a shoot for your friends at [he
named the place]. I hope you don't mind as I am shooting with
my party there on [and he named the date],' which was a couple
of days earlier than Bollinger's shoot. This would naturally have
completely ruined Bollinger's shoot. Bollinger, who as usual,
had helped himself liberally to the Viceregal champagne and
was feeling very good, flushed deeply and said, 'Well, Sir, all I
can say is, it isn't done!' The Viceroy, extremely annoyed, turned
away and Maclagan was, naturally, terribly embarrassed. Later, he
came back to Bollinger and said to him, 'Tollinton, the Viceroy is
very upset. He told me the only explanation he can offer himself
of your behaviour is that you were rather the worse for liquor.' To
which Bolinger replied, thrusting forward his chest, thumping it
hard, 'No ,Sir, rather the better for liquor!'

Sir Arthur Lothian, whom I first met during one of my
holidays in Gulmarg when he was Assistant Resident there, was
another good friend in the Service. He was in Delhi as Political
Secretary when I was in the Secretariat, and later still when I
was Prime Minister in Patiala from 1944 to 1947. We saw a lot
of each other, talking often openly about relations between our
two races. One day, he said to me, 'H.S., I am very puzzled about
something, perhaps you can help me. My Deputy Secretary is
a very decent chap and I like him, but sometimes he behaves
very oddly. He comes into my room, settles down in a chair
opposite me, pulls out his cigarette and altogether behaves in a
very uppish manner, which my British Deputy Secretary would
never dream of doing!' I told him, 'Arthur, you yourselves are
responsible for this. Don't forget that not so long ago you British
expected your junior officers, when they were Indians, to take
off their shoes before entering your room! This is just his way of
telling you that he is as good a man as you are!'

Another Briton whom I liked very much and developed a friendship with was Gainsford, then also serving in the Political Department in the Indian Government. I met him first on the golf course in Delhi, and Prakash and I began to see a lot of him and his wife socially. I was very impressed by his obvious robust health as well as his poise. A big man, he radiated well being. Nothing seemed to upset him, not even when he missed a short putt! He looked about ten years younger than his age. When I got to know him well, I asked him the secret of his excellent health and equable temper. He told me that it was because of yoga. Gainsford described how after he started studying yoga, he became so fascinated that he was afraid that if he continued his study of yoga he might be tempted to give up his present way of living, abandon his family and enter an ashram to attain spiritual perfection. That he was not prepared to face as he was a devoted family man with a loving wife and wonderful children so he deliberately confined himself to the physical exercises.

Two very important events took place in my family in these Delhi Secretariat years: one bringing us great joy, the other great sorrow and heartbreak. On August 19th 1935 our son Harmala, whom we affectionately called Mala, was born at the Portmore Nursing Home in Simla. Portmore was about six miles away from our house, not far from the Viceregal Lodge, while my office was about halfway between the lodge and the hospital. So, for the ten days Prakash was in hospital, I walked to the nursing home every morning, then back to the office and after office back to the nursing home to spend some time with my wife and son, then back home to Harji. The Scottish lady doctor looking after Prakash was an extraordinary character. Prakash's labour proved to be long and difficult, and her sister, Lilaji and I were in the corridor outside, waiting anxiously, when the doctor came out. To our amazement she told us that as the delivery was proving long and complicated, she would have to charge more than she had previously quoted. I was very worked up about what my wife was going through and felt like telling her to charge whatever she wanted and get on with it. But I controlled myself. Fortunately everything turned out happily.

The sad event was my father's death in May 1936 while we were in Simla. The telegram with the news came as a terrible shock because we were totally unprepared for his death. We knew that he had had an attack of malaria but at 73 he was fit and unusually strong for a man his age. Later, we learned that the family doctor who had been looking after him had been somewhat careless in his treatment. We were all heartbroken. I left immediately for Rawalpindi. My brothers were already there, and we did our best to console our dear mother, who with her wonderful faith, was amazingly brave and controlled. I found it difficult to control my grief and completely broke down when I saw him lying there, as if asleep. I had looked on him as a vigorous, strong man, always full of life, the very picture of *Char di Kala*, the expression we Sikhs repeat to ourselves often, which means 'High spirits! Victory!' and I could not bear to see him lifeless. I was thankful that he had come to Delhi in the winter months to spend a little time with us. He had been so happy to see our son whose coming he had looked forward to so greatly.

The funeral was a big affair. Practically the whole male population of the city followed the procession to pay tribute to a man whom they all respected for his integrity and courage, and who had done so much for them during his lifetime. People came up to us to tell us of their affection and respect for Father. For years, as a child, I had prayed that my life be taken before the lives of those I loved as I could not bear the thought of losing them. This was my first experience of losing someone whom I loved dearly and I found it hard to bear. I had enjoyed such a special relationship with Father, he had been such a profound influence in my life, had supported me in everything I wanted to do, and it was unthinkable that he was gone.

When I went back to Simla and we had a little prayer meeting at home, I broke down when I was taking the waak, the hymn from the Granth Sahib. Many years later my daughter Harji told me how shaken she was to see me because she had never seen me weep before.

CHAPTER 28

In 1937 the Government of India was considering the appointment of a Trade Commissioner in America. It was to be the first appointment from India in the United States. As Deputy Secretary in the Commerce Ministry I had been dealing with the file. It was a delicate matter because there was a good deal of public sentiment in the U.S. favouring Home Rule for India, and even President Franklin D. Roosevelt was known to be sympathetic. The British found this very irritating as they didn't want any comments on India from 'foreigners'. In New York they opened the British Library of Information whose main function was to counter anti-British propaganda in the United States through lectures throughout the country by prominent Englishmen, and by some Indians too. The single aim was to inform the American public of the wonderful job the British were doing in India. A number of Indian speakers, some of them quite distinguished, were enlisted for this campaign, including Mehr Chand Khanna who later transformed himself into an ardent Congressman, and was for several years a member of Pandit Nehru's Cabinet after Independence.

A great deal of correspondence was exchanged over the issue of this appointment between the Government of India, the Secretary of State for India in London, and the British Ambassador in Washington, Sir Ronald Lindsay, through the British Foreign Office. Lindsay took a strong line: in the first instance he objected to the whole idea of the proposed appointment. He felt that the work could be handled by the Commercial Section of the British Embassy in Washington. He also opposed it on political grounds, as he felt that such an officer, appointed by the Government of India, would be exploited by the anti-British elements in America, and this from Britain's point of view, would interfere with the good work being done by the British Library of Information. Lindsay was adamant that if the Government of India persisted in making this appointment over his objections then the incumbent must definitely be a Briton, not an Indian. He claimed that it would be difficult for an Indian to do the job because of the colour prejudice in America, and also, again, because of the greater danger of an Indian being exploited by the pro-Indian independence elements. He insisted, therefore, that a Britisher be appointed.

In our Secretariat, the Commerce Secretary, Hugh Dow, readily accepted Lindsay's arguments, and suggested the name of a British I.C.S. officer serving in another department. The file then came to the Executive Council Member, Sir Sultan Ahmed, who was officiating while Zafarullah Khan, the actual Member, was on leave. He was an eminent lawyer from Patna, with a mind of his own, and although also a Muslim like Zafarullah Khan, he was, unlike him, free from communal bias when it came to promotions and appointments. Instead of agreeing with the British Secretary and automatically sending the case on to the Viceroy for his approval, as was the general practice with the Indian Council Members, Sir Sultan walked into my office room one day and said, 'Malik, I don't agree with Dow, and I also disagree with the British Ambassador. I want to send an Indian and I think you are the right man for this job. Will you go? Being a Sikh there will be no question of you being mistaken for an American Negro!' I was completely taken aback. The possibility had never even occurred to me and I told him that I would like to think it over and consult my wife. Moreover, the terms and conditions of the appointment had yet to be decided. He said he hoped I would accept.

The idea of this posting was most appealing. I saw it as something challenging and interesting. Prakash also agreed, although we were very ignorant about America for in 1937 very little was known about America in India. In complete contrast to today, very few Indian students went to the U.S. for advanced studies, and apart from a handful of businessmen in New York and the Sikhs in California, along with a sprinkling of people who had settled down in the U.S. as professors or doctors, there were hardly any Indians in America.

I had not had much contact with Americans in the past. Apart from a few Rhode scholars and my friends, the Tookers, I knew no Americans. The idea of serving in America seemed like an adventure. This was the first time that an Indian was going to the States in a senior representative capacity, and I felt proud that a Sikh should be chosen for this honour. So, I told Sir Sultan that I would go. He said that he was still to get the Viceroy's approval but that he would insist on his recommendation being accepted. He didn't anticipate any problems. However, there was quite a battle, but finally the Viceroy agreed, and I was duly appointed.

In these days of routine air travel and easy telephone communication, it is difficult to remember that in 1937 America seemed very far because travel was only by sea. Letters took some weeks to arrive and telegrams were the only rapid means of communication. So, family members had their reservations, especially my mother and Prakash's parents. Harji, knowing nothing about America, had been all set to go to boarding school in England before my posting, because we had decided that schooling in India was not satisfactory. So she had been pouring over prospectuses of various schools and was disappointed. Prakash too had some qualms as she was expecting our third child in the autumn. But it all worked out and in the end we were all excited at the prospect.

I had been due eight months leave, and we had planned a trip to England and Europe, to leave Harji at school among other things. Instead, we spent a couple of months holidaying in Kashmir, mostly in Gulmarg. I had also to travel all around India visiting industries and meeting representatives of trade organizations to prepare for the new job. I found these travels to be extremely fascinating and a real education.

We left for New York via London in the spring of 1938 and for three pleasant months I was attached to the office of the High Commissioner in London for further briefing. It was a delightful period because we were able to see many dear friends again and, as usual, I also got in some cricket and golf.

We found a nice house in our old favourite area, Hampstead, in the Vale of Health. These were the years when the Jews were being persecuted in Hitler's Germany. It was the beginning of the Holocaust, and some friends of ours asked us if we would help a young German Jewish woman to escape to the United States by taking her as a governess for our three-and-a-half year old son, Harmala. We readily agreed. She was related to the great Sigmund Freud. But at the last moment she wasn't able to get her papers in time, and another young woman, Annemarie Hecht, came with us instead.

Travelling by the Cunard Line's flagship the *Queen Mary* was an enjoyable experience. What a contrast to the P&O! We were almost sorry it was such a short voyage. We arrived in New York on the 4th of July 1938 to a very warm reception by the Indian community in the city arranged by J.J. Singh, one of the prominent Indians settled in New York. J.J. was actively working for Indian independence through the India League of America of which he later became President. He felt that the arrival of the first Indian to represent the country in New York was a special occasion. Having lived in the U.S. for many years, he fully understood the importance of publicity in the country and saw this as a chance to give India prominence.

He boarded the ship as soon as we docked, bringing with him

some press photographers. So photograph after photograph was taken. Harji was very frustrated because she had been looking forward to photographing the famous New York skyline and instead ended up being snapped herself. However, she and my son Mala were absolutely thrilled when we were escorted to our hotel overlooking Central Park by a New York City Police motor cycle escort complete with a wailing siren!

Partly thanks to J.J.'s flair for publicity our arrival in New York attracted a good deal of interest. It was the first appointment of an Indian official representing India in the United States, and, in addition, because so little was really known of India, there was a good deal of curiosity. Our interviews and photographs appeared in several daily papers, while one of the Sunday newspapers carried a full-page article accompanied with full-page photographs. It painted an extremely extravagant portrait of us. Prakash was said to own hundreds of saris with sets of jewellery to match each one! This, of course, was complete nonsense. But Prakash told some of our friends later that she was quite alarmed at this report because she felt that people would believe that we were very wealthy which might tempt kidnappers. The terrible Lindbergh kidnapping story was still very fresh in people's minds, so there was some cause for concern.* Prakash and I were crossing Fifth Avenue the morning after the story on us appeared. The traffic policeman, recognizing us from our press photographs, held up the traffic to let us pass. I must confess we felt very important!

---

* The little son of Ann and Charles Lindbergh, the great aviation hero who had flown solo across the Atlantic, was kidnapped and found dead, making world headlines in 1932.

CHAPTER 29

The three years in America from July 1938 to January 1943 proved to be a great challenge, and a wonderful experience. I had the whole of the U.S., Canada and South America to cover! However, I found the United States and Canada a big enough parish, and to our great regret, later, largely because of the outbreak of World War Two, I never attempted to visit any country in South America.

In New York I was starting from scratch. Although I was able to take over the old Railways Mission office which had closed down—a fine location in the Rockefeller Centre in the heart of Manhattan—my work as Trade Commissioner broke entirely new ground. My first task was to contact various organizations concerned with the import trade with India, like the Jute and Shellac Asociations, all of which had their headquarters in New York. My good golf reputation came in very handy as an automatic introduction to a large circle of business people in and around New York as most of these associations held their own golf tournaments. In time, I visited big industrial and commercial centres, in both the United States and Canada, and met the Foreign Trade Councils in those cities.

I first called on the Mayor of New York, the dynamic, voluble Fiorello La Guardia, also called 'the Little Flower'—an Italian-American. I had, of course, to call on the British Library of Information, and realized immediately that I could not follow one of the main instructions from my Government which was to work in close collaboration with this institution whose main function was political propaganda where India was concerned. They assiduously carried out this work both in print and through lectures all over the country. Those Indians who were only too happy to visit the United States, even if it meant preaching the gospel of the benefits of British rule to Americans, were often heckled at such lectures, both by Americans, sympathetic to the demand for Indian independance, and by Indians settled in America, many of them staunch nationalists. This led to some amusing incidents.

The late Louis Fischer, the well known author who wrote a famous biography of Gandhi, was very active as a public speaker in those days, and frequently spoke from public platforms in favour of Indian independence. At one such meeting, he was being heckled by a British member in the audience who accused him of being rabidly anti-British. He retorted, 'No, my friend, I am not anti-British, I am merely anti-stupidity!' Another time Krishnalal Shridharani, in those days a student in New York and later a reputed author, was making a speech in New Orleans. He was being repeatedly heckled by the British Consul who was in the audience. Shridharani, known for his repartee, replied to the Consul's questions with hard-hitting rejoinders. The Consul finally lost his temper and said, 'You can't speak to me like this! I am His Majesty's Consul here!' to which Shridharani, without turning a hair, retorted, 'It's alright, my dear Sir, you need not apologize, we all have to earn our living one way or another!' The audience roared with laughter and the Consul asked no more questions.

I was determined not to collaborate with the British Library of Information. My job was trade and I would concentrate on that, eschewing all politics. If the Government of India disapproved of my attitude, I was prepared to be recalled to New Delhi. At the same time I was invited to become a member of the British Club in New York and attended many of their functions. I made good friends among the British residents, but made it very clear that while I was a good friend of Britain's, I was a staunch nationalist.

When I went to Washington to pay my formal respects to the British Ambassador, Sir Ronald Lindsay, I told him frankly that I was well aware of his strong opposition to an Indian being appointed as Trade Commissioner in New York, and assured him that I would do my best to prove him wrong. A dour Scot, a man of few words, Lindsay just grunted in return saying that it was still to be seen. India, as part of the British Empire, had no diplomatic representation in the United States, and the British Ambassador handled all India's foreign relations via the India Office and the Foreign Office in London.

I succeeded in winning Lindsay over a day later when he took me to call on Mr. Cordell Hull, the American Secretary of State at the time. Cordell Hull and Lindsay were good friends and after his first few formal introductions, Hull turned to Lindsay and said, 'Sir Ronald, I see that there is more trouble on the North West Frontier of India. I can't understand why the British Empire, with all its resources, can't deal with this handful of trouble makers.' Hull was pulling Lindsay's leg, but Lindsay, who had very little sense of humour, was obviously embarrassed, more so perhaps because I was there, and grew rather red in the face. I dared to intervene, 'Mr. Ambassador, if you will permit me, I would like to answer the Secretary of State's question.' Lindsay was uncertain of what I might say but could not very well decline, so I said to Mr. Hull, 'Sir, I can best answer your question by telling you a true story. In one of these frontier campaigns, the Indian regiment concerned captured two of the enemy. When they were brought before the British Colonel commanding the regiment, he recognized them as having served well under him. So addressing them by name, he asked them, "You rascals, you were fighting for me. What do you mean by fighting against me?" "Sahib", they replied, "We were with you for seven years, then you discharged us and sent us home. We have to fight, so as we couldn't fight for you, we fought against you!'" Hull had a good laugh while Lindsay looked relieved.

We were on good terms after that, and whenever I went to Washington we played golf together at his club, Burning Tree. My old Balliol friend, Victor Mallet, also a keen golfer, was Counselor at the British Embassy in those years and helped in bringing Lindsay and me together. Good relations were very important as I was working under him.

Our priority was to find a suitable house quickly as Prakash was expecting our third child in October. After looking around in the suburbs around New York—we did not want to live in the city—we found what was to be an ideal home for the next few years. It was the country house of a family which, having unfortunately suffered financially in the Depression, wanted to rent out their residence, fully furnished. It was adequate for us, containing four bedrooms and a large living and dining room, and staff quarters. Its greatest attraction, however, were the seven acres of ground. The cultivated garden was charming but most of the area was pleasantly wild. We could not have afforded to maintain such a garden but the owner of the house agreed to maintain most of it at her expense. Quarry Close Farm, as it was called was a very happy home for us, and the red cement tennis court, though rather ancient with its share of cracks, proved to be an absolute blessing. Prakash and I both played and Harji learned to love the game and became a good player, and had a great time inviting her school friends to play. The large grounds sloped down to the main road towards Long Island Sound, an estuary of the Atlantic Ocean. In the Connecticut winter the driveway proved to be a marvelous sleigh ride for us all, the new baby included, in the snow.

Prakash used the grounds to perfect her driving skills, almost essential for housewives with husbands commuting to New York every day, as I was. It was a 40-minute railway journey from Portchester, the nearest station, to New York and I became a regular commuter. Although we had a driver, when Prakash learned to drive, she took Harji, and later Mala, to and from school, as well as drove me to the station. She became such a good driver that she even drove the car in to New York City when we had evening engagements.

Anne Marie Hecht, the Austrian girl who had come with us from London, helped to look after our baby daughter, Veena, when she was born that October, making our family complete. But after a few months, Anne Marie went to Japan to join her Austrian fiancée who had settled there. So we arranged for a trained Scottish nurse, Miss Ross, to come from England to look after Veena. She and Veena shared one of the three bedrooms downstairs.

In 1938 domestic staff was easy to find unlike the situation once the war began. Being totally unfamiliar with American staff conditions, we took the advice of friends and engaged a couple to help us—the husband to work as a valet and chauffeur, the wife as cook and housemaid. With Miss Ross and the couple, Prakash was able to manage well. The problem, however, was to find suitable couples, who would stay. We soon learned how totally different expectations of American staff were from Indian ones and our couple had a well furnished suite of rooms beyond the kitchen. We had many experiences, some amusing in retrospect, others very frustrating. All lessons in human behaviour! All of which was a great headache for Prakash, especially for the several months before and after our baby's arrival when she was not physically very strong.

Our house was on the border between New York State and Connecticut, and we lived there very happily for about three years. I was made a member of the exclusive Round Hill Golf Club in the nearby town of Greenwich, one of New York's most beautiful suburbs. Later, I joined the famous Apawamis Golf Club at Rye, nearer our home, and made many friends there, some of whom grew to be close friends with whom I played regularly. Many happy hours were spent on the course and in the Club House at the 19th Hole. Ellis won the American Seniors Championship year after year, and when I was in America in 1970, we thoroughly enjoyed playing again at Apawamis.

Our daughter Harji joined Rosemary Hall, a famous girls' school in Greenwich, established many years earlier by two English suffragettes on the lines of an English public school. We found that the girls' winter uniforms and even their shoes came from England! Rosemary had an excellent academic reputation. Harji was very happy there, made many long lasting friends and did extremely well, generally standing at the head of her class. In her senior year, she won the highest award in school, the Optima Medal, the winner of which was chosen by both the faculty and the students. Never can Prakash and I forget that moment. It was during what Americans call the Commencement Ceremony, the annual convocation when school degrees and prizes are awarded. All the parents, students and school staff were there, of course, and after the usual reports and speeches, the prize distribution began. Harji's name went up four times to receive prizes in various subjects. Prakash and I had been overjoyed by Harji receiving so many prizes, but with the Optima Announcement we were overcome with emotion.

CHAPTER 30

In 1938 American ignorance about India was abysmal. Americans looked on India as the land of maharajahs, fortune tellers, naked fakirs, snakes and tigers and, of course, the Indian rope trick.* Soon after we arrived, we were dining at the Waldorf Astoria. A party of young Americans at a nearby table seemed inordinately interested in our little group. Finally, unable to repress their curiosity, one of the girls walked over to us and asked to join us. I politely pulled up a chair for her. To my consternation, she stared earnestly at me and said, 'Can you tell me what is going to happen to me?' Taken aback, I quickly realized that because I wore a turban, she thought I must be a fortune teller! When we explained who we were, she was profusely apologetic.

Another time Harji and I were driving into New York for the premiere of the film 'Marie Antoinette', and were stuck in a traffic jam in the city. People looking in the window, pointed at me, saying, 'A magician! A magician!'

On another occasion, in Philadelphia, at a dinner hosted by the Foreign Trade Association, one of the members sitting near me at cocktails leaned over and said, 'Congratulations, sir! I see that your King has had a son!' I was very puzzled until I remembered that a day or two earlier the newspapers had

---

* This was the magic associated with India where a fakir, a holy man, supposedly threw a rope up into the air where it stayed suspended in space. He then sent a little boy to climb up, who then disappeared.

mentioned that Egypt's King Farouk had had a son! When I explained that he was perhaps referring to the King of Egypt, he said, 'Yes, I know, but Egypt and India are the same, aren't they?' He was a businessman, a member of the Foreign Trade Association, so I thought he must be joking, but he was serious. One must remember, however, that in those days the rest of the world was equally ignorant about America. When we were moving to the U.S., a good English friend of ours presented us with a book on gangsters warning us of what we were getting into. And he was being quite serious!

My turban and beard lead to other amusing experiences. When I showed up for the first time on any golf course, the caddies would look highly amused, and uninhibited as most Americans are, they made no attempt to hide their amusement until I took my driver and started to swing. I always had a very smooth, easy swing described to my delight years ago by the English writer, Charles Graves, in London's *Daily Mail* as 'the best swing in the world'. Watching my swing the caddies fell silent. And soon sniggers changed to surprised approval.

The first major event I entered was the North versus South Golf Tournament at Pinehurst in North Carolina. The night before the tournament Prakash and I were dining with George Dunlap a well known American amateur golfer whom I had met at Prestwick in Scotland some years earlier when he came over to play in the British Amateur Championship. After dinner in his home the children's nurse came in with the local paper, the *Pinehurst Chronicle*, and gave it to George. It read: *By far the most interesting entry this year is the swarthy swell from India, Sardar Hardit Singh Malik. It is said that he has 90 wives! However, he showed up with only one!* I was highly amused but totally aghast, and told our host that I didn't know who had written this fantastic nonsense. I had not met any journalists since we arrived in Pinehurst. George said he knew the local writer and could arrange for us to meet. So we had a friendly meeting, and I said to him, 'Apart from the fact that you have got the facts all wrong about my wives, I hope you realize that you are paying me a great compliment, for I have neither the means nor the constitution!' Some years later, in Washington, I told this story to a syndicated columnist, George Dixon, and he found it so amusing that he included it in his column which appeared all over the United States and I had my leg pulled many times over this!

1939, the year after we arrived, was the year of the World Fair in New York. This was quite a sensation with exhibits of the latest technological innovations from all over the world. Various countries competed to display the most spectacular pavilions and the fair turned into a major international attraction. The man in charge, Grover Whalen, was a tremendous showman and publicist, so a large number of official functions were held in order to bring additional publicity to the fair. These included visits by a great many VIPs, including a visit by King George VI of Great Britain and Queen Elizabeth.* The Foreign Consuls and Trade Commissioners based in New York were invited to most of these functions, and Prakash and I had a busy time socially, some of which was a lot of fun, much of it quite boring.

One incident in particular gave us a good laugh. The old Maharajah of Kapurthala, Jagatjit Singh, who was well known in America since he travelled extensively all over the world, came to New York to see the Fair and asked me to arrange for an official visit. This I was able to do. Such a visit included a Guard of Honour of the U.S. Marines and a gun salute to receive him. Grover Whalen asked me how many guns were required. In India strict protocol was meticulously observed about the number of guns. As Kapurthala, was one of the smaller states, the Maharajah was entitled only to a 12 to 15 guns salute. In New York, however, I felt the number didn't really matter so

* Queen Elizabeth II's mother.

I suggested a 22 gun salute, which was agreed to. When the Maharajah and I were discussing the arrangements for his visit, I suggested that he should wear an achkan and a turban. He did not like this idea and insisted on wearing a morning coat and top hat because he said that if he wore a turban he would be taken for a fortune teller! I didn't want to insist but I still advised him to wear Indian dress. All went well at the formal luncheon. Our party was received by Grover Whalen, the Guard of Honour and the 22 gun salute. So the Maharajah, in his top hat, was delighted. But, when after lunch, we visited the various stands and pavilions, the people who received us there thought I was the Maharjah because I was wearing a turban, and the gentleman in the top hat was my secretary! The Maharajah soon realized his mistake, so I told him that I would retire from the party, and my American assistant accompanied him for the rest of the visit, and there was no further embarrassment.

The World Fair was to be the last great show for many years to come for later that year the Germans attacked Poland and the Second World War began.

In the six years we spent in the United States we found people extremely warm and friendly, and formed many friendships which have lasted through the years. To us, Americans seemed, on the whole, essentially simple and direct, with a wholesome curiosity which at times was almost childlike. It was a welcome change from the smugness of Europeans, especially the British.

Certainly the Americans worshipped success, and the self-made man, far from being considered an outsider was admired for his hard work. This trait in the Americans, while it could be offensive in some cases, was generally admirable. Each man was considered as good as any other, very different from the social system in England and Europe, where class distinctions were extremely difficult to overcome, irrespective of how much money a man had or what he had achieved on his own.

We were shocked, however, with the attitude of our American friends towards the Jewish people. In Greenwich, for instance, it was impossible for a Jew to even rent a house, much less own property. So Greenwich was called a restricted area. Golf Clubs in this area would not allow memberships to Jews. The Jews, in retaliation, formed a purely Jewish golf club in Connecticut called Quaker Ridge.

The Rosenthals, an extremely wealthy family, the owners of Sears Roebuck and Co., one of the biggest department stores in the country, lived across the road from us. In fact, they had bought the big house of which our Quarry Close was just the cottage. They were charming people, cultured and sophisticated, and we went over to their home sometimes for lunch or dinner or a tennis party, and they came over to ours. To return their hospitality, we thought we would invite them for tennis and a meal at my club, Apawamis, instead of playing on our somewhat ancient court with its cracks in the cement. When we casually mentioned our plan to some friends, we were warned that we could not take the Rosenthals to the club as guests. We also received hints from some of our non-Jewish friends not to invite them to our home together with the Rosenthals. We were horrified at this racial intolerance by an otherwise friendly and warm-hearted people, and we never really got over it. Harji too ran into anti-semetic sentiments at college.

We had been warned that Americans were very mercenary. We did not find them so at all, quite the contrary. Certainly they were money conscious, but most generous. My dentist in Greenwich, Dr. William Hillis, was a very fine human being and we became good friends as we were equally devoted to golf.* While looking after my teeth he found that I needed a special procedure and advised me to consult a New York dentist who was a specialist in

---

* H.S. Malik: A happy memory is when the two of us together won the Open Invitation Foursomes Tournament at Apawamis.

the field. I told Bill that he must be very expensive and beyond my means. Bill said that he would speak to him. I agreed, and underwent the rather lengthy treatment, awaiting the bill with some trepidation. But I was only charged the nominal fee of a hundred dollars.

Several years later when I revisited Greenwich Bill and I played golf together like old times. He insisted on having a look at my teeth for free. When I refused, instead of driving straight to the station to put me on my train to New York, he stopped en route to buy a beautiful present for Prakash who was in India.

Another unforgettable instance of this kind of the American generosity was the way Harji was treated by her college friend, Hoppy Rossmassler and her family when she stayed behind in America for over a year to complete her college education while the rest of us had to return to India. Hoppy's mother, a typical, large-hearted American, took our daughter into her family, and Harji, who became truly devoted to them, spent a great deal of time with them as a part of their family until her return to India.

My job required me to travel all over the country. My first visit to the West Coast was a memorable experience. The journey itself was impressive, four days by train, in the luxury of a compartment all to myself, with excellent food served to me there. I spent many hours in the Observation Car at the rear of the train, enjoying the superb views through the Rockies and the western states. On the way to San Franciso I stopped over in Chicago to renew an old Oxford friendship with Jim Douglass, who had played golf for Cambridge in 1921 when I had played for Oxford.*

In San Francisco, one of the most beautiful cities in the world, the usual lunch meeting had been arranged by the Foreign Trade Council, where I spoke about India. After the meeting one of the journalists present asked if he could accompany me to my

---

* James Douglass was General Eisenhower's Secretary in the Eisenhower Presidency.

hotel as he wanted to ask some more questions about India. He was an amenable young man, just out of university. We had a pleasant chat on the way back to the hotel and I asked him in for a drink. When we sat down he said, 'Mr. Malik, your talk about trade and commerce was very interesting but the general public is more interested in the mystic and spiritual aspects of Indian life. Can you tell me something about yoga?' In a weak moment I confessed that I was a strong believer in yoga exercises. He jumped at this. 'That is exactly what I want to know about.' He was so enthused that I fell for it, and waxed eloquent about the exercises, explaining how they were the best way I knew for acquiring physical well being and mental poise. I told him about the Sees Asna, the head stance, explaining that ten minutes of this asna in the evening ensured complete recovery from fatigue. He left, satisfied. In the evening paper, there was a large headline: 'Malik says "Stand on Your Head!"' along with my photograph, and a brief account of the luncheon meeting and a much longer article on my views on yoga.

In San Francisco I ran into Lionel Tennyson, grandson of Alfred Lord Tennyson, the famous poet. I had met him when I was playing cricket for Sussex and he captained Hampshire, and later England. He was a good fighting Captain in those days, but in 1938-39 he had put on a lot of weight and was drinking heavily. He had married a charming American girl from Santa Barbara and they were living in California. It was sad to see Lionel in that state, and indeed, he died soon after.

From San Francisco I went on to Los Angeles, stopping on the way at the spectacular Monterey Penninsula with its two great golf courses, Cypress Point and Pebble Beach. I stayed at The Lodge, a small hotel just off the 18th green at Pebble—about the best hotel of its kind in the country, and played those wonderful courses.

During my years as Trade Commissioner in New York, I visited Los Angeles three times, and although each visit was interesting, the first one was really memorable, for apart from

the commercial community whom I met, I was introduced to the
Hollywood crowd through Pardee Erdman, a well known local
personality who knew all the movie stars like Bing Crosby, Bob
Hope and many others. He took me to the famous MGM studios
where I watched films being shot and also saw the sets where the
Tarzan films were made and the film which won two Oscars, 'All
Quiet on the Western Front'. I was amazed to find these tiny sets
and appreciated, for the first time, the skill involved in creating
the illusion of space in films from these sets. For instance, the
great lake into which Tarzan dives was just a tiny pond!

Pardee took me to the Golf Club favoured by all the big stars
where he had fixed up a game of golf for me with Bing Crosby
and Bob Hope. Both were fine players! It was weird to see in
the lounge famous figures such as Humphry Bogart, Johnny
Weismuller, Ronald Colman and other stars whom one had seen
so often on the screen but had, of course, never met in real life. I
felt like shaking them by the hand before I was even introduced
as they seemed to be old friends! The game with Bing Crosby and
Bob Hope was enjoyable enough, but the spontaneous wit of Bob
Hope made it the most entertaining game I have ever played!

I also met some of the famous stars at dinner parties, a
particularly memorable one being at the house of the British
Consul General. Among the guests were Mr. and Mrs. Ronald
Colman, Joan Fontaine and her husband, and a very tall woman
from New Zealand who struck me as quite a personality. But the
name, Beryl Markham, meant nothing to me. I was particularly
thrilled to meet Joan Fontaine who, along with Greta Garbo and
Norma Shearer, were my favourites on the screen. During the
course of our conversation after dinner Joan Fontaine asked me if
I had met the New Zealander. I said I had but we had not talked.
'You must meet her,' she told me. 'You were a pilot in the war and
she is also a pilot.' And she took me over to her saying, 'She is very
modest and will not talk about herself, but you make her. You
will be fascinated.' So I did, and although she was most reluctant,

on my pressing her, she told me the story of her flight across
the Atlantic from Abingdon, near Oxford, to Newfoundland in
a small, single-engine plane. She flew solo and non-stop, in 22
hours and 25 minutes! I asked her how she was able to keep
awake for such a long time and she explained that for most of
the time the weather was bad with low clouds and rain, she was
therefore forced to fly very low and there was never a moment
when she could relax, so she never felt sleepy. She had coffee
with her and a few sandwiches but she could not carry much as
she had to take on such a heavy load of petrol. She sipped coffee
from time to time and had a bite of sandwich to keep going. I
was amazed at the fantastic story of her feat, which seemed to
be more ground breaking than Lindbergh's famous flight across
the Atlantic in the Spirit of St. Louis.* Yet her extraordinary feat,
achieved just a few years earlier, had been forgotten and I felt
guilty that the name Beryl Markham had meant nothing to me.

Aldous Huxley, whom I had known at Balliol, had settled
down in Hollywood. He had been commissioned by MGM to
write the script for *Pride and Prejudice* which was then being
filmed. I had lunch with him at the studios and he told me that
he was having some difficulty about the final scene and had not
yet made up his mind about how it should be. Aldous Huxley
and Jane Austen, it could only happen in Hollywood! That night
at dinner I met Greer Garson, the leading lady in the film and
told her about my lunch with Aldous Huxley and the problem
he was facing. She gave me her famous smile, saying, 'Please
tell him not to worry! We finished the last scene today!' When
I returned home my daughter, Harji, listened, fascinated, to the
tales of my Hollywood odyssey!

* Charles Augustus Lindbergh (1902–74) was the American aviator, author,
inventor and explorer. In 1927, Lindbergh emerged from virtual obscurity to
almost instantaneous world fame as the result of his Orteig Prize-winning solo
non-stop flight from Roosevelt Field on Long Island to Le Bourget Field in Paris
in the single-seat, single-engine monoplane Spirit of St. Louis.

CHAPTER 31

During my tenure in the States I was a member of the Indian delegation in a number of international conferences. There were two of particular interest: the Food and Agriculture Conference in 1942, and the United Nations Relief and Rehabilitation Administration Conference (UNRRA) in 1943.

The first of these, held in Hot Springs, Virginia, was called by the American President, Franklin D. Roosevelt, who, with his tremendous vision, realized that the main cause for the Great Depression of 1929 was the fall in world prices of food and agricultural products which drastically reduced the incomes of primary producers. This triggered off the cycle of falling demands which in turn led to trading restrictions all over the world.

The main aim of the Hot Springs Conference was to ensure a price floor for food and agricultural products in the future so as to guarantee a minimum to the producers. The tendency in the more advanced countries until then was only to ensure that manufacturers got the raw materials they required at the lowest possible prices entirely ignoring the interests and the buying power of the primary producers. While the conference failed to achieve all that it set out to do, it did succeed in highlighting the fact that primary producers and manufacturers shared a common interest in ensuring that the former could maintain and expand their purchasing power, which, in turn would help to maintain world demand for manufactured goods. It was what we now call a trend setter.

The conference was unique in one respect. All the delegates

were housed in one hotel and the schedule was arranged in such a way as to allow them to relax and get to know each other socially. There were arrangements for tennis, golf and riding while every evening we had a concert or dancing. The result was to create a warm, friendly atmosphere among the various national delegations, a camaraderie which had been the President's explicit intention. Many prominent and influential persons participated in the conference including Dean Acheson, later American Secretary of State Lester Pearson, who became Prime Minister of Canada and a leading international statesman, along with a number of ambassadors heading their countries' delegations. Among them was the Norwegian Ambassador in Washington, Mr. Morgenstern. We got to know each other quite well. He had two attractive female secretaries, and we often made a group together in the evenings with my old friend, Andy Brennan, from the South African delegation and Scotty Campbell from the U.S. delegation. One evening I told Mr. Morgenstern, 'Mr. Ambassador, your secretaries are really beautiful, I have a very good looking son who we think is a really good specimen of what India can produce, just as your girls are of Norway. Wouldn't it be wonderful if they met and my son fell in love and got married? Just think of the children they would have!' The Ambassador responded enthusiastically, 'Excellent idea! You send your son to me and I will see what can be arranged!' We all had a good laugh when I told him that my son was only eight years old and we would have to wait a while! Little did I know then that our son, Harmala, would marry a blonde, but from France, not Norway.

The conference aroused a lot of interest in the media and *Fortune*, the major business journal of the country, had a big write-up on Hot Springs. To our amusement the article also contained a wonderful cartoon of me, a caricature of a many-armed Indian deity holding a tennis racquet in one arm. Turbans and beards make great material for cartoonists!

The second meeting, the UNRRA Conference, held in Atlantic City in 1943, was a very different story. By then the Government in New Delhi had appointed an Agent General in Washington to work under the British Ambassador and deal with matters regarding India. It was a somewhat anomalous position since as India was a colony it had no diplomatic representation. But he was the official Indian representative in Washington and the Trade Commissioner was, therefore, under his jurisdiction. The Agent General was Sir Girja Shankar Bajpai, a brilliant, I.C.S. officer, with a reputation of taking his position very seriously.

1943 was the year of the great Bengal Famine when millions of people lost their lives. The UNRRA Conference was just the organization that could have come to India's rescue. However, as it turned out India received no help. The two member Indian delegation consisted of Sir Girija as the delegate, and me as the alternate. When the conference opened, everyone there who knew about the terrible conditions of the famine with thousands dying on the streets of Calcutta itself, wanted to help India by sending supplies immediately to meet the crisis. However, the official stand of Winston Churchill's British Government, represented at the conference by Britain's Food Minister, G. Llewellyn Davies, was that there was in fact no famine, and that the Indian National Congress had only created this fiction to defame the British administration in India as part of their effort to make the British quit India. Therefore, the British declared that India needed no help.

In 1942 the political situation in India had taken a violent turn with the Congress Quit India resolution leading to serious disturbances, and with the New Delhi government putting all the Congress leaders, including Mahatma Gandhi and Pandit Nehru, in jail. Consequently, Indo-British relations were at a very low point which may have been responsible for Britain's callous, criminal, foolish and short-sighted position.

To my horror, I found Bajpai, who was closeted with Llewellyn most of the time, ready and willing to play the British game. He confirmed the British version of conditions in India to the delegates of other countries during private conversations. Several of them whom I knew well, including the Commonwealth delegates who were waiting for India to make an appeal for help, came to me greatly perplexed as they were given a completely different picture from the press and by me. So, while the delegations were anxious and ready to give assistance, they could do nothing, because the Indian delegate, supporting Great Britain's stand, told the members of the Conference that no help was required.

My arguments with Bajpai were of no use. Officially I was helpless. Being the alternate delegate, I could speak at the Conference only if Bajpai was absent, which he made sure he never was. I was furious and told him plainly, in private, that by hiding the truth he was responsible in a way for the death of millions of our people whose lives could be saved with help from the Conference.

When Bajpai sent off a telegram to New Delhi stating that there was no hope of getting any help from the Conference, I told him brusquely that not only was he lying to the delegations by saying that there was no famine taking place in Calcutta but he was misrepresenting the situation at the Conference to our Government in New Delhi and misleading them by stating that there was no help coming, when in actual fact all delegations, with the exception of the British, were eager to help. He just shrugged his shoulders and told me I was too inexperienced to understand. I, in turn, said that I understood perfectly and that I would not be a party to his deceit, and I left the Conference early to return to New York.

The late K.C. Mahindra, who later established Mahindra and Mahindra, and was then Head of the India's Supply Mission in Washington, fully shared my anger and indignation, as did

Bajpai's own Military Adviser, Major Altaf Qadir. But we were all helpless.* J.J.Singh, then President of the India League of America, came to Atlantic City and held a press conference there exposing Bajpai's duplicity but even this had no effect. When Bajpai asked me to write the official report on the Conference, I could not hide my disgust and told him to do his own dirty work.

Of course, he was furious and I heard later that he had reported me to Lord Halifax, the British Ambassador in Washington. He, in turn, had written to the Viceroy, Lord Wavell, in New Delhi asking for my recall. In fact, within a few weeks following the Conference, I received orders recalling me to India in the middle of the Second World War, despite the fact that I had previously been told that I was to stay in the States. My recall involved an extremely hazardous journey by sea for my family and me, exposed as we were for six long weeks to submarine and aerial attack.

In all fairness to Bajpai, I must admit that his intellectual ability and clarity of thought and expression were remarkable. Many years later, as Secretary General of the Ministry of External Affairs, I found him brilliant at our Ambassadors' meetings with Pandit Nehru in Europe. Pandit Nehru, recognizing his intellectual qualities had appointed him to the post. The story went that when someone remonstrated with Panditji pointing out Bajpai's reputation, Nehru remarked that he had always served his masters well, at one time the British and now India. Nehru said, 'He will serve us!'

A conference held by the Institute of Pacific Relations (IPR) in Cleveland, Ohio in December 1941 was as dramatic as the

---

* H.S. Malik: He was the brother of Manzoor Qadir, Pakistan's distinguished Foreign Secretary. He later became General in the Pakistan Army after Partition.

UNRRA Conference. The IPR, then in the hands of its able, energetic Secretary General, Edward Carter, used to arrange periodic conferences to which I was invited. I found them interesting because of the erudite participants. Amongst them was Dr. Jessup, subsequently elected as Judge to the International Court at The Hague. At the Cleveland Conference the subject to be discussed was the prospect of Japan entering World War Two. It was a two-day meeting and the participants were men and women from varied fields, all with special knowledge of Japan. Among those who spoke were experts from the State Department, the Army, Navy and Air Force, and well known journalists, senators, congressmen and diplomats. On the opening day, December 6th, we discussed various items on the agenda, and the experts all agreed on one thing: Japan would never come into the war and face the combined forces of the Allies and the United States.

The main argument put forward supporting this view, particularly by the representatives of the armed forces, ran something like this: The naval forces were bound to play a very important role in such a war and while Japan has a good navy, in these times a navy can operate only if it has an efficient Air Force to work with it; the Japanese Air Force is no good because the Japanese pilots all have poor eyesight and are, therefore, ineffective. This was the argument put forward seriously by experts, one of whom I recall being Hugh Bias, a journalist for *The New York Times* known to be an expert on Japan.

On the following day, 7th December, the meeting in the forenoon was to be followed by lunch with the final session of the Conference scheduled for the afternoon. At the morning session the views expressed the day before were repeated and sustained. Then we adjourned for lunch. While we were at the table, the Chairman was handed a message. After reading it, he got up and announced somberly, 'Ladies and gentlemen, I have just been informed that the Japanese have bombed Pearl

Harbour. We are now at war with Japan.' There was total shock
and consternation. It was true, however, and the conference
ended abruptly.

   Harji told us later that the evening of Pearl Harbour, on 7th
December, Vincent Sheehan, the famous author and foreign
correspondent, who was later to write the extraordinary book
on Mahatma Gandhi, *Lead Kindly Light*, was scheduled to speak
at her College, Bryn Mawr. He came straight from Washington
where he had been summoned and was over two hours late.
Everyone, already agitated by the war situation, became even
more worked up waiting for him. When he finally addressed
the students he told them that most of the U.S. Navy had been
destroyed at Pearl Harbour and that the West Coast of the United
States was in danger of bombardment! He caused near panic,
and with his dramatic dash from Washington, his talk carried a
feel of authenticity. His words were immediately played down
by the college staff, but in fact he had told the truth, which of
course the American Government would not divulge for many
months, even years. The story that unofficially went around
amongst Bryn Mawr students was that Sheehan, who enjoyed
his drinks, had had one too many!

CHAPTER 32

My routine work as Trade Commissioner continued during the six years we were in the States. In Washington Lord Lothian succeeded Lindsay as British Ambassador and I got to know and like him. Charming and unassuming, he was a true liberal at heart and much as he loathed the Nazis, he was afraid that they would win the war because they were so totally disciplined and dedicated to their National Socialism while the people of the great democracies were somewhat complacent. Sadly, he died before he could see the total defeat of Hitler and see his fears unfounded. I went to Washington for his funeral and was deeply disappointed at the formality of the ceremony, all perfectly arranged and dignified, but totally lacking in soul. In the church, I got the strange feeling that in spite of the service and the tributes that were being paid to him there seemed to be the absence of real grief when looking at his body in its pathetic little wooden casket. And yet grief there was for this man was genuinely liked and respected by many. Maybe I got this impression because the congregation was made up of officials and dignitaries of state, diplomats, and generally people from well-to-do backgrounds who are usually not prone to show their emotions. It was also certainly due to the absence of any close relatives as Lord Lothian's sisters were in England.

Lord Lothian was succeeded by Lord Halifax who I had known as Lord Irwin, Viceroy of India, in the 1920s. He was very different from his predecessor. A man of fine character, deeply religious and sincere, as Viceroy he had been very reserved, almost shy around people. However, there are few people in the world who adapt themselves to changing conditions as readily as the British do, and everyone who had known Lord Halifax as Lord Irwin in India, was amazed at the way in which his whole mannerism changed when he came as Ambassador to Washington. This naturally retiring, reserved member of the British aristocracy transformed himself into a hearty back-slapping extrovert, almost like an American politician.

We had known each other in Delhi and when I called on him in Washington he was very friendly. I used to keep a diary at the time in which I used to make entries sporadically. It reads: *Met Lord Halifax, the new British Ambassador in Washington last month. He asked me to lunch; others present were Haggard, the British Consul General in New York, Arthur Sulzberger, the owner of the* New York Times, *Childs, the Press Chief at the Embassy and an American General whose name I did not catch and found him quite impersonal! Halifax in a reminiscent mood talked about Baldwin and Chamberlain. He said, 'In 1936 I tried to persuade Baldwin to ask for 300 million pounds sterling for rearmament and Baldwin said, "The House will certainly shout me down if I do and the country will turn us out. That in itself is not important, but if we go, Labour will form the Government and Labour is even more pacific than we are and will do less."' Halifax, who had an engaging way of detaching himself from what he was participating in, and observing it as if from the outside, continues, 'Looking back at it now I can see it was a mistake. Baldwin should have told the House the truth. The Conservatives would have been turned out and Labour would have come in. Labour was peace minded it is true, but after Baldwin's exit, they would have been forced to follow the advice of the General Staff and army.' I tentatively interjected a remark in the form of a question, 'Did you realize at that time that Hitler was a menace?' Halifax looks at me with that frank searching, introspective look and replies, 'True, we did not. At that time we believed that he had no ambitions beyond liberating his own people in Czechoslovakia and Poland.'*

And then Halifax goes on about Chamberlain, 'When Chamberlain returned to London from Munich there was so much popular enthusiasm and cheering that it was difficult to say anything to him. During our drive from Croydon to London I did, however, tell him, 'There are two important things that you must attend to immediately. The first is that now at the height of your popularity your friends will press you to have a snap election so that you may be returned to Parliament with an even greater majority. You must resist this. And the second thing is you have a wonderful opportunity now to form a National Government. Ask Labour to join you.' But Chamberlain would not agree. Churchill would have done it, but Chamberlain could not. I often wonder what the outcome would have been if Chamberlain had won the cooperation of Labour at that time. It was an enjoyable and extremely interesting lunch.

Halifax had hardly changed at all since I had last seen him in India eleven years ago, in spite of the tremendous strain he must have been in under the last few years. The secret I am sure is poise and balance which come with faith and religion. Lothian had it too in full measure. A great support in times of difficulty.

When the United States entered the war, I was asked to stay on in my post until the end of the war. Our families at home were not happy with this situation and Prakash and I also worried about my mother and her parents but we had no choice. We were happy enough but those family concerns were always there. Meanwhile our children were growing up. Harji was at college, at Bryn Mawr, Pennsylvania, Mala was enjoying his school and our little daughter, Veena, was still our 'baby'.

In the United States, spared as it was from any invasion or bombing of its territory, the war's tragedy was confined to the heavy casualties suffered by many American families and, as always the terrible aftermath of those left maimed and crippled. Rationing came into force for petrol and many food items and although it was nothing compared with the deprivation suffered by Britain and Europe, it was something very new for the Americans, used as they were to a life of unrestricted plenty.

We were equally affected and it was my wife who bore the brunt of it because staff became almost impossible to find. The war industries demanded as much man and woman power as was available and Prakash faced tasks she had never handled before in the many times she was without any help. Being the youngest in the family and married so young she had, unlike most young Indian women of that time, never learned to cook, but, with a family to feed, she rose to the occasion without complaint, acting as chauffeur, governess, cook and housemaid at times! Petite as she was she even shovelled coal into our old fashioned furnace in the cellar!

To add to her difficulties I had to travel to Washington frequently during these times leaving her alone to cope. But she found time to drive in to New York and attend meetings of the India League of America which carried on its support for Indian independence throughout. I, of course, could not attend these meetings but she never let that stop her. Together we did attend one most impressive, meeting in Madison Square Gardens when Madame Chiang Kai Shek, very elegant and chic, complete with sparkling emerald earrings, addressed thousands of Americans appealing for support for China. These were the years when Chaing Kai Shek was battling against Mao and his followers and the United States was staunchly supporting the Nationalist Chinese.

We anxiously followed the news from India through those years and Prakash's sporadic diary notes in August 1942: *'They have arrested Gandhiji, Nehru and other Congress members'*—*'Riots have broken out at home and the British have started shooting'*— *'News from home tragic. They have started whipping people.'* But news was sparse and it was frustrating to be out of the country at such times.

CHAPTER 33

Soon after the UNRRA Conference I was recalled to India. In 1938, I was posted to New York for a three-year term but with the war breaking out the Government asked me to stay on for the duration, but then I was asked to return to India in the autumn of 1943, at the height of the war. It was two years after Pearl Harbour and the American entry into the war.

The only way my family and I could travel was by sea and under the prevailing conditions it was impossible to find passage. We had given up our house in Greenwich since we had no definite dates for departure, so we lived a nomadic existence for three months, first camping at the Apawamis Club and finally, for the last fortnight, in the Gotham Hotel in New York. These were difficult months, full of uncertainty as we tried to find passage on a ship. One day, we were told of a possibility, only to find a few days later that nothing was available. Harji, of course, was in college but with eight-year-old Mala and Veena who was just over five, it was a harrowing time for us. Finally, and only through the personal intervention of Mr. Hambro, who represented Norway in New York for shipping, was I able to secure passages for the four of us, on a Norwegian freighter, the *Aida Bakki*. The ship was part of a convoy of 100 vessels carrying war supplies and stores, and we finally sailed from New York in December 1943.

After agonizing over whether Harji should stay back for eighteen months and complete college or come back with us, we decided she should finish at Bryn Mawr where she was doing well, having been elected President of the Undergraduate

Association for her final year. We were somewhat comforted to know that our good American friends would take care of her and one of them, Vivien Kellems, became her guardian while she remained in the States. Had we had any inkling about the kind of journey we were undertaking, I don't think Harji would have stayed behind!

An alarming drama took place just before we were to leave! We were staying in the Gotham Hotel on Fifth Avenue, on the 5th floor. Prakash and I had gone out for some last-minute shopping for a couple of hours. When we returned to the hotel the manager met us in the lobby, looking very grave and concerned. He told us a terrible catastrophe had been avoided. While we were out a policeman on the Fifth Avenue beat outside the hotel spotted two children walking along the ledge outside our 5th floor suite! Showing great presence of mind, he entered the hotel, went up to our suite, climbed out of the window, walked out onto the ledge and very quietly brought the two youngsters back inside. Mala, quite unperturbed, explained to us that while playing with his toy bow and arrow, he had shot an arrow out of the window on to the ledge, so without giving it a thought, he climbed out of the window to retrieve the arrow, and Veena followed him on to the ledge! It was at this point that the cop saw them. What a merciful escape it was from what could so easily have ended in the most horrible tragedy.

This reminds me of two other incidents during our stay in America which could also easily have ended tragically. The first occurred in Greenwich on a Christmas Day during the coldest winter we had ever experienced. We were all enjoying our Christmas turkey at lunch when we heard a terrific explosion in the cellar. I rushed downstairs to find a great fire raging in the coal furnace where the boiler had burst due to the frozen pipes. A couple of buckets of water were always lying handy in the cellar for times of emergency and, without thinking I immediately threw a bucket of water into the fire. Fortunately for me, by sheer instinct, I stood to one side while doing so, for a huge tongue of flame shot out of the fire as the water hit it. Had I been standing facing the fire I would have been burned to a cinder!

The second incident, equally trivial in itself, could also have finished me off but for the grace of God. While walking from my office in the Rockefeller Centre in New York to Grand Central Station at the end of the day to catch my train to Greenwich, I heard a tremendous crash just behind me. A bucketful of building materials of some kind had fallen from the 20th floor from a scaffolding where some men were working. It missed my head literally by a split second. Had it fallen a moment earlier, I would have been completely crushed. How the strange vagaries of fate determine our lives!

The same good luck held for us through the six-week sea voyage to India, a journey which in peacetime would have taken three weeks, but which in wartime took twice as long. We arrived safely in Bombay in January 1944 but what a nightmare that six-week journey was! In a convoy of 100 ships our speed naturally had to be the speed of the slowest ship in the convoy, just four to five knots, and in the Mediterranean, then controlled by the Germans, with German subs all around, we were like sitting ducks!

At the start of our voyage we found the Norwegian Captain rather unfriendly. However, when he got to know us better he warmed towards us, and explained his initial coldness. He was strongly opposed to having women on his ship, he said, as on a previous occasion he had some missionary ladies as passengers. During an air attack, these ladies had panicked, making things very difficult for him and his crew by interfering with the gunners firing their anti-aircraft guns at the planes! So, when he found we were being forced on him by his Government, as the Norwegian Minister of Shipping had personally intervened to secure our passages, he was furious. He told me that Prakash and our five-year-old Veena were the only women in the entire convoy of 100 ships! I reassured him that my women would not behave like the missionary ladies. Later, he also told me, in strict confidence, that the other reason for his reluctance to take us was because his ship was loaded with ammunition. If we were hit by a torpedo or from the air, the whole ship would blow up with no question of taking to the lifeboats!

I kept this information to myself and told Prakash only after we sighted Bombay. I was not overly perturbed by what the Captain told me as I felt that if we were to go, it would be better to go that way than die slowly in open boats at sea at that time of the year.

In many ways the voyage turned out to be not too uncomfortable. We were lucky with the weather. It was pleasant after the first two or three days, and we gradually got used to the unusual conditions. Across the Atlantic there was a sense of security knowing that our convoy was protected by an aircraft carrier and four destroyers of the U.S Navy right up to our arrival at Gibraltar. There the U.S. Navy handed us over to Britain's Royal Navy which by that stage of the war was in difficult straits and could spare only one small sloop for the entire convoy. The protection was laughable, for in the Mediterranean we were actually attacked from the air, and while our convoy was crossing another, we saw two ships in that convoy sink after a submarine attack. For the two following days we were expecting submarine attacks at any time, and went to bed fully dressed, ready to evacuate ship, although, of course, I knew that if we were hit there was no question of evacuation! Prakash was not only the picture of calmness herself during these days but made a game of the whole situation with the children, so they were not at all frightened. She told Veena that even her doll must keep her suitcase ready. When I finally told my wife about the ship's cargo she was quite angry with me for not having told her earlier.

There were some things about this memorable voyage we would never forget—the beautiful moonlit nights when we came out on deck, with not a ripple on the ocean, not a light anywhere because of the strict blackout, the sky full of stars, extra brilliant in the pitch darkness. Our ship sailed so slowly that at times we seemed not to be moving at all, and yet we were conscious of the other ships all around us, the destroyers moving up and down on the flanks of the convoy. We would lean over the rails gazing at the water, watching for every little sign of life on the surface of the ocean which was so calm it might have been oil. A ripple, the slightest break in the smooth surface and we wondered if it could be the periscope of a submarine, or merely a porpoise or perhaps a flying fish. The combination of the calm, the blackness of night, the near complete silence—for our turbines were turning over so slowly you could hardly hear them—was eerie, and yet, extraordinarily beautiful.

The efficiency and calm discipline of our Norwegian crew was impressive. There was no clicking of heels, no unnecessary saluting, yet one constantly sensed how the crew respected the officers. Equally impressive was seeing how individual members of the crew carried out their respective duties, quietly and coolly under such dangerous conditions.

There was, of course, the monotony of a long voyage but this was eased by the inevitable tension of wartime conditions and the constant sense of danger. During the day we read or played with the children, and in the evenings I played *vingt et un*, commonly known as pontoon, with the three other passengers on board and one or two of the officers.

What a tremendous relief it was to reach Port Said! From there for the first time we were able to send a cable to Harji in the States to tell her that we were safe. She had, of course, been terribly worried about our fate as she had read in the papers about a convoy being attacked in the Mediterranean just about the time we might have been there, as indeed it proved to be true.

In Port Said our convoy broke up and the *Aida Bakki* could go on her own through the Suez Canal on to the Red Sea and the Arabian Sea. She was a fast ship and we had no escort, but the Captain, who had felt very frustrated at the slow speed of the convoy making his ship an easy target for a submarine, explained that he was happier without an escort as by constantly zigzagging instead of keeping on a straight course, he felt he had a good chance of getting away from any Japanese submarines that may have been lurking around waiting for us.

These tactics worked and we finally arrived in Bombay after spending a night in Aden to find that we had to anchor outside the harbour, fully exposed to Japanese submarine attack, instead of being allowed inside where we would have been fully protected. It turned out that the British Harbour Master had left office early before we arrived, to have an early dinner so nothing could be done! Our Captain was livid.

Our relief at reaching Bombay safely was beyond words and we were full of gratitude to Satguruji as we sincerely felt that it was thanks to the prayers of loved ones that we had come through this ordeal unscathed.

Throughout the six weeks at sea we were made to observe a complete blackout. So we could not send any messages of any sort to anyone, apart from the brief cable to Harji from Port Said. No one, therefore, knew of our arrival in Bombay, so naturally there was no one to meet us. Soon after landing I telephoned my service colleague, Sir Benegal Rama Rau, who was then Governor of the Reserve Bank, and informed him that we had just arrived in Bombay. He very kindly came over to the docks himself and took us back to his house where we all stayed for several days as his guests.

Rama Rau told me he knew about my being recalled and said that there was talk that I was in for a real dressing down from the Viceroy, Lord Wavell. I told him the entire story about my fight with Bajpai at the UNRRA Conference and assured him that I had done only what I felt was my duty, and if the Viceroy condemned me for it, I would not tolerate the reprimand and would resign from the Service rather than accept censure. Lady Rama Rau, Dhan, who was an active social worker, also participated in the conversation which naturally turned to the nationalist struggle and to the British sensitivity on the subject of American public opinion.

Our little daughter, Veena, who, of course, had never been to India, was extremely intrigued at everything she saw in Bombay, particularly the crowds in the streets, and could not get over seeing so many people walking the streets barefoot. We were most amused when she asked us if my brother T.S. who was coming to Bombay to meet us would also be barefooted. We had a tearful reunion as it had been five years since we had last seen each other. And, together we left for Delhi. On our way to the capital we stopped over for a few days in Jaipur where my brother and his family were living. He had been asked to come to Jaipur by Sir Mirza Ismail, the Prime Minister of Jaipur State, to take over as Development Minister and help him carry out some of his schemes for improving and beautifying Jaipur city. This was our first visit to Jaipur and we did a lot of sightseeing, admiring the old fort and its wonderful museum, and the famous Amber Palace which I have always found to be one of the most picturesque and interesting old palaces in what was then Rajputana. For someone who had always lived in British India the colourful turbans of the often startlingly handsome men with their beards and curling moustaches, and the beautiful swirling skirts of the women in fantastic bright colours were something from another world.

CHAPTER 34

Very soon after we arrived in Delhi I was summoned by the Viceroy, Lord Wavell. I went prepared for the worst, ready to hand in my resignation. But when I met him, I was pleasantly surprised to find him most friendly. He never mentioned a word about my work in America or my recall. Instead, he told me that he wanted me to go to the princely state of Patiala as Prime Minister! I was completely taken aback at this unexpected development. He explained that the young Maharajah, Yadavindra Singh, was a very promising ruler and Wavell felt that I could be of real service in helping him modernize and improve conditions in the state. In fact, the Maharajah had asked for my services. I told the Viceroy that I did not know the Maharajah at all, but had known his father, Maharajah Bhupendra Singh in the old days, and from what I knew of conditions in the state, I didn't think that I was the right person for the job. Wavell, however, refused to take no for an answer, and we finally agreed that I would give him my final word only after I had met the Maharajah himself.

When we met we had an extremely frank and comprehensive talk and I told him of my misgivings as I had no experience of the Indian states. I found him very friendly and most charming. He assured me that I need have no apprehensions as he was determined to set up an efficient administration and modernize the state in every way, and he felt I would be able to help him in carrying out his plans. Very graciously he referred to my ability and experience, making it very clear that he wanted my services. Finally I said to him, 'Your Highness, it would be a pleasure and privilege to come and help in all that you want to do for your people, but I will come only if I have your complete confidence and trust, in spite of the intrigue that I am told is the normal condition in the Indian states. In other words, although I will be serving you, you will have to treat me more like an elder brother, because of my experience and age, than as merely your Prime Minister.' He assured me that this was exactly what he intended to do and I should have no doubts on that score. So it was agreed that my services would be lent by the Government of India to Patiala for three years.

The relationship between the Government of India and the Princely States, which did not form part of British India, was unique, as was the position of these states in the Indian sub-continent. India was divided into two entities, British India— with its different provinces, administered by the Viceroy and Governor General, and his Council, with Governors and Lieutenant Governors, under the control of the Viceroy—and Princely India, consisting of over 600 states, ruled by Princes, each of whom had an individual treaty with the King Emperor for all matters dealing with these states.

The states varied greatly in size and importance. There were large states, such as Hyderabad, Mysore, Baroda and others, large in area and population with correspondingly important revenue. There were others, smaller even than tehsils.* To give an idea of the size and revenue of such tiny states, Dujana State which adjoined Rohtak District, where I was Deputy Commissioner, was ruled by an immature fourteen-year old boy. The revenues were very small but the state had its own army, consisting of a Commander-in-Chief in a resplendent uniform, and three Privates. Similarly, there was a State Police Force comprising an Inspector General of Police, a Superintendent of Police and a total force of three or

* A tehsil was a small administrative unit in a district in British India.

four constables. It was a farcical situation but still the Nawab of
Dujana was a ruling Prince! In between the very large states and
the tiny ones, states such as Gwalior, Kashmir, Jaipur, Patiala and
many others had large populations, area and revenue.

Conditions varied greatly in these states. Hyderabad, Mysore
and Baroda were well administered. It was claimed that in
matters such as education, medicine and urban amenities, the
people there were better off than in British India. In these areas
a fair portion of the state revenue was spent on public works of
various kinds. But there were many other states, backward and
almost totally feudal, where the ruling Princes were notorious for
their autocratic, irresponsible and selfish behaviour. Everything
depended on the whims of the ruler.

In Princely India, the ruler had absolute power within his
state. He could appropriate for himself the major portion of
the state's revenue, leaving little for financing services for his
subjects, behave most unjustly, sometimes with extreme cruelty,
towards them. His people had no means of redress. If they rose
in revolt against the ruler's malpractices, the revolt would be
crushed, either by the ruler's own armed forces, or under the
terms of his treaty with the British Crown. British India's armed
forces were ordered to go to the ruler's rescue by the Viceroy. A
bad ruler, therefore, often got away with impunity for all kinds
of misbehaviour towards his own people.

In striking contrast, if the ruler did anything that questioned
his loyalty to the King Emperor or the British authority in any
way, the Viceroy would immediately intervene. This was the
anomaly of Princely India. So no action was taken against the
thoroughly dissolute and depraved Maharajah of Alwar who
was responsible for acts of great cruelty and injustice towards his
subjects. The Viceroy asked no questions. However, the moment
any ruler was caught in an intrigue against the British Raj, he was
arbitrarily deposed, banished from the state and his successor
quickly placed on the gaddi by the British Government.

The general perception in India was that the Princely States had been created deliberately by the British as part of their colonial policy of 'divide and rule' so that these privileged rulers would act as a buffer against Indian aspirations for independence, since the British could always count on the Princes to oppose the Indian national movement and remain loyal to the British. It was also a practical solution to help the British govern a vast country like India. And so they left the governance of a large part of the country in the hands of the Princes.

One of the amusing, somewhat pathetic characteristics of the Princes was that while they put on a great show of arrogance and pride with their own subjects as well as with Indians in British India, whom they regarded as commoners, when it came to dealing with the British they were incorrigible sycophants! I was quite shocked when I heard in New Delhi that one of the most distinguished and important princes had literally begged the Military Secretary to the Viceroy to be allowed to stand next to the Viceroy when the latter took a salute at a ceremonial parade! And who can ever forget the humiliation we felt at seeing the young princes of one of the larger states sitting at the feet of Queen Victoria in official photographs of the Imperial Dewan in Delhi! The irony of it was that the parents of the boys actually looked on this as a great honour. Indeed, even the rulers of major states sought eagerly to be ADCs to the King Emperor!

When many of the senior people I knew, men like Sir Jogendra Singh and Raja Daljit Singh, who had had personal experience of serving in the Indian states, heard I was going to Patiala, they warned me that I would not last there more than six months. I told them that I had promised the Maharajah to serve him and the state for three years and, come what may, I would serve my term.

And I did! It was hard going at times—an extraordinary experience in many ways. I have never worked so hard, for after office hours I invariably had to see people at home till late hours, nor has Prakash ever had greater anxiety about my welfare. The last few months of those three years were very trying indeed but I stuck it out till the end. On the whole, it was an interesting and challenging, and in many ways a rewarding experience.

For more than two years the Maharajah kept his word. We worked together as a team and were able to get some good things done. Towards the end, however, he was misled by certain vested interests in the state, and by his own inability to discriminate between those who were really loyal to his interests and those, the inevitable sycophants, who flattered him for their own personal gain. This was a failing common to most Indian princes, due partly to their upbringing surrounded by the usual atmosphere of flattery and intrigue. I had been warned specifically about this, and ultimately it created difficulties between the Maharajah and I. So when the time came for me to leave it was a relief to us both!

I found Maharajah Yadavindra Singh a complicated personality. Tall—he was six feet four and appeared even taller in his Patiala-style turban—a striking figure, extremely handsome, with great presence and natural charm, a fine athlete and an outstanding sportsman. With all the social graces, he was extremely fond of music, loved to dance, was a good singer and could play the guitar and the piano. Highly intelligent, he had a good mind so that whatever he turned his mind to, he could do well. Intensely interested in botany and horticulture, he created gardens and farms which won great praise. And, on mountaineering treks he collected plants to add to his collection. He also had a talent for painting.

When I got to know him I felt that with all these assets, as the premier Sikh ruler he was the natural leader of the Sikh community destined to play a decisive role in the critical days that lay ahead of us with India changing over from a colony to an independent sovereign state. I put my faith in him and worked hard alongside him, giving him all my loyalty in the belief that this was the best service that I could render to my country and community. Unfortunately, this could not be achieved because of the mutual jealousies and selfishness of the Sikh leaders and the tragic inability of every one of them to accept any one leader. I tried to explain to them that in the coming times great changes lay ahead which would vitally affect the future of all the various communities, particularly the minority communities. The future of the Sikhs, the part they were to play in the upcoming negotiations and their stance, required serious study. I urged them to form a small study group of competent people who would apply their minds to the problems that were likely to arise, so that our leaders would have the necessary material at their disposal to help them during the negotiations.

I spoke about this idea to various leaders, including Master Tara Singh, Sardar Baldev Singh—who was to be the first Minister for Defence in independent India—and the three Sikh Maharajahs, Patiala, Nabha and Faridkot. Individually they all thought it an excellent idea, however, they would not get together to put it into action.

In Patiala the conditions in which I worked were a totally new experience. In many ways I found them both stimulating and even exciting. From the first contact I had with people of Patiala, particularly the Sardars, some of whom I had known in the past, I saw what I would have to contend with. Factions and 'parties' were the norm in Patiala life and the Sardars soon began dropping broad hints to me to form a Prime Minister's Party. I was told that all past prime ministers had done this and had used the considerable secret funds, placed at their disposal, to strengthen their position in the state. I put an immediate stop to these attempts by letting it be known that I was not asking for such secret funds, that for me there was only one party in the state, and that was the party that worked loyally for the ruler and the good of the people of the state. This, naturally, did not find favour with the old guard.

My relations with the Maharajah were excellent. He was always accessible to me, and apart from the hours set aside for routine work when I submitted various matters to him for his approval, we met frequently, either on the tennis court, cricket field or at parties, mostly at Motibagh Palace, and at other social occasions when I had plenty of opportunity to get to know him. On one of these occasions, soon after I arrived in Patiala, the Maharajah remarked, 'One thing you will find here, all our people eat well and dress well.' I replied, 'Yes, Your Highness, I have noticed this and I wonder how they do it, certainly not on the salaries that they are paid because these are very low.' 'You mean they make money in other ways? Corruption?' he asked, to which I replied that I feared it was so. He then asked me to do all I could to stop corruption, as he was most anxious to have a good, honest administration. I told him that I would do my best but that nothing could be done until the salary scales were revised and salaries raised. He immediately authorized me to look into the matter with the Finance Minister and put up proposals. At daily meetings with the Finance Minister we worked out new salary scales that would not upset the economies of the state in anyway, and yet would provide more reasonable incomes for all grades of state servants from the highest to the lowest paid whose salary was only Rs. 8 per month! Only the Prime Minister's salary, set by the Government of India, on service scale remained unchanged! The Maharajah approved the proposals and the new scales came into operation immediately, an important reform was achieved in a couple of months which would have taken at least two years in British India.

We were anxious to set up industries in the state and I spread the word to industrialists that we would provide facilities for this purpose. Before long Seth R.K. Dalmia approached me. At that time he was one of the leading Indian industrialists. He said that he wanted to invest ten crores of rupees, in 1945 that was a very large sum of money, to establish industries in the state. I told him that he would be most welcome and we would help him in every way we could in matters such as acquisition of land. However, when we started to discuss the proposal, he explained that he would come in only on one condition: that he should be at liberty to deal with labour without, as he put it, 'any troublesome laws' regarding labour. I told him that he would have to comply with the existing laws as they applied to all industries in the state. He explained to me that industry in India could only flourish on the lowest possible wage level and he didn't want to have to deal with any silly labour laws! I told him that I had just returned from America after spending six years there and I had seen what Ford, for example, had been able to do by raising prevailing low wages. I emphasized that I was convinced that one of the principal obstacles to Indian industrialization was the poor purchasing power of the people which made any great increase in demand impossible, and that the crying need in India was for a higher wage level. He said nothing but looked at me as if I didn't know what I was talking about. The negotiations ended abruptly and I had my first taste of the mentality of Marwari businessmen.

CHAPTER 35

During summer in those Raj days the entire Government of India, and some provincial governments, moved up to the hills to escape the heat. And so the bureaucracy and their fortunate office staff escaped the misery of summer in the plains. Democratic India could not afford this imperialistic extravagance and after 1947 the bureaucracy had to suffer the sweltering temperatures along with lesser mortals, although, very soon, many a Minister and Members of Parliament found that urgent work called them overseas in the summer!

In 1944, however, the Government of India still migrated from New Delhi to Simla in hot weather and, in Patiala, the Maharajah and his staff moved up to Chail, the small hill station in Patiala State. A charming little town set in a beautiful forest, Chail was situated across a broad valley from Simla and on a clear night the twinkling lights of Simla were clearly visible. Accommodation in Chail was limited so I, as Prime Minister, moved to Simla where the state owned some houses. Other Ministers would come up from Patiala for cabinet meetings in Chail, or to Simla to meet me. Simla and Chail were connected by a fairly good road, so I went to Chail frequently while the Maharajah who had a palatial house in Simla also visited Simla often to meet the Viceroy or for social functions.

Between 1944 and 1945 many American service people were still stationed in Delhi. We got to know some of them well through Scottie Campbell, our friend from Hot Springs, who had been transferred to Delhi. We became good friends with the hospitable George Merrel, American representative in Delhi and his sister, Ruth. George loved entertaining at his pleasant home on Tughlaq Road in Lutyens Delhi. It was built around an open courtyard—a perfect venue for many delightful informal parties. These American friends frequently came up to Chail where they livened up the otherwise rather quiet, limited Patiala social life.

The Maharajah enjoyed entertaining at his charming cottage at Dochi, a few miles down the mountain road from Chail, where with his considerable skill as a horticulturist and landscaper, he had created a beautiful terraced garden below the cottage, overlooking a valley, facing the high Himalayas. It was a fairytale setting for an evening party with the usual excellent food and drinks. Music was played by the state band conducted by the rotund Austrian Max Geiger, always beaming like a cherub, as the sound of the waltz floated across the garden. I wrote to Harji in America describing one of these evenings. It was almost magical, with the sun slowly setting across the valley behind the mountains as the moon rose in the sky behind us, with music playing in the background.

Our American friends also came to Patiala when the Maharajah invited them to attend what was to be his last Durbar, the traditional annual ceremony on his birthday when he received the tribute from his subjects. It was a colourful, truly mediaeval show, with the Maharajah dressed in his achkan of rich magnificently bejewelled brocade, wearing some of the fabled Patiala jewels. A lesser man might have looked somewhat ridiculous amongst all this pomp and splendour of bygone days, but with his looks, his personality and his bearing he carried it all off magnificently. When Harji came back from America in 1946, she witnessed this Durbar and when she saw the Maharajah, in full regalia, walking in procession, followed by his Ministers and ADCs, she most irreverently let out a loud wolf whistle, American style, before he actually entered the Durbar! The evening before she had jokingly warned him she would do this. It says much for the Maharajah's sense of humour and sporting spirit that he responded with a smile.

In Patiala and in Chail we met all the local notables, the Sardars of the state. In addition, there were the Maharajah's personal relations and his large number of half-brothers, for his father is said to have sired 55 children; a few from from his wives who were officially recognized as Maharanis, others from women who though married to him in some sort of ceremony were not given the status of Maharanis. But most of the women belonged to his harem and were referred to as his keeps. The children were graded according to the status of their mothers and the boys referred to respectively as Rajah, Kanwar and Kaka. This huge family imposed a very heavy responsibility—both financial and otherwise—on the Maharajah and later the Maharani, which he tried his best to fulfill. But there were many problems, and inevitably, much resentment and dissatisfaction, for all these offsprings of the late Maharajah considered themselves part of the Patiala royal family. There was a great deal of bitterness especially after the Princes' Privy Purses were abolished by the Government of India in 1971 and the Maharajah had to make drastic financial adjustments.

The half-brothers, closest to the Maharajah were Peter and Michael, both Rajahs, and there was Billy, a Kanwar. The English pet names were given by their English and Anglo-Indian governesses. The only one who has participated in public life since Independence is Rajah Bhalindra Singh (Peter) who involved himself in sports and served as President of the Indian Olympic Association for some years. The Maharajah had no real brothers, only one sister, Princess Honey, who married Rajah Surendar Singh of Nalagarh, a small state in the Punjab hills. Nalagarh, somewhat of a playboy before 1947, made a name for himself in agriculture in independent India, and became very knowledgeable in the subject, and was largely responsible for setting up the National Seed Farms. Unfortunately, he died young, very suddenly, putting an end to a promising career.

General Jogindar Singh, known as 'Jaggo', and Brigadier Jaswant Singh, nicknamed 'Jasso', veterans of the once famous Patiala polo team, were present regularly at the Maharajah's social evenings. They were interesting reminders of the fabulous past of the Maharajah's father, Maharajah Bhupendar Singh. It was said that these great polo players, all of whom led active lives until they died at a ripe old age, used to start their mornings with champagne or even brandy and liquors, continuing to drink the rest of the day! Normally such high living results in short lives but they played polo all day, sweating out the poison from their systems.

Particularly enjoyable in both Patiala and Chail were the cooking parties where all the food was cooked by the Maharajah and Maharani, assisted by some of their guests. Patiala's royal kitchens had a fabulous reputation and the Maharajah was an expert cook, a skill he had taught his young Maharani. The three-minute chicken, cooked by the Maharajah in exactly three minutes by the watch, was famous at these parties. Unbelievable, but true, and most succulent and delicious! Prakash learned the secret later but was made to swear never to divulge it.

Life in the state was an extraordinary mixture of the modern democratic processes, encouraged by the Maharajah in many matters, and the feudal, mediaeval ways which persisted in others, at times surfacing dramatically. But, on the whole, we developed a modern administration. It was not merely a façade in spite of some glaring anomalies. One particularly bad case fortunately came to my notice. While I was in Simla a lady from Patiala and her son asked to see me. I told my secretary to tell them that I could not see the lady as all the Patiala ladies from good families observed purdah, but I would see her son. The young man told me a story which I found hard to believe. He belonged to a well known Sardar family in the state and had married the daughter of a General in the Patiala State Forces, a famous polo player, known to be very friendly with both the late Maharajah and the present one. The marriage was not a success and after some time the bride returned to her own family who felt this was a disgrace. Being extremely influential, they initiated a false case against the young man, and he was convicted and sent to jail. His family appealed to the Patiala High Court which quashed the conviction, and he was freed. This occurred during Maharajah Yadavindra Singh's rule. The bride's father was furious and again, because of his influence persuaded the Maharajah to issue an executive order confiscating all his son-in-law's property and confining him to his village. The young man explained that he had escaped and come to me to ask me to intervene and have the orders against him revoked. I assured him that I would look into his case and that he should return to his village and await further orders.

I was shocked by this story, and when I immediately took steps to verify the facts, I found them all to be true. So I took up the case with the Maharajah and told him that I had refused to believe this story initially because I could not comprehend why the Maharaja, who had set up the High Court himself, would do anything to nullify the orders passed by that Court after a proper hearing in a criminal case. The Maharajah confirmed that what I had been told was absolutely true and that he had acted only to protect the honour of an old, loyal servant of his father's. I requested him not to flout the laws that were being administered in his own court. He at once realized the seriousness of the matter and we discussed what could be done. My advice was for him to cancel his previous order, but he said he could not do that. However, he authorized me to do so, and I immediately issued the necessary order. The young man was freed and his confiscated property restored.

Another striking instance of the hold which his late father, who had been a very dominating personality, exerted on the Maharajah even after his death came to my notice after I had been in Patiala for about a year. I learned that the residence in Patiala of the Maharani's father, Sardar Harchand Singh Jayjee, was in the possession of the state. The late Maharajah had confiscated it because Sardar Jayjee, one of the leading Patiala Sardars, had refused to comply with the Maharajah's orders whereby all the Sardars in the state were to tie up their beards as he did instead of allowing them to remain open and flowing. Sardar Jayjee, himself a man of very strong principles, felt, rightly, that the Maharajah had no right to order his subjects how to keep their beards, and he, who always kept his beard untied, refused to obey. To avoid being sent to prison he immediately fled the state and settled in Lahore, but all his property in Patiala State was confiscated and remained so even after Maharajah Yadavindra Singh had married Sardar Jayjee's daughter. In fact, Sardar Jayjee was unable even to have an audience with his son-in-law! The Maharjah was reluctant to cancel any order passed by his father even where his own father-in-law was concerned. However, I was able to persuade him in this case and the property was restored to the family. These instances were typical of the autocratic, feudal functioning of the states under the Raj.

CHAPTER 36

M aharajah Bhupindar Singh, who left his indelible mark on the State of Patiala was indeed a remarkable man. Charles Barry, my first Deputy Commissioner, once recounted an incident which illustrated the Maharajah's powerful personality. Barry was in charge of a sub-division adjacent to Patiala State. On one occasion the Maharajah was riding through a part of Barry's domain which, of course, was in British India. Barry met the Maharajah at the border and started riding alongside him. The Maharajah at once signalled to him to ride behind him. Barry told me, 'I knew that the Maharajah had no right to do this. I, as head of the sub-division, was the Representative of the King Emperor, and in my own territory I had every right to ride alongside the Maharajah. However, by sheer force of his personality he got away with it and I continued to ride *behind* him!'

The difference between the Maharajah and is father is graphically illustrated by an incident which occurred while we were in Patiala. It also demonstrates how subservient the Indian Princes were to the Raj. The Resident of Patiala, as the Representative of the Viceroy dealing with the Maharajah's relations with the British Government of India, presided when an investiture ceremony was held in the state to present the honours and decorations conferred on state subjects by the Viceroy, similar to the Honours List in British India. The first time I attended such a ceremony, I noticed that the Maharajah, the Head of the State, stood next to the Resident, like an aide, and handed him the decoration which the Resident then pinned on the recipient's breast or placed around his neck. Both Prakash and I found this to be disrespectful to the monarch. So I told the Maharajah that if he approved I would try and persuade the Resident to reverse the order in the future, so that the Resident would hand the decoration to the Maharajah to present to the recipient. The Maharajah agreed and I told Thompson, the Resident, whom I personally found most friendly and reasonable, that it would be much appreciated if in future he agreed to follow the procedure I proposed, as the people of Patiala would value their decorations more if their own ruler was presenting them. Thompson diplomatically saw the point and agreed. At the next investiture, the new procedure was followed and much appreciated. However, in my third year in Patiala I was abroad at the time of the ceremony, and to my disappointment, Prakash told me on my return, that during my absence they had reverted to the old procedure!

I was soon put to the test in Patiala when our police misused its authority by going into a village to extort money, beating up innocent villagers for this purpose. The incident was reported to me and I had the facts verified by a magisterial enquiry. I then recommended to the Maharajah that the police officer concerned, a Sub-Inspector, along with two head constables and some others be dismissed, and that the villagers, who were the victims, be given adequate compensation. Moreover, I added that the Inspector General of Police should personally visit the village, apologize on behalf of the police and inform the villagers of the disciplinary action taken. The Maharajah was taken aback for such official reaction was unprecedented in the state. However, he promised to speak about it to the I.G. of Police, Hamilton Harding who had been employed by the state on retiring from the Indian police before I came to Patiala.

The Maharajah informed me that Hamilton Harding would not agree to my proposal as he feared that such action would seriously affect the prestige of our whole administration and the maintenance of law and order in that part of the state. The Maharajah added that Hamilton Harding had told him that he would resign if I persisted in my recommendations. I told the Maharajah to let him resign. I was the one responsible for law and order in the state. Hamilton Harding was obligated to follow my orders. I was convinced that if action was taken as I proposed, the prestige of the Administration, far from suffering, would be enhanced as people would know that justice was done. I hinted that I would resign on this issue and that the Maharajah must choose between me and Hamilton Harding. The Maharajah then told Harding that the action proposed by the Prime Minister was to be followed. Harding did not resign and the law and order situation did not deteriorate. On the contrary, the whole incident enhanced people's faith in the administration.

The Maharajah seldom came into contact with ordinary villagers. The Sardars, many of them landlords with bad relations with their tenants, were able with the help of the local police and revenue officials who were often in their pay, to commit all sorts of excesses with impunity. They naturally did not want the Maharajah to come into direct contact with their villager tenants. I, however, felt that if the Maharajah visited villages and met his people, he would be very popular with them. This would have an excellent effect on villagers who felt that the Administration supported the landlords in their ill-treatment of the people.

The Maharajah was persuaded to hold a couple of durbars in the rural areas for the first time. These proved very successful as village headmen expressed their concerns directly, and the Maharajah talked to the people in simple Punjabi. He had the perfect personality for this kind of interaction. The direct contact made a great impression on the villagers who showed tremendous respect and devotion to their ruler. The Sardars, however, became alarmed and campaigned against me, accusing me of encouraging the villagers who they alleged were Communists and would rise in revolt with such encouragement. They even hinted that I was a Communist myself! Unfortunately, the Maharajah, vulnerable to such talk as I had been warned, was misled by such propaganda and the rural durbars came to an end.

Much of the area owned by the Sardars was cultivated by 'occupancy tenants'. They were peasant farmers who had been occupying the land for generations and felt they had ownership rights. Under the law they did enjoy special rights, as for example immunity from eviction. However, the powerful Sardars had evicted those who proved difficult, so there was great discontent in some areas which proved to be fertile ground for the Communists. I found violent incidents were frequent in these areas with the Sardars often unable to live on their estates. After consulting the Maharajah I proposed a compromise to the Sardars which would restore peace. But the reactionaries among these landowners opposed any such solution and ultimately as I had warned, the tenants successfully claimed all the lands.

The Patiala Sardars in their short-sightedness opposed setting up relief camps in the state for the refugees who fled the Muslim attacks in the Punjab districts of Cambellpur, Rawalpindi, Gujrat, Jhelum and others in the early months of 1947. There were terrible tales of the atrocities perpetrated against them. I strongly advised the Maharajah to intervene and warned him that if Patiala turned these refugees away our name in the Punjab and amongst the Sikhs would forever be disgraced. I reminded him that Guru Gobind Singh, whose personal arms were venerated in the Patiala Fort, had blessed the Patiala family with the words, 'Tera Gha Mera Se', 'Your House is My House' when the Guru, who sought shelter with them from the Mughals, had left Patiala. Wisely and generously the Maharajah set up the relief camps, run most efficiently by the Army.

Prakash enlisted the help of the Maharani and Patiala Sardarnis to help in the relief work, and we heard later that in Partition days the Maharani came totally out of purdah bringing the Sardarnis with the younger ones actually drivings jeeps to work!

CHAPTER 37

India was on the threshold of Independence and as Prime Minister of Patiala State I was inevitably drawn into the major question of the future position of the Princely States in new India. As the Vice Chancellor of the Chamber of Princes, the body of which all the Princes were members, the Maharajah of Patiala was, of course, deeply concerned about what action the Princes should take. The Chamber, however, was unable to play any important role in the eventual agreement that was reached because some of the biggest states like Hyderabad, Mysore, Kashmir and Travancore took no interest in the Chamber, thinking they could negotiate on their own. Other states among them Baroda, Gwalior, Patiala and Bikaner were not at all happy about the close relationship between the Muslim Nawab of Bhopal and Muhammad Ali Jinnah, head of the Muslim League who was demanding the creation of Pakistan, a separate country for Muslims. The Nawab's objective appeared to be to create a Princely India comprising all the Princely States spread throughout various parts of undivided India including what was visualized as Pakistan. This concept, which appeared to suit Jinnah, was quietly promoted in certain British circles.

Ultimately, the entire burden of negotiations between the Government of India and the Princes fell on a small committee consisting of the Maharajahs of Patiala, Baroda, Bikaner, Gwalior, the Jam Sahib of Navanagar and one or two others. As a result of several meetings between this group and Pandit Nehru, then Prime Minister, Home Minister Sardar Vallabhbhai Patel and Maulana Abul Kalam Azad an understanding was finally hammered in 1946.

Before the start of the discussions I called on Sardar Patel. I had not known him before but we had a very frank talk and I told him that I felt that the Congress was not making enough of an effort to win over the Princes, an effort which I thought was well worthwhile as it was vital that an understanding be reached. He asked for my opinion on what the Congress should do. I told him that to me two things seemed of major importance—one: an assurance to the Princes that the Congress would no longer create problems for them in their states through the Praja Mandals,* and two: a further reassurance regarding some form of dynastic succession. Sardar Patel said that the Congress was ready to give these assurances. I told him that in that case I would ask the Maharajah of Patiala to come and see him so that Sardar Patel could tell him so in person. To my surprise he refused to do so explaining that while he trusted me, he was not certain that the Maharajah would keep this information confidential and not share it with the Nawab of Bhopal. His reaction was typical of the mutual mistrust between the Princes and the Congress leaders. I assured him that the Maharajah's loyalty to India was beyond question and that the Sardar could trust him. He then agreed to a meeting with the Maharajah. This was my first meeting with Sardar Patel, and he struck me as a very strong character, very pragmatic and direct, but somewhat cold, unmoved by sentiment.

Soon after this in 1946 our small group was formed. We held a number of meetings among ourselves in which the Jam Sahib, Sir B.L. Mitter on behalf of the Maharajah of Baroda; Sardar K.M. Pannikar on behalf of Bikaner; Srinivasan, adviser to Gwalior,

* The Praja Mandals were the People's Parties that the Congress had established in many states as their contribution to the freedom struggle in order to establish democratic reforms.

and I on behalf of Patiala participated actively. Our first meeting with Sardar Patel and Maulana Azad was arranged followed by a succession of such meetings where various issues were frankly thrashed out. These were then followed by a conclusive meeting at which Pandit Nehru as Prime Minister was also present, and after further long discussions an understanding was finally reached. We all dined together as guests of the Maharajah of Bikaner to celebrate the settlement and everyone left satisfied that such a difficult issue had been resolved with good sense prevailing on all sides.

However, the next day the Maharajah of Gwalior sent a message to say that he still wanted clarification on one or two points. He explained his objections and suggested another meeting with the Prime Minister and his colleagues. The general feeling amongst us was that Gwalior's points were not important enough to warrant such a meeting and those, like Pannikar, who knew Pandit Nehru and his quick temper were extremely apprehensive about his reaction. They were, therefore, loath to approach him, but Gwalior insisted. Pannikar was asked to see Pandit Nehru and request this meeting. He refused to go alone, and it was decided that I should accompany him.

The next day, we called on the Prime Minister and Pannikar hesitatingly explained the need for another meeting. At the mention of this Nehru flew into a rage refusing categorically to agree to such a request. He said angrily that he had spent three whole days discussing everything in detail and an agreement had been reached. He would not go over it again. Didn't the Princes know that the Congress was being very generous with them? Didn't they realize that Congress could make things so difficult for them that they would be driven out of their states by their own people? He continued in this vein while Pannikar and I listened in silence. Nehru's reaction was typical of the Congress attitude towards the Princes, whom they looked upon as anachronisms created deliberately by the British to assist them in controlling the Indian people, and who should be done away with as soon as possible.

Inadvertently I must have had a little smile on my face, as I was indeed rather amused at Nehru's outburst, for he suddenly turned on me and said abruptly, 'What are you laughing at?' I was completely taken aback and explained, 'I am sorry, Sir, I meant no disrespect, and I certainly agree that today you have the power to make things very difficult for the Princes in their states. But it strikes me that this would also mean a lot of trouble for you, so is it not worthwhile having a brief meeting to save us all this trouble?' To my relief, Nehru at once agreed to have a meeting. The meeting was duly held and a final settlement reached. I learned later that Nehru's quick temper and equally quick recovery in the face of a reasonable suggestion were typical of the man, and was one of his loveable qualities.

This was in fact my first face-to-face meeting with Nehru, and I came away greatly impressed. I had always admired him for his great services to India, but this incident made a deep impression on me.

This basic understanding with the Princes was invaluable as there was at that time talk about India being split up into three countries: India, Pakistan and Princely India. Some rulers of large states even had ambitions to set up separate kingdoms. In our group we felt that it was bad enough to have India split into two by the creation of Pakistan, if there was further partition it would be a total catastrophe. I remember having an earnest talk with the Chief Ministers of two important states, both renowned and highly intelligent administrators, who were seriously working towards creating separate kingdoms for their states—Sir Ramaswamy Mudaliar of Mysore and Sir C.P. Ramaswamy Iyer, Dewan of Travancore. Their plans were quietly encouraged by some senior British officers in the Political Service who dealt with the Princes. At one time, even the Viceroy's efforts had been concentrated on getting the Princes to form the proposed Federation of India.

When I warned these eminent men that this plan could lead to a disastrous 'balkanization' of the country, they called me inexperienced in such matters. I told them while I was inexperienced, I was wise enough to know that their people would disown them and foil their plans. As it turned out my instincts were right and they were thrown out by their own people, one of them under somewhat violent circumstances.

Before the creation of Pakistan became an accepted fact, Jinnah tried his best to win over the Sikhs. He had made all kinds of offers to the Sikh leaders but with no success. In the middle of 1946 he sent a message to the Maharajah of Patiala in his capacity as a leader of the Sikh community asking him for a meeting. Jinnah suggested that the Maharajah come and see him. The Maharajah asked my advice and I suggested that the Maharajah should certainly meet him but to have Jinnah come to Patiala. This was conveyed to Jinnah who regretted that he could not come to Patiala, so it was finally agreed that they should meet in Delhi, but on neutral ground, and the meeting took place at my brother, Teja Singh Malik's house, 4 Bhagwandas Road.

It was a historic meeting, one of the most interesting I have ever attended. Jinnah came alone, unaccompanied by any adviser, while on our side there were the Maharajah, the Akali leaders, Tara Singh and Giani Kartar Singh and I. I was to be the spokesman for our party. When Jinnah arrived, he began by saying that he was most anxious to have the support of the Sikhs in his demand for Pakistan and was prepared to offer them any concessions they wanted if they would agree to remain in Pakistan. I asked him if he would kindly tell us what concessions he had in mind. His reply was that it was for us to make up our minds on what we wanted.

I insisted that he speak first on what would be the Sikh share in a Government, a Cabinet, in the armed forces, in the Civil Service. He still insisted that we must tell him our terms. He then told us the story of Zaghlul Pasha, Prime Minister of Egypt in 1924, and the Copts, the Christian minority in Egypt. According to Jinnah, the Copts, who were a small but flourishing community, were nervous about how the Muslim majority would treat them in a free Egypt—this was at a time when Egypt was in transition from being a British protectorate to an independent, sovereign nation. The Copts, therefore, went to Zaghlul Pasha, then the most powerful statesman in Egypt, and asked him for special privileges in the new constitution. Zaghlul advised them to go home, think things over carefully and put their demands on paper, and then return to him. This they did. Zaghlul then took the paper, and, without reading it, wrote: *I agree.*

Pausing at the end of his story, Jinnah added, 'That is how I will treat the Sikhs.' This put us in a very difficult position and, for a few minutes, no one knew what to say. After a pause, however, I asked him, 'Mr. Jinnah, you are being very generous, but, God forbid, supposing you are no longer with us when the time comes to implement your promises. What then?'* Jinnah's reaction was immediate. His eyes flashing, he declared, 'Mr. Malik, my word in Pakistan is like the word of God; no one will dare to go back on it!'

The meeting broke up soon after this. I couldn't help thinking that this was colossal vanity! Such egoism was near madness. Our main concern now was to act immediately and let it be known to the Indian public that the Sikhs were totally opposed to the creation of Pakistan. We feared that this meeting could be used by parties with vested interests in all sorts of ways, damaging both to Indian interests and to those of the Sikh community. I, therefore, approached my old friend of the Associated Press, Sir Usha Nath Sen, and made an urgent request. I told him about our meeting with Jinnah and asked him whether it was possible

* H.S. Malik: According to most accounts Jinnah was already a very sick man at that time.

for the next day's newspaper to print this headline: 'The Sikhs Will Under No Circumstances Accept Pakistan'. Sen agreed and we got the story with the headline we wanted in the morning papers.

Jinnah must have felt that his demand for Pakistan would be irrefutable if he could persuade the Sikhs to be a part of Pakistan. He seemed to ignore history. He forgot the impact of Muslim tyranny over the Hindu population, the forcible conversions and other oppressive acts inflicted on and finally overcome by the Sikhs who secured freedom from Mughal rule in Northern India. The Sikhs' checkered past with Muslims, along with their role in the defense of India during British rule, and their contribution to the economic development of the Punjab, made the idea of a Sikh union with Muslim Pakistan totally unrealistic.

Independence finally came at the cost of partition of the country for which Congress, in its impatience to get the British out of India in order to take over power, will have to accept its share of blame in history. It was the Sikhs who suffered the most in having to abandon not only some of their most venerated gurudwaras but also vast areas of rich and prosperous agricultural lands they had developed in those districts of the old Punjab which went to Pakistan. The canal lands of the districts of Lyallpur, Gujranwala, Sialkot, Multan, Lahore, Sheikhapura, which they had colonized into fertile fields, were all left behind in Pakistan at the time of the migration of populations in 1947.

CHAPTER 38

When my three-year term in Patiala was over, I expected to return to the Punjab. But the coming of Independence was imminent and the Indian Foreign Service was being established. Pandit Nehru sent me a message in Patiala asking me if I would like to go to Japan as India's first Ambassador. I replied that I would be happy to do so. However, within a few days, I was told that Nehru had decided to send Rama Rao to Japan and to send me to Canada as High Commissioner instead. I was very happy about this appointment as I had friends in Canada who I had served with during the First World War in the Royal Air Force. I was also aware that a number of our people who had settled down in Canada suffered from racial discrimination, and it would be a challenge to try and do something about this.

But immediately after I finished my three years tenure in Patiala, I was asked to go to Geneva to attend a trade conference and from there proceed directly to Canada. Therefore, to my great disappointment I was not in Delhi to join in the celebrations when India gained independence. I was also spared seeing the horrors of the pre-Partition riots but heard from my family, who were in India throughout, of the terrible happenings in Patiala where the authorities were unable to control the situation. Patiala had a fairly large population of Muslims. Sikhs and Muslims had lived peaceably side by side through generations but when the rioting broke out the refugees from West Punjab, who had come to Patiala in 1946, were at the forefront of the killings.

* * *

While still in Patiala I was made a member of the Indian delegation to the Preparatory Committee to establish the International Trade Organisation Conference. It met in London and I was elected Chairman of the Economic Committee. The Conference was held in Geneva in 1946 with follow-ups in Havana, Cuba in 1947-48. In Havana, I took over as leader of the Indian Delegation. I was then serving as High Commissioner for India in Canada from August 1947.

The objective of the Geneva Conference was to encourage international trade by eliminating import restrictions, quotas and other such practices in the different countries, and although the charter, born of this conference, was never put into operation, it served a useful purpose, for the charter that in turn gave birth to GATT, General Agreement on Tariffs and Trade. GATT did extremely useful work. These assignments were a most interesting experience.

I took up my appointment in Canada in August 1947, and was able to celebrate India's first Independence Day in Ottawa. In Canada, both the Government and the press received me warmly for there was a great deal of interest and friendliness for the new India. The papers all carried leading articles about my appointment, giving a resume of my career, my service during World War One, and my association with Canadians during that war. I arrived in Ottawa alone, without any staff, because the Government of India wanted India to be represented in Canada without any delay. The Indian members of the staff followed some months later. Fortunately, I found an excellent secretary, Mrs. Bertha Brocklesby, the wife of a Canadian official. Her many contacts in Ottawa combined with her efficiency, practical sense and total reliability, proved her to be of invaluable help in setting up the office.

Prakash and the children joined me after a somewhat adventurous TWA flight which took nine days instead of the scheduled 48 hours thanks to a series of mechanical problems in the aircraft. After a good deal of house hunting, we moved into a charming house in Ottawa's beautiful Rockcliffe Park.

Shortly after I arrived in Canada, the Canadian Club in Ottawa arranged a luncheon meeting attended by the Prime Minister, Mr. William Mackenzie King along with several of his Cabinet Ministers and other prominent Canadians. I spoke about India and Canada, and received a standing ovation, a measure of the interest and friendliness the new India evoked in Canadians. The press' accounts too were very complimentary, and when, as a routine matter, I sent copies of the articles to New Delhi, Pandit Nehru, who was also Foreign Minister, wrote personally to me saying that I had obviously made a strong impression.

With no really major problems between India and Canada, relations were very cordial, but I took the first opportunity to visit British Columbia, where practically all the immigrants from India had settled to see at first hand if there were any problems. It was to be an unforgettable visit. Prakash, my daughter Harji, and I travelled by the Canadian Pacific Railway across the entire breadth of the country, stopping at various provincial capitals along the way to meet a variety of Canadians and members of the Government. We stopped at Saskatoon, Edmonton, Calgary, Banff, Lake Louise, before we reached Vancouver in British Columbia. Wherever we went we were received with warmth and friendly curiosity about India.

The vastness of the countryside, the beauty of the scenery, particularly through Ontario with its wealth of forests and lakes was spectacular. The Canadian Rockies was breathtaking too and we spent many enjoyable hours in the train's observation car.

In Calgary we met a fine Sikh family, the Haris, who had migrated from Patiala some years earlier and established a large dairy farm outside Calgary. They were a striking family, tall and good looking.

At a very moving ceremony I was presented a Sword of Honours by Canada's Calgary Regiment which had fought alongside a Mahatta regiment in the Battle of the Rapido River in Italy in World War Two. The sword was to be given to the Indian regiment.

When our train pulled in at Vancouver, we found that almost the entire Indian population of British Columbia was at the railway station to welcome us. The genuine warmth of their welcome deeply moved all of us, and we felt overwhelmed by their affection. Among them were many old Sikhs with flowing white beards, some of whom had played a part in India's freedom struggle in the Ghadr Movement.*

The Sikhs had also contributed generously to support the struggle for freedom in India. For all of them, therefore, it was a moment of tremendous personal pride and joy to see free India represented by an Indian in Vancouver. As the majority were Sikhs, it only added to their joy that the Indian was a Sikh. Many of them wept openly. It was an emotionally charged moment for them and for us.

From the station they took us in a great procession—a cavalcade of a hundred cars was followed by a large number of Sikhs on foot, some with grey flowing beards, with swords drawn, accompanied by two bands—through the streets of Vancouver, holding up traffic. A plane overhead, draped with the Indian tri-colour, showered flowers on our open car! It was truly unforgettable. Our cavalcade stopped first at the gurudwara, where there was a brief service, and then we were escorted to our hotel.

We spent several days in Vancouver and Victoria. The area was like one beautiful garden with its wealth of flowers, shrubs

* 'Ghadr' means revolt and was the name given to the party of Sikh revolutionaries prepared and trained in Canada and the United States for anti-British activities in 1914 who returned to India with the objective of throwing out the British. The movement was ruthlessly suppressed by the British authorities. Their treatment of the Ghadrites led to much resentment in the Punjab and the Ghadr members were hailed as freedom fighters.

and trees. We visited two of the biggest lumber mills and forests that were owned by our people, most of whom were from the districts of Hoshiarpur and Jalandhar.

The most successful of these 'new Canadians' was Kapur Singh, slightly built, modest, and extremely soft-spoken who had arrived early in the 1900s like so many others seeking work on the construction of the Canadian Pacific Railway. By 1947, Kapur Singh, who had been the only literate Indian among them, known as Babuji for he kept all their accounts, had become an extremely wealthy man, owning hundreds of acres of forestland and his own lumber mills. But he lived very simply in Vancouver city with his wife who in spite of her many years in Canada still looked as if she had just arrived from her village in the Punjab. The following day Kapur Singh took us out to his lumber mills and to see his estate. We were standing on a hilltop looking across at hillside after hillside of forest and I asked him where his land extended to. Very quietly he pointed to the horizon encompassing all we could see.

Kapur Singh described what tremendous difficulties they had faced when they first arrived in Canada. They could hardly speak English and, of course, felt totally alien in a foreign land. I asked him whether it had been easy for them to find work. The general impression was that Indians were ready to work for much lower wages than immigrants from Europe. To my surprise, he said emphatically that they did not accept lower wages. In fact, Indians demanded higher wages. He said it was so because Indians worked harder than the immigrants from Italy, Spain and other countries.

These immigrants had originally come in the early 1900s to work on the building of the two great railroads, the Canadian Pacific and the Canadian National. At that time, there were no more than a thousand Indians settled in Canada, and one rarely came across them outside British Columbia. Some of them settled down in Canada, while others had moved south to California.

Naturally, they were drawn into the freedom struggle. The famous Komagatamaru incident when they were refused landing in Calcutta and forced to return to British Colombia is part of nationalist history. It was the Sikhs returning from Canada who were among some of the bravest members of the Babbar Akali Movement which inspired so much terror in the Indian police during the freedom struggle.

When we arrived in Canada my brief was to try and remove the restrictions that were still imposed on Indian-Canadians and to secure the same status for them as was accorded by the Canadian Government to immigrants from European countries who had settled in Canada and become Canadian citizens.

Fortunately, Mr. Lester Pearson, who subsequently became Prime Minister of Canada, was then at the Foreign Office as Under-Secretary of State. I had known him for several years as we were both at Oxford at the same time, and subsequently were both in the Royal Air Force during World War One. I had always found him very friendly. In Ottawa, he was extremely sympathetic towards this matter and willing to help in every way possible. The question I raised informally with Canadian friends in the Government was a simple one: the immigrants from India, once settled in Canada eventually acquired Canadian citizenship and along with it responsibilities of citizenship including the liability to be drafted into the fighting services, how then could the Government deny them all the rights of citizenship? Where was the justice in restricting certain rights? Unlike European immigrants they were refused the rights to bring in certain grades of relatives into Canada to help them on their farms or in their businesses. I then learnt that the labour organizations in British Columbia were opposed to any further concessions being given to Indian immigrants, who, of course, were serious competition to local labour. However, eventually justice was done and our people got full rights of citizenship.

CHAPTER 39

During my two years in Canada I was asked to speak at many meetings to a wide variety of organizations including even church groups as independent India inspired tremendous interest. This allowed me to present India's case to a representative section of professional and business people, a very useful exercise in correcting the false propaganda against our country. As India had taken the lead for the liberation of colonial countries, I faced attentive audiences who were really interested in the subject. I received such a large number of invitations to speak in those first days of independence that I asked Harji to speak at many of the women's clubs and church groups. One particularly interesting and challenging meeting for her was when she addressed a large group of high schools, and was made to answer many questions. She seemed to have been an effective speaker although she confessed later that her knees were shaking while talking to this young audience!

In 1948 Lord and Lady Mountbatten visited Canada. From India's point of view this turned out to be an extremely useful visit as they both took every opportunity of showing India in a very favourable light to the Canadians. As the Mountbattens were held in high esteem by the Canadians, this made a strong impact. At one of the important meetings in Ottawa held in their honour, where the Prime Minister also spoke, Mountbatten devoted a good part of his speech to India, and we were deeply impressed by his reference to the Indian leaders when he said he was amazed at the generosity and greatness of men like

Mahatma Gandhi and Pandit Nehru. He said, 'We put them in jail from time to time, and then released them whenever it suited us, and then the time came when we had to negotiate with them the terms of our departure from India. If you Canadians or we British had been treated in this way we would have been bitter, and we would have said in reply, "To hell with you!" These great men did nothing of the kind. They forgot their bitterness, took in friendship the hand that was held out to them and forgot about the past.' His words greatly impressed this important Canadian audience.

On another occasion during Mountbatten's visit the Canadian Government held a banquet in honour of the Mountbattens to which most of the prominent personalities of Ottawa and many heads of mission were invited. After dinner Mountbatten came up to me and asked me to come along with him to discuss the difficulties I was facing in securing arms from Canada with the Prime Minister. We went up to Mackenzie King and Mountbatten said to him, 'Mr. Prime Minister, the High Commissioner tells me that you will not permit the shipment of arms to India unless similar quantities are sent to Pakistan.' Mackenzie King professed his surprise and signalled to Lester Pearson to join us. He asked him why they were not permitting the shipment of arms to India. Mike Pearson was visibly embarrassed and explained that there had been some misunderstanding. The Prime Minister then asked him to see that everything was put right. Later, Pearson took me aside, and said in jest, 'Look at the old rascal! He was the person responsible for this order and now he pretends he knows nothing about it!' Following this incident, we had no problem in securing arms.

We witnessed Mountbatten's tact and quick wit at a very formal affair hosted in his honour by the Governor General, Lord Alexander. According to custom, at the end of dinner, the ladies left the table to move into the drawing room, leaving the men to their port and cigars. As each lady left the room, she curtsied to the Governor General as the representative of the Queen. This included Lady Alexander herself. My wife, a woman of very strong character and principles had never curtsied to anyone, even to Queen Mary herself at the Buckingham Palace garden party many years ago, so when it came her turn to make the formal curtsey, she put her hands together in the Indian namaskar while looking at Lord Alexander. There was a moment's hush which might have been embarrassing but Mountbatten immediately said in a loud voice, 'I have always found this Indian way of greeting so charming.'

A few months after arriving in Ottawa, I was deputed to lead the Indian delegation at the International Trade Organization Conference in Havana, Cuba. I had already participated in its earliest stages in London and Geneva. It turned out to be a rewarding, most interesting experience. It was also a welcome opportunity for renewing friendships with members of delegations from other countries whom I had met previously. Among these was Walter Nash, the distinguished leader of the New Zealand Delegation whom I had known in America when he was Ambassador in Washington. At one time Prime Minister of New Zealand, Nash was an exceptional human being, a prominent figure at many international conferences. Unlike a great many distinguished men in politics, he was very forthright in expressing his views. He was basically liberal and tolerant. I took a great liking to him and always found him helpful and understanding at the many international conferences in which we participated.

The ITO Conference succeeded in drawing up a charter which aimed at removing trade and quota barriers plus other obstacles to free trade, thereby liberalizing and expanding world exchange of goods and services. For various reasons, however, the provisions of the charter could not be implemented so its success was qualified. The charter remained a dead letter until it finally gave birth to United Nations Conference on Trade and Development (UNCTAD), which continues to be active and has achieved a great deal in removing some barriers to world trade.

Much social activity took place during the conference. The functions were arranged by the host country's delegation led by Sergio Clarke, the President of the Conference. The visit in those days of King Leopold of Belgium and his wife, the Princess de Rethy gave a big boost both to the social life and to tourism in Havana. For me, personally, this was a great pleasure because I was able to renew my real friendship with King Leopold which we had formed earlier in Geneva. This was, of course, before the Castro Revolution when Cuba was a very different place from Castro's Cuba

In those three months in Havana I saw the prevailing conditions in Cuba. The great wealth of the big Spanish families, like Sergio Clarke, who owned great plantations, was in stark contrast to the tremendous poverty and miserable state in which the natives of Cuba lived. The big American companies who monopolized the rich trade in tobacco, sugar and other Cuban resources had accumulated immense power and wealth and controlled the country in many ways. In addition to this corruption was rampant among politicians and in the Government services, and no attempt was being made to provide social services to the common people. These conditions explained why Castro was able to seize power and then both consolidate and preserve it in the face of the open U.S. hostility and the obvious deterioration of economic conditions through many years because Cuba was entirely dependant on trade with the United States.

In 1948 the External Affairs Ministry deputed me to join the Indian delegation to the General Assembly of the United Nations. It was my first experience of the U.N. I was naturally curious to see this body at work. I came away disappointed with the feeling that there was far too much talking and too little action. The long, sometimes eloquent, speeches in both the Assembly and the Security Council were generally heard in semi-somnolence and boredom, bringing home to me forcefully the fact that great eloquence in public speaking may be pleasing to the speaker, occasionally entertaining for the audience but all too often has little value and is indeed overrated. I described the events in a letter to my daughter: *The work itself has not been inspiring. In fact, there is an air of unreality about the whole business, much horse trading, a great deal of cynicism, a great deal of name calling, very little idealism and faith, or goodwill.*

Some years later when our representative, V.K. Krishna Menon was making his marathon speech at the Security Council on the Kashmir question and earning much merit among his admirers and friends, the general impression in the U.N., and among diplomats in general, was that far from winning over people to our stand on the issue, he had succeeded in making more enemies at the U.N. than any representative of India had ever done.

The Hyderabad action* which had provoked much criticism of India in many countries occurred while I was on tour in Nova Scotia. Rushing back to Ottawa, I called a press conference to put forward India's case. Fortunately, this meeting received full publicity in the Canadian press, so we were able to undo a good deal of the damage done to us particularly by the propaganda carried out by Pakistan and its friends.

We had presumed that we would be staying in Canada for three years, the usual length of time for a normal posting, but towards the end of 1945 the Ministry of External Affairs wrote to me stating that the Prime Minister was thinking of sending

---

* The Nizam of Hyderabad had declared that he would not join India or Pakistan in June 1947, and for a year he kept a decision pending, at the same time toying with the idea of 'independence'. In September 1948 the Indian army took police action against the Nizam's forces and the state was integrated into the Indian Union.

me as Ambassador to Italy. I was being asked how I felt about this. I replied that I would go with pleasure anywhere Pandit Nehru wanted to send me, but I felt that I should be allowed to stay on in Canada for another six months as there were still one or two matters I wanted to complete before leaving. In this letter to my old friend, K.P.S. Menon, then Foreign Secretary, I added a postscript, more as a joke, that if the Prime Minister had suggested Paris, my reaction might have been different. After a couple of months, I received a telegram from New Delhi informing me that the Prime Minister had decided to send me to Paris as India's first Ambassador to France!

In 1949, when the time came to leave Ottawa, I called on the Prime Minister, Monsieur St. Laurent, an extremely fine man, to bid him farewell. Expressing his regret at my departure, he added that while there was a real bond between our two countries, in France I would find things to be very different especially in dealing with French settlements in India, that of Pondicherry and others. And then he added with a twinkle in his eye that there would also be the problem of Rita Hayworth! At that time the Prince Aly Khan, son of the Aga Khan, was having a dalliance with the lady.

We left Canada after a happy, fruitful period of service, with the satisfaction of having secured full citizenship rights for our people settled in Canada. Personally, I was able to meet several old friends with whom I had served in the First World War—among them were Air Marshall Mike McEwan, popularly known as Black Mike, Dr. Neil Blacklock, a dentist in Montreal, and Colonel Bell-Irving, my old flight instructor. Unfortunately, my friend and colleague, Flight Commander Barker, had been killed in an air accident some years earlier.

We thoroughly enjoyed our stay in Ottawa. We even enjoyed the long Canadian winter with our three children skiing on the Gatineau hills around Ottawa. We made many new friends, finding Canadians extremely warm and friendly, and we were sorry to leave so soon, still not having visited many parts of this magnificent country.

I was touched by the leading article in a Canadian daily on the eve of our departure. *Diplomats by profession are wanderers. It was perhaps inevitable that Sardar Hardit Singh Malik should eventually be appointed to another post. In a few days he will leave for Paris. Those who have heard him speak will know that Canada has lost a wise counselor. Those who have encountered his redoubtable skill on the golf links will regret the departure of so sturdy an opponent. And all Canadians will have lost a friend.*

CHAPTER 40

We left for France, via New York, in the second week of July in 1949 on the famous Cunard liner, the *Queen Elizabeth*. Three years earlier Harji and I had travelled from New York to Southampton on the same ship when she had been fitted out as a troopship in World War Two ferrying American soldiers to England. We then had a cabin with eight bunks, and Harji had remarked that we could change bunks every night. In 1946, the *Queen* was the height of comfort and luxury. While Prakash, the three children and I thoroughly enjoyed the voyage, a very important member of our family, Rajah, our handsome and much-loved Collie, did not. He was the sole occupant of the ship's kennels, and in spite of our frequent visits, he was very lonely and miserable. To add to his unhappiness, the kennels were situated just below the enormous funnels of the ship, and when they hooted, letting out a tremendous noise, he was absolutely terrified.

We arrived in Cherbourg but because of the extensive damage to the port during the war, we had to anchor outside and go in by tugboat. The Embassy had been opened earlier under a Charge d'Affaires, and Vasant Bhide, one of the officers, had come to receive us. Vasant was from the Indian Railways and had been selected for service in the Embassy. Although I was never told exactly what his assignment was, I gathered he was there to keep a check on the Embassy staff. I would not have approved of this. However, he settled down to the normal work of a Second Secretary and was an exemplary officer. We became close friends with him and his wife, Indira. But on that first encounter he must have found us a very peculiar family. He had come out on the tug to receive us, and almost as soon as he had greeted us, the tug let out a loud hoot, and Rajah, restrained on a leash by our daughter, Veena, bolted in panic, with the Malik family, including the Ambassador-designate, chasing after him, fearful that he would leap into the sea. On the train journey to Paris we had a compartment with six seats. Rajah, like all dogs was very sensitive to vibrations and refused to sit on the floor. He occupied one first class seat while our son and daughter, Mala and Veena were crammed in together on another! Vasant was too polite to display any reaction to this unorthodox behaviour. In the Paris papers the next morning marking our arrival in the city, Rajah was most prominent, sitting with us on the seat, getting his first view of the city looking out of the car window.

I confess to being tremendously thrilled arriving in Paris as India's first Ambassador to France. Having served in the French Army 33 years earlier, it was like a dream come true to find myself in Paris as Ambassador for my country. My enthusiasm was further strengthened by the reception I received in France from the President, M. Vincent Auriol, when I presented my credentials to him. Exceptionally warm-hearted and friendly, President Auriol, in his formal speech welcoming me said, 'Anyone coming from your great country to represent it in France would be welcome, but you, Mr. Ambassador, are more than welcome, because you have shed your blood for France.' This, of course, was a reference to my having been wounded in aerial combat in France. I was deeply moved as he embraced me.

While posting me to France Pandit Nehru had told me that he was sending me there because of my war record. He felt that I was the best man to persuade the French to return the French settlements in India to us. I told Panditji that I would do my best, but at the same time I felt that my position would be very difficult because while we were rightly opposed to French colonial policies, we had nothing to offer France except criticism. Until these policies were changed I would thus be faced with the problem of asking the French to return the French settlements to us without offering anything in return, except our opposition to their policies! Panditji smiled, in his own rather whimsical fashion, saying that I would just have to do the best I could.

This assignment had to be accomplished with great patience and tact. The Portuguese were being openly hostile toward us, refusing even to discuss the question of Goa. France, of course, knew this. I began feeling my way with extreme caution before putting forward any demand or request. My great advantage was that the French knew I was a friend, that I had known the country for so many years and loved it, and therefore they were willing to accept from me more by way of good humoured criticism than from someone else, and I made full use of this advantage.

I remember my first conversation on the subject with the Foreign Minister at that time, M. Robert Schumann, a man of great character and integrity, deeply religious, honest and sincere. One evening, after dinner at the Embassy, when I briefly mentioned the subject of Pondicherry, he said, 'Mr. Ambassador, we appreciate your wish to have French India back now that the British have left, but you must realize that the people of these French settlements have become French by culture and education. They speak French and they are really a part of our country. We cannot suddenly tell them that we are leaving and that in the future they will be part of India. After all, they have been with us for 200 years.' This was a wonderful opening and I responded, 'I am delighted to hear you express these sentiments, Mr. Minister, because feeling as you do, you will be able to appreciate *our* sentiments. The people of these parts were with us for 2000 years before you came!' He saw the point immediately and laughed good humouredly.

In Paris I had the opportunity to get to know the President of France. Apart from official meetings and social functions, he invited me and a few other Ambassadors for pheasant shoots at his official country residence in the forest of Rambouillet. These smaller get-togethers presented a chance to talk to him privately and at length. At one such gathering in Rambouillet we were only about a dozen people. We shot pheasant in the forest in the morning and then met for lunch. Over coffee President Auriol turned to me and asked why I was always talking to them about returning French India back to India, and why did the Indian Government not concentrate on getting Goa back from the Portugese. This was said in jest because everyone knew that the Portuguese were extremely hostile about their Indian possessions. I responded to the President that in India France is always looked upon as a great country, as the most advanced and the most civilized in the West in many ways. Above all, France is respected and loved for its part in the struggle for human liberty. The French Revolution is looked upon as one of the great landmarks in the fight for equality and freedom. I added that if I were to go and tell my people that this great country was waiting for a lead from an insignificant, reactionary country like Portugal, what would they say? President Auriol broke into a great laugh and said no more on the subject that day.

Another, most unusual incident occurred when Dr. Radhakrishnan, then our Vice President, came to Paris and called on President Auriol. I accompanied him to the Elysée Palace. M. Auriol was prepared for this visit and was expecting Dr. Radhakrishnan to talk about Pondicherry and the other French possessions. Dr. Radhakrishnan did, in fact, mention the subject, and as soon as he did, the President picked up a book from a table by his side, turned over a few pages and said, 'Mr. Vice-President, I have here Article so and so of the French Constitution which says that no part of the French Commonwealth can be given away without the consent of the people concerned.' It would have been alright if the President had stopped there, but he went on to talk about how France had always stood for freedom and liberty, and referred to the French Revolution. Dr. Radhakrishnan, sharp as a knife, immediately seized the opportunity to say, 'Ah, Mr. President, in 1789 you had to break the Constitution!'

Gradually, I was able to work on the most influential men in France to try and get them round to our point of view. In a free and independent India it was not possible to have foreign powers in possession of Indian territories. I had spoken from time to time to members of the Cabinet whom I knew well, like M. René Pleven, at one time Minister for Defence in the Cabinet. We became friends because his daughters, Françoise and Nicole, had been in America during the Second World War, attending the same college as Harji and they had maintained their friendship. I had been able to secure Pleven's support, and through him the support of several other members of the Cabinet. I found a sympathetic ear in Pierre Mendès when he became Prime Minister. He was a man of liberal views. He completely understood India's demand for the return of the French possessions, and it was during his term in office that we were able at arrive at a settlement on this issue.

To my great satisfaction, we came to an agreement without any bitterness and with goodwill on both sides. France agreed to hand over the French possessions to us and we, in turn, agreed to preserve, as far as possible, the French culture there. It was an extremely difficult negotiation, and made more difficult by the fact that the French Ambassador in New Delhi at that time, an highly astute and shrewd diplomat, who had the ear of some top people in the Ministry of External Affairs, was not in favour of the transfer, and repeatedly delayed matters. At one point, I felt constrained to write to the Ministry asking them whether they were listening to their Ambassador in France about the situation regarding the French possessions or to the French Ambassador in India! But in the end the French Ambassador's efforts came to nothing.

I was rather irked when, after succeeding in persuading the French Government to hand over their possessions with such goodwill, Pandit Nehru, instead of appointing me to head the team to negotiate the actual terms of the treaty to effect the transfer, entrusted R.K. Nehru, then Foreign Secretary, with this task. I wrote to Panditji in protest. I told him that under the circumstances as it would be embarrassing for me to be in Paris while the terms were being negotiated. I would, therefore, arrange to be out of the capital. I pointed out that the settlement had been reached as a result of my efforts during the last three years, and it seemed very strange, that I not be entrusted to handle the negotiations. I felt that the French Government would probably feel the same way. I preferred, therefore, to absent myself from Paris. The Prime Minister replied that far from side-stepping me his intention was that I be in Paris throughout the negotiations to guide R.K. Nehru. This was the role I eventually played. It was R.K., however, who conducted the negotiations.

Some months later, my wife was watching the Independence Day Parade in Delhi. When the float depicting the return of Pondicherry to India came past Prakash was most amused to hear Rajan Nehru, R.K.'s wife, who was sitting quite near her, turn to a friend sitting next to her and exclaim in excitement, 'Ratan's Pondicherry, my dear!' Then she caught Prakash's eye and, rather sheepishly, looked away.

I consider myself extremely fortunate to have been able to complete the assignments both in Canada and in France during my tenure. As a rule, the fate of ambassadors is to start work on some problems and then be transferred to another post before finishing the job. In Canada, of course, two years were sufficient to obtain full citizenship for the Indian immigrants. But in France, where I faced a far more difficult problem, it required more time and I was fortunate to be left there long enough to have been able to see the French possessions returned to India.

CHAPTER 41

The French were very proud of what they had achieved in their colonial 'empire' and I was keen to visit Morocco and see the conditions of French rule for myself. Although the Sultan of Morocco was the ruler, the control of the country was in the hands of the French Resident General who exercised great powers through provincial Governors. After some initial reluctance the French Government approved my visit. But it was insisted that I should be the guest of the French Government throughout. I, on my part, said that I must also meet the nationalist leaders.

Prakash and I left for Morocco in early 1952 accompanied by M. Emmanuel Pouchepadas, the Press Officer in the Embassy who spoke perfect French and had contacts with the nationalist leaders. From the very start of our visit a senior French official was with us constantly. His principle duty was to make sure that wherever we went we met Moroccans who were full of praise for the blessings of French rule. In Casablanca, the Representative of the Resident General explained to us how France had 'unified' a tribal Morocco split between the Berbers and the Arabs, and how together France and Morocco were exploiting the wealth of the country. But he confessed that there was little social contact between the two communities and that the Arabs and the French had a different legal system.

In Rabat, the capital city, where we stayed with the Governor General, General Guillaume, he briefed me on what he described as the Sultan's theocratic attitude towards governance, adding that while Morocco must move forward, there was danger in going too fast before the Moroccans had learned to manage their own affairs. Until then the Sultan could only rule with French protection, he said, otherwise the powerful Berber Pasha of Marrakesh, El Glaoui, could dethrone him. The Pasha, a great friend of Winston Churchill, was loyal to the French. This was all too reminiscent of the British 'divide and rule' policy in the Raj days! No Frenchmen we met during the entire visit had anything good to say about the Sultan. In contrast, the Arabs, even those not too politically involved, blamed the French for 'manufacturing' the Arab-Berber differences to preserve their own rule, and there was great respect for the Sultan.

When I told General Guillaume that I would like to pay my respects to the Sultan he said it would take many days to arrange it, so I told him that in that case I would go and sign the Sultan's book at the Palace because my failure to do so would be misunderstood by the people of both Morocco and India. The French suspected the Sultan of quietly encouraging the nationalist Istiqlal Party which was demanding Home Rule, hence the General's reluctance. But seeing I was determined the meeting was arranged.

I was received with full honours at the Palace and greeted by the Sultan in the Grand Salon as a special sign of friendship for India. I was also told later that the Sultan had met me without the dark glasses which he always wore while receiving people at the Palace, and this was also a special honour. In his very cordial speech he referred to Mohammad Iqbal and Mahatma Gandhi who he said were respected and admired throughout Morocco. To my great surprise, he then decorated me with the highest Moroccan Order, the Order of the Grand Croix de l'Ouissam Alouite. I mentioned to him that my wife was accompanying me and would be greatly honoured if the Sultana would receive her, and also it would be a privilege for us to attend the Prayer Meeting on Friday. He immediately said both could be arranged.

A couple of days later, Prakash was received with great warmth by the Sultana and her ladies and, to her surprise, the Sultan joined them for tea. He had a long talk with her, and mentioned that he had heard that we were to visit Marrakesh where El Glaoui was arranging a big party in our honour. The Sultan told Prakash about El Glaoui's disloyalty to him and added that he would greatly appreciate it if we somehow managed to avoid the Pasha's hospitality. Earlier the Sultan had also sent a message proposing a private meeting without a French presence in Casablanca on our way back to Paris.

The Prayer Meeting when the Sultan went to the Mosque to offer prayers in public was striking evidence of how the people loved and respected him for several thousands had come to pay their respects to him. Dressed simply in a white jalaba, the Moroccan costume, a fez on his head, the Sultan came on horseback with his mounted bodyguard. As he passed where we were standing he removed his dark glasses, and smiled at us, making the same gesture on his return. The crowd noticed this, and after he had passed, they crowded around us, kissing my hands and my clothes, shouting, 'India, India! Gandhi, Gandhi!' This overwhelming demonstration of affection for the country and its leaders was deeply moving for us.

From Rabat we went to Meknes passing through very fertile country mostly the farms of the French colons, settlers. This colonization of the best land by the French was one of the chief causes for Moroccan bitterness. The beautiful old city of Fez, the ancient capital of Morocco, is the religious and cultural centre of Morocco, the only city which had a university. Our host there, the French Governor, although said to be genuinely devoted to the country told me that it would be 20 years or more before the Moroccans were ready for self-government. When I met one of the most respected, venerable Moroccan leaders the next day he asked me to tell the Governor that on behalf of the people of his country he accepted the offer! Little did either of them imagine that because of the French mishandling of the situation independence would be conceded within five years.

We then went to Marrakesh but only for one night, a change of plans with the excuse that I had been recalled to Paris earlier than planned. The Moroccans we met everywhere told us that the colons had expropriated huge areas from the peasants at nominal rates and that a reign of terror prevailed. No one dared criticize the administration, there was no freedom of the press, and they welcomed India's support in their struggle for freedom. I was told that everyone knew the real reason why I changed our Marrakesh plans.

Back in Casablanca the private meeting with the Sultan had been arranged. That evening a car arrived to take me to his palace with a Moroccan officer who asked me to put on a jalabah which completely covered me. We were driven at a furious pace in a zig-zag course, James Bond style, to a place where I was transferred to another car and we raced off again to yet another waiting car with a new driver and then on to the Palace. Removing the jalabah, I was taken to a back door which was opened immediately by the Crown Prince himself and taken to the Sultan. The three of us sat talking for nearly two hours. No servants were present and the Crown Prince himself served coffee and fruit, so the French would not hear of the meeting.

We talked of France and India and the world generally. Then he told me that the main reason for him arranging this meeting was him to ask my advice on his future action vis a vis the French. He was debating over whether he should accept Dominion Status if it was offered. He wanted to know about the Indian experience. I told him that Dominion Status would result in independence in a very short time and advised him to accept it.

I came away deeply impressed by the Sultans personality, his intelligence and integrity and his genuine desire to have a friendly settlement with France in spite of the intrigues of

Frenchmen such as Marechal Juin and Georges Bidault, who were irrevocably opposed to Moroccan independence. I was also convinced that the Sultan, revered as the spiritual and political head of the country, was the only man who could negotiate with the French. I felt that perhaps with the good relations I enjoyed with the French Government I might be able to play a useful role in bringing about a real understanding between Morocco and France. How wrong I was!

A few months after our visit, the reactionary Georges Bidault became France's Foreign Minister. Under his influence and that of Marechal Juin the French Government decided to throw the Sultan Mohammad V into exile, ousting him and his family unceremoniously, without warning, from his Palace which was surrounded by French tanks on the pretext that they were 'saving' his life from El Glaoui. Shocked and convinced that the French had made a monumental mistake I called on M. Bidault. I told him I had come to see him as a friend of France, not as an Ambassador to tell him that the Sultan was a friend of France, and was the only man who could reach a peaceful settlement. I told him that I was convinced that one day they would ask him to return from exile to reach such a settlement. Bidault was furious and told me that if I had come and spoken to him like this as Ambassador of India, he would have asked me to leave. But as I had come as a friend, he could only tell me I was mistaken and they had acted to protect the Sultan.

History records how the Sultan had to be brought back from Madagascar, how El Glaoui literally crawled on his knees before him to beg forgiveness and how the French ultimately came to a settlement and conceded Home Rule to Morocco. When the Sultan came to Paris after his exile, I impulsively, decided to call on him while coming back from playing golf at St. Germain for he was staying at a villa in St. Germain. I was driving myself not in the official car and explained who I was to the security staff. They sent a message to the Sultan who received me graciously.

He promised to come to our Embassy on his next visit and he did so for an informal tea party accompanied by his Prime Minister, the ex-officer in the French Army, Si Bokkai, a very fine man whom I had met in Fez. Sadly, for his people and for Morocco, the Sultan did not live long after his restoration.

Among France's colonies in North Africa: Morocco, Tunisia and Algeria, it was Algeria that was administered very differently from the other two. It was always l'Algérie Française with the French insisting that there was no difference between the French and the Algerian people. They could never believe that Algeria could wish to separate from France, so the Algerian revolt came as a great shock to the French people, which is why the Algerian fight for freedom was so bitter, and lasted for so many years. In 1958, General de Gaulle finally enforced his decision that Algeria would be independent on the mutinous French settlers, the colons of Algeria. The colons were supported by powerful elements in France, including those in the army itself. At one time there was even talk of rebel French forces landing in Algeria and taking over the government. The demoralizing effect on the French of the Algerian war was very similar to the way in which the war in Vietnam divided the American nation. In Tunisia, in contrast, independence was won relatively peacefully with the French and other foreign settlers accepting Tunisian nationality and staying on in the country.

CHAPTER 42

During my years in Paris Pandit Nehru paid several official visits to France. During one of these he called a conference in Paris of all the Indian Ambassadors in Europe. Our Embassy was a beautiful house, however, at that time, living accommodation was very limited with only three proper bedrooms and a small room which was formerly Mme. Barzin's maid's room. The house had been refurbished many years ago for Madame Barzin, the former Cornelia Vanderbilt, by her French husband, Jaques Barzin. The Prime Minister was therefore put in our bedroom while Mrs. Indira Gandhi, who accompanied him with her two young sons, Rajiv and Sanjay, were accommodated in the bedroom normally occupied by our son, Mala, when he was home on vacation from school in Scotland. It was otherwise used as a guest bedroom. Prakash, Veena and I, all piled into Harji's bedroom.

Before the Paris visit I had been instructed that Pandit Nehru did not want too full a programme as he wished to rest part of the time. I had, accordingly, arranged a comparatively light schedule for him. There were, of course, the usual official visits to the President of France and the Prime Minister, and a big reception in his honour at the Embassy. But apart from that, as he had instructed, his time was kept comparatively free.

However, when he arrived in Paris and saw the programme, he complained that I had not arranged enough work for him! He kept silent when I said that I had merely followed his instructions. He had also mentioned in his letter to me prior to his visit that he wanted to spend one day in the country and go riding. I had learned that one of the members of the Rothschild family had a country house with stables and excellent horses not too far from Paris. I made all the arrangements with Guy de Rothschild and kept one day free for this purpose.

On the day concerned, young Rothschild arrived at the Embassy to drive the Prime Minister to his home. He had never met Panditji before and, being rather shy, was a bit nervous. Prakash, who was in the same car with Panditji and Rothschild on their drive to the country, told me afterwards that Panditji was in no mood to talk, so for the first few minutes there was total silence. Rothschild must have felt that he should say something and he began by apologizing for what he described as his 'humble house' to which he was taking the Prime Minister. Instead of replying graciously, Panditji said rather brusquely, 'What difference does it make to me whether you have a big house or humble house?' The conversation came to an abrupt end. Prakash, embarrassed at this impoliteness, coaxed Rothschild into a conversation, asking him where he had spent his time as a prisoner of war. Rothschild explained that he had been captured by the Germans and had been a POW in Germany. As soon as Panditji heard this, he turned to Rothschild and started to talk to him in a most friendly fashion, asking him all kinds of questions about his experiences as a POW. The ice was broken, the situation saved, and the visit was a total success! And the Prime Minister thoroughly enjoyed his day in the country.

This was the first such meeting of the Indian Ambassadors in Western Europe. The purpose of the conference was to have informal discussions on foreign policy, obtain feedback from the different countries and allow the Prime Minister, also functioning as the Foreign Minister, and the Secretary General of the External Affairs Ministry, Sir Girija Shankar Bajpai, to brief the Ambassadors. Before coming to Paris Pandit Nehru had been in London and had had meetings with V.K. Krishna Menon, our High Commissioner there, so Krishna Menon was not expected in Paris. Much to my surprise, however, he arrived, unannounced at the Embassy late one evening, and went up to meet the Prime Minister.

The next morning Krishna Menon joined the Ambassadors as we waited for the Prime Minister who had appointments with one or two visitors before the meeting. Suddenly, Menon got up and interrupted the Prime Minister and his visitors. This was typical of Menon who always wanted to advertise his close relationship with the Prime Minister. He then came out of the room and I met him in the hall. He told me that he had arranged for the Prime Minister to meet certain people in Paris. I was most annoyed as he had no business to interfere with arrangements which we at the Embassy had made with great care, and I told him rather angrily that he had no business interfering here as he had already spent a whole week with the Prime Minister in London. I added that if he wished to take over Paris as well, he was free to ask the Prime Minister! But as long as I was here, he should keep his nose out of my business! As I said this, Panditji came out of the room and immediately saw that there was some argument taking place. He looked at me but before he could say anything, I said, 'It's alright, Sir, don't worry. I am not going to hit him. I would like to as he has no business to interfere with my arrangements, but I won't.' Panditji, knowing Menon, understood and said nothing, and Krishna Menon tried to explain. Nothing more was said about it, and there was no further interference!

After the conference was over and the Prime Minister had left for India, Harji and some of my staff told me that all the time Panditji was in Paris, Krishna Menon appeared to be very unwell, physically weak, leaning on someone for support as if he was not able to walk on his own, and that on more than one occasion Panditji had shown concern. But, they said, with amusement, that as soon as the Prime Minister had emplaned, Krishna Menon straightened up, seemed full of beans, and actually invited Rajah Dinesh Singh, 2nd Secretary in Paris who had served under Menon in London, to tea at a famous tearoom!

Krishna Menon, who had been appointed in London, presumably as a reward for his contribution to the Nationalist Movement, as he had no real qualification for such an important post, had a habit of calling attention in public to his special relationship with the Prime Minister. He would take him aside at public gatherings and whisper in his ear. To our surprise, Panditji, normally so impatient with this kind of behaviour, would never stop him, and this led to speculation that Menon had some special hold over Nehru.

While Menon was in charge of London and I, of Paris, quite a number of incidents took place between us. I first met Menon when I was passing through London in 1947 on my way to take up my appointment in Canada. He was most friendly, came to receive me personally at the airport, and accompanied me to the Savoy Hotel where I was staying. We had a pleasant conversation over tea, and he told me that I was an experienced administrator while he had been made High Commissioner in London without having any experience of administration. He would be grateful, therefore, if I would give him some advice. I told him that I was quite sure he would handle the situation well, and the only advice I would venture to offer was that he should spend the first few months in observation to get to know the ropes before taking any important action.

We did not meet for the next two years. During our next encounter in London, when I had taken over in Paris, I found him a very different person. Now, confident of the Prime Minister's never failing support, he had become arrogant and difficult to get along with. In due course, we ran into problems when I discovered that he was trying to control the supplies of arms and other equipment purchased by India in France from London. I was concerned with his attempt to handle the supplies from France to India through his nominees in London. I was determined not to permit this as I was convinced that apart from it being totally unnecessary and unwarranted, it would mean extra expenditure by India, amounting to several crores of rupees.

The Prime Minister had been told by India House in London that we could get nothing from the French except through intermediaries in London. Seeing through this ruse, I had taken the precaution of securing the agreement of the French Government to supply us armaments, including airplanes, tanks and other equipment, direct on a Government to Government basis, without the services of any intermediaries. I obtained this assurance in writing from the Minister of Defence in the French Government. When I was suddenly summoned to India specifically to appear before a Cabinet Committee which had been appointed to look into this whole question, I took this letter from the Minister with me, along with relevant files.

On arrival at Delhi I was called almost immediately by the Prime Minister. He expressed his concern about India being unable to get arms from the French without intervention of London. I asked him where he had got this information from, and assured him that it was incorrect. Panditji asked me somewhat angrily what I meant as he had been told about this both by the Defence Secretary and Krishna Menon. I then produced the letter from the French Defence Minister and asked the Prime Minister to read it. He did, and then asked if I had shown this to Krishna Menon and the Defence Secretary. I told him I had done just that. It was obvious that the Prime Minister had been misled, but he said nothing, and after a couple of days I was told that I could return to my post in Paris. I was not asked to appear before the Cabinet Committee although I had been called to Delhi specifically for this purpose.

It was often wondered why the Prime Minister protected

Krishna Menon, and I myself have been asked this question many times. The only explanation that I can find is that Panditji had a very genuine affection for Menon, going back to the time when Krishna Menon, as President of the India League in London, worked earnestly for India's freedom.

I recall one occasion when Krishna Menon had been unable to attend to his duties in London for a considerable period because of illness. Work was held up because he would not allow anyone else in his office to do take on the task. I suggested to the Prime Minister that Menon take a leave of absence so that the work of the Government could carry on, or that he be sent somewhere else and the Ministry replace him in London with a fitter man. Panditji's only answer was that while he was aware of the situation, he feared that if he shifted Krishna Menon from London, he would die, and he did not want that to happen.

At that moment the important thing was that I won my point. Orders were issued that supplies from France to India were to be channelled through the Embassy in Paris, not through the High Commission in London. We did get a very reasonable price—the French had agreed to supply us at prices which they charged to their own services—for airplanes, tanks, guns and other weapons which were urgently required in India. Krishna Menon was finally forced to resign as Defence Minister after the Chinese attack in 1962.

I have often been asked about my personal impressions of Pandit Nehru. To me he was a great man. Of course, all great men have their own weaknesses and he had his. But I admired him very much for he had done tremendous service to our country, something one could never forget. He was a man of vision with tremendous powers of leadership, and great character. But administration was not one of his strengths. I think he had a strong will; once he had made up his mind nothing could stop him. But these little human weaknesses are prevalent in everyone. The lives of great men reveal certain aspects of their personality which are not in keeping with the rest of their character. Panditji was no exception. As a man he was vain, could be most charming if he wanted to be, but almost unpleasant at times through sheer lack of consideration. As an architect of foreign policy he had a very fine sense of India's position internationally, and I think the policy he laid down for India was the only one we could follow at that time. The struggle for India's independence, the need for Indian leadership after Independence, gave him the opportunities to rise to the highest stature. He took that opportunity and he rose to the occasion.

CHAPTER 43

These years in France were, in a way, full of sadness for me. The France of 1949 was a very different country from the France I had known during the First World War. Then people were proud, and rightly so, of the part they had played in defeating Germany after a heroic struggle. In 1939, let down by its politicians, France gave up the battle without a fight. That humiliation was something the French people could never forget. Apart from the stand taken by General Charles de Gaulle and the heroic work of the Resistance, the people on the whole were very conscious of the feeble struggle they had put up under the leadership of General Pétain. They were, therefore, sensitive and very much on the defensive.

Many years of political instability after the war accentuated this malaise. Governments constantly fell to be followed by new equally short-lived governments. As my chauffeur, Louis, a typical Frenchman, described it to me once on my return from India, 'No change, except for new faces in the Government!' Politicians had earned a bad name throughout the country. The result was a thoroughly demoralizing, widespread cynicism. Being an extremely proud, intelligent people, these political developments disillusioned and disgusted the French to the point where they lost faith in everything, even in themselves—a sad state for any people to be in.

While I was in Paris I was accredited as Minister to Norway. This was a somewhat unusual posting as we had an Ambassador in

Sweden who could also have been accredited to neighbouring Norway. However, the Norwegians, who still remembered the time when they were under the rule of the Swedish King—a time of strife and bitterness between the two countries—were sensitive on this point, and preferred to have India's Ambassador in Paris look after Norway until India could open an independent mission there.

For me and my family this was a pleasant arrangement because it allowed us to see something of the Scandinavian countries. What added to my pleasure was that the Crown Prince of Norway was also from Balliol College. So it was a great pleasure for me to get to know him. It was considered sufficient for me and a couple of my officers to visit Oslo from time to time and pay our respects to members of the Government and of the Diplomatic Corps. So we did not open an office in Oslo.

In those years the main activity between our two countries was India's import of Norwegian newsprint. Subsequently, Norway played an extremely helpful role in developing fisheries in India. The accreditation to Norway gave us the opportunity to see some of the spectacular fjords north of Oslo, although we missed seeing the 'Land of the Midnight Sun' as while we were en route to this destination, I was recalled to Paris on urgent business.

I was in Paris during the post-war reconstruction of Western Europe, particularly France and Germany, which was devastated by the war. It was truly remarkable to see the scale and pace of the reconstruction. The tremendous task was made possible only through the generous help provided by the United States by way of funds under the Marshall Plan. In France, damage to the main ports such as Marseilles, Brest, Le Havre, Toulon and Cherbourg was repaired in record time. Not only were the facilities at these ports rebuilt but they were also modernized and expanded.

In West Germany, which I visited from time to time, where the destruction was massive—cities like Cologne and Hamburg were virtually razed to the ground—reconstruction work was taken up with typical perseverance by the Germans, and completed within an unbelievably short period. For the Germans it was a matter of personal pride to rebuild their shattered cities as fast as was humanly possible. We witnessed how in Cologne which was almost levelled to the ground workers worked literally day and night with tremendous fervour to achieve the 'German miracle'. In Germany in particular, during reconstruction, facilities were modernized, and in the case of industries, new plants and modern techniques were incorporated to ensure that reconstructed industries were far superior to those badly damaged or destroyed in the war. Ironically, it was noted with some bitterness in France and Britain, that the reconstructed industries were far superior to those in France and Britain! This reconstruction led to West Germany's economic superiority in a short time.

It is yet another irony of human experience that in spite of the United States' generous contribution to post-war reconstruction, the Americans were popular neither in West Germany nor in France. Graffiti on the streets read 'Americans Go Home!' I remember talking to some German friends about this, and when I mentioned America's assistance in rebuilding German cities, their only response was, 'Well, they were the ones who destroyed them!'

NATO was created at this time and the whole movement for the integration of Western Europe began. Paris was, therefore, a great centre for gatherings of national leaders both from America and Europe. This made for endless opportunities for exchange of ideas and opinions with a great many well informed and influential men. General Eisenhower was the first head of Supreme Headquarters Allied Powers Europe (SHAPE), the military instrument for implementing NATO policies. We were both members of the same Golf Club and, therefore, I had the opportunity of meeting him from time to time and saw something of the great courtesy and tact which had made him such a successful supreme commander of the Allied Forces.

But it was General Laurie Norstadt, who commanded SHAPE later, who I got to know much more intimately. A man most efficient in his work, retaining all the enthusiasm and keenness of youth, he became a really good friend, and Prakash and I saw a great deal of him and his charming wife.

It was Laurie Norstadt who arranged an enjoyable and unusual golf game when he got the great Ben Hogan—then at the peak of his career having just won the British Open—to Paris to play an exhibition match at the golf course of St. Germain. Ben Hogan partnered me against Sir Christopher Steele, the British Ambassador to NATO and Colonel Conrad, the U.S. Army champion in Europe. I have never seen a greater performance of golf than Hogan's in that match! As his partner, I went round the course in par, and never came in at a single hole! An unforgettable experience for any golfer.

CHAPTER 44

NATO had a Defence Officers' Club in Paris consisting of very senior officers of the NATO countries and its members, and I was asked to lunch to speak on India. I explained India's position vis a vis Pakistan very frankly, particularly in regard to Kashmir. Most of the people present sympathized with Pakistan despite our belief that India was the one constantly provoked by Pakistan while we on our part demonstrated our will to live in peace. I expected to be heckled after my 45-minute talk, and hoped for many provocative questions, particularly from the senior American officers so I was prepared with answers. However, I received a standing ovation and no questions were asked. I only hope that it was because I had convinced them, and not just out of politeness!

My luncheon meeting with the Press Club in Paris where I spoke on India and Pakistan was different in nature. I spoke very frankly and there were plenty of questions which I was happy to answer. A couple of days later the Pakistan Ambassador, a fine man and a friend, Sardar Shah Nawaz Khan of Kot, said to me, 'Malik Sahib, what have you gone and done? We were living quite happily here. Now you have made a speech at the Press Club and my Government has asked me to reply to it.' I asked him if there was anything in my speech which he found objectionable. He replied, 'No, actually, Pandit Nehru has said the same things more than once and nobody has objected, but between you and me, we have no leadership in our country comparable to the leadership of Pandit Nehru and they will not be satisfied unless I give a reply.' All I could do was to tell him that he must do whatever he felt necessary. But nothing ever came of it.

The Ambassador's wife, a very dignified, traditional and cultured Muslim lady, called on Prakash. It was a purely courtesy visit, and according to protocol, to last a few minutes. I had made a point of being away from home at the time as I knew she observed purdah. But because she stayed on for a long time I returned to the house before she had left. My wife sent me a message that the begum had expressed a wish to meet me too—she was so charmed by Prakash that she ignored her purdah—so I joined them at tea. Prakash told me later that they had had a very pleasant talk during which Begum Sahib expressed her sorrow at the partition of India, saying that it was a shame, adding that a lot of Muslim riff-raff had come over to Pakistan from India! No good had come from the Partition she said. My wife heartily agreed reminding her very gently that India had never wanted the partition to take place. Unfortunately the Ambassador was transferred soon after this.

I was invited to address the British Empire Club in Paris at their annual Empire Day luncheon. Lord Alfred Duff Cooper, formerly First Lord of the Admiralty and later the British Ambassador in Paris, was the President of the Club and came to invite me. He told me that the previous year Field Marshall Montgomery had addressed the Club and this year his Committee wanted me to come. I tried to excuse myself but he insisted. I agreed on condition that they take what I was going to say in good spirit and not bear me any ill will as I proposed to talk frankly about relations between India and Great Britain in the past. Duff Cooper accepted my condition assuring me that I would receive a warm welcome.

The lunch was well attended and I sat with my wife and Lady Diana Duff Cooper at the head table. I spoke at some length on Indo-British relations—the mistakes made by the British in the past and of the eventual happy outcome as their departure from India was effected without bitterness but with goodwill on both sides. Duff Cooper, who was presiding, got up and said, with considerable emotion that there were two things he wished to say about my speech: the first was that as a great and personal friend of Winston Churchill, and a confirmed Conservative, he had felt at the time that the British had made a great mistake in giving up their rule in India; the second was that he had listened to many speeches but had never been converted by any speech. 'Today I have been converted by a speech. I realize now that by leaving India, we did not lose India, rather we won India.'

In 1950 the United Nations General Assembly was held in Paris. I was a member of the Indian delegation led by that fine statesman, Sir. B.N. Rau. When he was appointed a judge to the International Court at the Hague, I was appointed leader of the delegation. The Security Council also met in Paris at this time and the subject of Kashmir came up for discussion.

At the Assembly I got an unexpected opportunity to express India's sentiments on the South African Government's racial policies. Although it had been previously decided that we would not enter any acrimonious debate with the South African spokesman, when he attacked India bitterly in his speech, we decided to hit back. When my turn to speak came I said that we had no desire to cover up the discriminations that still persisted in our country but we were trying to eradicate them, as indeed were the Americans and all decent people everywhere. I further stated that the Government of South Africa was unique. Far from being ashamed, they were proud of what they were doing. The day of judgment was to come. General Thimmaya, in Paris for the Security Council debate on Kashmir, told me later, 'With your turban and grey beard you were like an oracle from the Old Testament!'

* * *

While we were in France we saw something of the Duke and Duchess of Windsor as they were living in Paris, and had a chance to see how this strange marriage was working out!* The Duke and I played golf together and, although he loved the game and was a keen golfer he was never very good at it. One day when we were playing at La Boulie near Paris we were on the tee of a longish par three. The Duke played a fine shot, landing on the green and was utterly overjoyed. He threw his club on the ground, came and hugged me, saying with glee, like a schoolboy, 'That's the first time I've ever driven this green!'

He loved gardening too and was very proud of the garden he had created at their farm, but the Duchess was not interested in either golf or gardening. She loved entertaining and being entertained and, like the gentleman he was, he went along with her. Were they happy? It was very difficult to say because he was completely loyal to her, never by way of word or behaviour letting on that he regretted the past. But she gave the impression of being very inconsiderate of him and rather selfish.

One evening while dining with us, the Duke and I had been reminiscing over a drink after dinner. He was obviously thoroughly relaxed and enjoying himself when the Duchess decided it was time to leave. Without even allowing him to finish his drink she got up, and said, 'Come on, David'. In the middle of our conversation, he put down his unfinished drink and meekly obeyed! Another time, when we were dining at their home in the Bois de Boulogne, I was sitting next to her and she asked me all of a sudden, 'Mr. Malik, you are an old friend of my husband, do you think I have made him happy?' Totally taken aback, I managed to murmur, not very convincingly, 'Of course, Your Highness.' But no more was said.

Another time when Prakash and I were driving back from a

* King Edward VIII abdicated the throne in 1936 to marry the twice-divorcee, American socialite Wallis Simpson. This caused a constitutional crisis in the United Kingdom.

lunch with them in their farm outside Paris, my wife told me that when the Duchess took her and a couple of other ladies to her private apartment, Prakash noticed that on one of the small cushions on a chair were embroidered the words 'Don't worry, it never happens'. The Duchess noticed my wife looking at the cushion and murmured to herself: 'But it does happen sometimes you know.' Prakash was very intrigued but, of course, could not ask any questions.

As a family we had been deeply moved by the events which led to the Duke's abdication after his short reign as Edward VIII. We were in Delhi at the time, and as we had no radio in our home, Harji, then eleven years old, and I walked over in the dark around 2 a.m. next door to my brother, Sir Teja Singh's house, to hear the abdication speech on the radio. Harji, while at school in England when he was Prince of Wales had been an admirer of the Duke. So, with tears rolling down her face, she listened to him tell the world that he could not carry on without the help of 'the woman I love'!

CHAPTER 45

In 1954 my orders came to return to India after my five years posting in France. So we packed up, said our farewells to our many friends and left for home. Harji and Veena had sailed earlier, taking all our baggage and Prakash and I flew back. We planned to stay a few days in Bombay, and to our great surprise we were entertained by the Bombay Pradesh Congress Committee and its Chairman, Mr. S.K. Patil who was extremely friendly. At the same time we received a number of invitations from prominent personalities in Bombay who were mere acquaintances. We were greatly mystified by all this but later we discovered the reason behind this warm welcome. There was evidently a strong rumour that I was coming to Bombay as Governor! This was confirmed when I met Pandit Nehru after I arrived in Delhi. He informed me that he had called me back from Paris to appoint me as Governor of Bombay. However, Mr. Morarji Desai, who was the Chief Minister of Maharashtra at the time, had objected to the appointment of a civil servant.

Panditji explained that the appointment of a Governor was in his hands and if I wanted to go to Bombay he could insist on my appointment. He then asked me how I felt about it. I told him that it would be most undesirable to have a Governor who was at odds with the Chief Minister as it would involve constant friction and unpleasantness. I therefore preferred not to be in Bombay if the Chief Minister did not want me there.*

* When I finally returned to India at the end of 1956, I paid courtesy calls on all the important Cabinet Ministers, including Mr. Morarji Desai, who was

The Prime Minister said that in that case he would send me to Argentina as Ambassador. I asked if it was possible for me to return to Paris for my remaining service period. He said that it could be rather embarrassing as I had already said goodbye to the President of France. I requested Panditji to leave that to me because, strictly speaking, according to the rules, I continued to be Ambassador in Paris until my successor had presented his credentials and taken charge of the post. Since my successor, K.M. Pannikar, had been appointed, but had not yet arrived in Paris, nor had the French given their formal agreement to his posting, it would be perfectly acceptable for me to return to Paris. Panditji finally agreed, as did the French who, graciously, reinstated me in the same position on the list of precedence of Foreign Ambassadors which I had occupied before I left.

So, we returned to Paris to the delight of all our family and our friends in France. In 1955 when the Prime Minister was visiting Paris again, he brought up the question of a Governorship, and told me that he had a post for me in India if I wanted to come back. I told him that I was very grateful to him but I had thought the matter over very carefully and was really interested only in two Governorships: the one of Punjab, the other of Assam—Punjab, because it was my home state and Assam because the Governor had a great deal of solid work to do in that state. It seemed to me that under our present Constitution, the Governor was largely

---

then in the Cabinet. After a few minutes talk I got up to leave. He asked me to sit down and said, 'I want to talk to you.' He was surprised when I told him I probably knew what he wanted to talk to me about. I said I knew of his refusal to have me as Governor of Bombay. He was quite taken aback and asked who had told me this. I explained that it had been the Prime Minister himself. He then explained, 'Mr. Malik, I would like to tell you that I had nothing personal against you, but in Bombay we had some trouble with the previous Governor, who was a Service man, and we felt that it would be easier if someone from a political background came as Governor, particularly as we had plenty of administrative experience in Bombay.' He added that I would have been among the first in his choice if he had wanted a Service man.

a figurehead, the main power in the state being in the hands of the Chief Minister. In Assam the situation was different and the Governor had a role to play which is why I had mentioned Assam as I felt that I had still real service left in me. He explained that neither Punjab nor Assam was available at that time. He did not want to send a Sikh to Punjab and someone had just been appointed in Assam. He had intended to give me Rajasthan. I asked Panditji if, given the circumstances, I might be allowed to decline his offer. He was somewhat surprised but did not mention the matter again.

Meanwhile, I had been approached by a couple of important British companies to join them in India after I retired from the diplomatic service. I showed the letters I had received from these companies to the Prime Minister and explained to him that with the experience that I had, and with my knowledge of the British and American people, I felt that at this stage of India's economic development I could play a useful part as a representative of these companies in their negotiations with the Government of India. Panditji was good enough to say that since I had not had anything to do with these companies during my service, and had been out of the country since 1947, there would be no objection to my joining them. But, he added, that he would have to consult his Cabinet ministers before giving me permission. Subsequently, he wrote to me stating there was no objection to my joining any one of these companies, and after retirement I did so.

In December 1956, having said our final farewells to France, we returned to India. Very soon after that I retired from the Indian Civil Service after 55 years, to enter a new phase of my life. I was to be involved in the corporate sector for the first time.

It was very different from the I.C.S. and the Diplomatic Service but in a way turned out to be exciting, a new sort of challenge. At that stage of the country's development the big story was industrialization, and I proved to be useful in such areas. I was greatly impressed by the British businessmen I had met in England with whom I was to be associated. Trevor Peppercorn, on the Board of Directors of Dunlop's, was one of them. We formed a lasting friendship, for he was one of those rare people with a brilliant mind, a wide and tolerant outlook, and a man of great integrity. Simon Carves Ltd., the other company I was to join, had been actively associated with the steel industry in India for many years, having built most of the coke ovens for Tata's and the Indian Iron and Steel Co. Ltd. The head of the company was Lord Simon of Withenshawe, one of Britain's leading industrialists, but the Managing Director who first approached me was an old friend, Rupert Potter, whom I had met in France. He was a charming man and a forceful, dynamic industrialist. He told me they intended to start a branch of the Company in India and wanted me to be its chairman. I felt I could play a useful part and accepted. Later, I was also to join the Metal Box Company who had an interesting operation in India, Union Carbide and May & Baker, the pharmaceutical firm. So I found myself involved in a wide spectrum of industrial development. As an 'outside' Director I also enjoyed my association with Mahindra and Mahindra, whose Chairman, K.C. Mahindra was a very dear friend, a friendship going back to when he was head of the Indian Supply Mission in Washington and I was Trade Commissioner in New York.

At times there was excitement and achievement but unfortunately, because of the License Raj, more often there was tremendous frustration resulting from the inability to get things done because of the hurdles put up by the bureaucratic systems. I found I could play a useful role as a liaison officer between the companies and the Government, and came into contact with some remarkable men, both in the corporate world and with the ministers and bureaucrats dealing with them.

* * *

As I could speak frankly to British and American executives, and I knew the senior officers in some Ministries, I was able to help to bring about a better mutual understanding.

As soon as I joined Dunlop's, their Managing Director in Calcutta, Cecil Stack, told me about the unfortunate misunderstanding between Dunlop's and Mr. T.T. Krishnamachari, then Finance Minister. Apparently Stack's predecessor had been extremely tactless in dealing with the Minister and the latter, greatly annoyed, made it clear that he would not see any of the Dunlop's officers.

The head of Dunlop's, an extremely important figure in world industry, had come to Delhi especially to see Mr. Krishnamachari in this connection, but the Minister refused to receive him. After going through the case file I told Stack that the company had been in the wrong and it seemed to me that they must apologize to the Minister. He assured me that they realized their mistake and were prepared to apologize. I then went to see Mr. Krishnamachari, whom I had met casually a couple of times, and told him that it was most unfortunate that such bad blood had developed between him and this important company, that they had realized their mistake and wished to apologize. I asked him if he was prepared to forgive them. I pointed out that Dunlop's could play an important role in the country's economic development, but because of the stupidity of their former Managing Director, who had since left the country, they were unable to make any progress. The Minister was good enough to agree, and I took Stack to see him and everything was patched up after the apology. The company's considerable expansion plans, which had been stalled, were soon approved.

In connection with my work, I frequently visited both England and America to meet the directors of the parent companies and discuss plans for expansion as well as any problems their Indian counterpart faced. I was told by the Managing Directors of the Indian companies that the men at the top in America

and the United Kingdom, who had subsidiaries in many parts
of the world, were always being approached by their subsidiaries
for finance, and they had to decide where to make the larger
commitments as the funds available were limited. My colleagues
in India felt my intercession with the parent companies was
helpful because we were able to build a strong case, with the
stable conditions in India and the potentialities for expansion
in comparison with other developing countries.

In the summer of 1966 I was invited to visit America by Union
Carbide for consultations and since Prakash too was invited,
we took the opportunity to travel through Europe and England
to visit old friends. We also went to San Francisco and were
extremely interested to see the great change that had taken place
in the standing of the Sikh community which had settled in
California since I had last visited the state over 25 years ago.
In those days the Sikh community, mostly peasants from the
Punjab, was confined almost entirely to the Sacramento Valley.
Being generally ill-educated, a great many of them married
Mexican girls, and were socially backward and not accepted
by most Americans living in the area, even though they were
doing well. During this visit we found a great many Sikhs
occupying prominent positions in the American community
as well respected doctors, engineers, technicians, businessmen
and professionals. It was interesting to learn that while the old
peasant settlers were shedding their old traditions, the new lot,
justifiably proud of their traditions, was holding on to them.
This gave the entire Sikh community in California a much better
name and enhanced its standing in the public eye—a most
refreshing and encouraging change.

On the last day of our visit we met an outstanding young
couple, Dr. and Mrs. Narendar Kapany. A prominent scientist and
artist Kapany had done remarkably well and been recognized
as 'the father of fibre optics'. He was head of an outstanding

company in its field, Optics Technology. He himself had done brilliant research in the field of laser beams and was the author of many technical publications and responsible for several inventions in laser technology. Kapany went on to be prominent in the Sikh Foundation in California and endowed a Chair of Sikh Studies at the University of California.

CHAPTER 46

We visited Honolulu, Japan and Bangkok on the way to India. Honolulu was disappointing, very touristy, not at all what we had expected but we were told that several other places in the Hawaiian Islands were extremely beautiful. Unfortunately, we did not have the time to visit them. Japan, however, I found fascinating. I had been there twice before with K.C. Mahindra on business trips. However, this was Prakash's first experience of Japan and she was totally charmed. On a previous visit I had met Mr. Iwai, head of one of the big trading companies in Japan. From the very start we had got along very well and had kept in touch. He was a most interesting person. He had been educated in England, France and Germany and was extremely well informed, with a broad liberal outlook. He and I spent interesting evenings together.

Before leaving India I had written to him about our upcoming visit, asking for his advice on the best way to spend two weeks in his country. He replied saying he was looking forward to our visit and would look after us. On arriving in Tokyo we were met by one of his people who acted as our guide throughout our stay. After a couple of days in Tokyo we went to Osaka where Mr. Iwai met us. He entertained us at his home and we met his wife, a typical Japanese lady, who was very friendly, in spite of the difficulty we had communicating with each other as she spoke only Japanese. The Iwais were most hospitable and kind and took us out to eat at some typical Japanese restaurants with excellent food and immaculate service.

We visited beautiful temples, palaces and gardens. We were
then were taken to a monastery which had been established by
the donation from Mr. Iwai's late father. Our Japanese host told
us the fascinating story of this unusual monastery. His father,
who had found success early in life, found that around the age of
35 his health was beginning to fail. He had become a bundle of
nerves, had no taste for food and suffered badly from insomnia.
The doctors could do nothing for him and he became desperate.
At this critical time in his life he met a Buddhist monk who
persuaded him to change his way of life completely. While Mr.
Iwai continued to work, he devoted a good deal of his time to
meditation in which the monk initiated him. In a few years his life
was totally transformed. He gained poise and calm, shed all his
nervous tension, began to sleep and eat well, and became a normal
human being again. At the same time he continued to work hard
to build a most flourishing business. He died after having lived a
healthy life leaving in his will a large sum of money to establish
a monastery where, in addition to the monks, there would be
a number of students who, while studying at the neighbouring
Osaka University on post-graduate research and other studies,
would live in the monastery and also pursue religious studies and
practices like the monks there. They would be subjected to the
same rigid rules of discipline and conduct as the monks.

After hearing Mr. Iwai's story we were keen to visit the
monastery as this combination of higher academic studies
and spiritual development seemed to be the answer to many
of the problems faced by humanity today. Our host took us
to the monastery situated a few miles from the city of Osaka.
The buildings were simple but adequate: a chapel, very simply
furnished with cushions for the worshippers to kneel on, living
quarters, austere but immaculately clean for the monks and
students, all set in a beautiful garden. The atmosphere of purity
and simplicity of the place, with its peace and serenity, made a
deep impression on both of us.

We were received by the Abbot, a fine looking, ascetic old man. After he had shown us around the monastery, he took us to his room where we sat down for a chat and a cup of tea. At our request he asked one of the monks to chant a Buddhist hymn and my wife responded by singing one of our shabads. Our Japanese friends appreciated this. Unfortunately we could not meet any of the students as they were away attending their classes at the university. He added, that since the life was very hard, with the young men having to do both their work at the university and carry on their religious studies in the monastery, the monastery was finding it difficult to fill all the vacancies despite the fact that board and lodging was entirely free. As we took leave of the Abbot he said to me, 'You, Sir, have been holding positions of honour and responsibility in the service of your country, and have had a successful life, but I see that you attach much importance to spiritual matters. I wish you would see our Prime Minister and other Ministers and tell them about this.' I smiled in thanks.

As on my two previous visits I found Japan fascinating. Its natural beauty was striking, if one leaves out big cities particularly like Tokyo, which has so little to commend it, in spite of the beauty of the Emperor's Palace and its grounds, and some of the public parks. Tokyo indeed outdoes some of the great cities in America and Europe which are spoiled through overbuilding, overcrowding, transport congestion and pollution and noise. But Tokyo lacks qualities which in these other cities compensate for the evils of urbanization—the dramatic quality of New York, the unique atmosphere of London, the charm of Paris.

Despite large scale industrialization the Japanese countryside retained great charm, as did some of the smaller cities like Kyoto, a city with which Prakash fell in love, and Osaka. As we travelled by road we were extremely impressed by the beautifully maintained gardens, even small cottages, with their neat little plots, full of flowers, vegetables and fruit. At the same time I was amazed at the tremendous progress post-war Japan had made which was rapidly making it one of the most advanced countries in the world—progress brought about in the absence of any great natural resources. Progress was achieved by the industry and skill of its people but above all by the pragmatic, practical policies of Governments which changed their political make-up from time to time but remained consistent in their attitude towards business and industry. The entire Government machinery was geared to help growth. It is this cooperation between Government and industry that has enabled Japan to make the enormous strides, both in the technical and managerial fields, which have earned the country this enviable position in international commerce and trade.

We visited America again in 1970 and found New York greatly changed. The pollution made me feel generally unwell and the insecurity of the city, which we had heard about, was brought home to us when, one evening, we decided to walk back to our hotel from the Radio City Music Hall where we had gone for old times' sake! Not only were the streets previously so lively and crowded with people almost deserted but our lift attendant at the hotel, told us we were lucky to have got home safely without being mugged.

On our way back home we visited Nairobi, Kenya, a part of the world quite new to us for the first time. The fortnight in Kenya was both interesting and enjoyable. We were guests of Acchru and Krishna Kapila, to whom we had been introduced in India. Acchru's sister, Kanta Advani, was a good friend of our family. After our Kenya fortnight a new friendship was forged. Acchru was a leading lawyer in Nairobi and he and his wife had taken on Kenyan nationality. He was a member of the team of lawyers who defended Jomo Kenyatta, the President of Kenya in 1970 when he was prosecuted by the British for his connection with the revolutionary Mau-Mau Movement. Because of this role

Acchru enjoyed excellent relations with the Government at that time but later fell into disfavour with the new regime. Our hosts saw to it that we saw some of this beautiful country including the great game sanctuaries for which Kenya is famous.

From Nairobi we had a pleasant flight back to India and to our new home, finally a home of our own after over 50 years my wife and I had been together! And one that was built according to our own wishes.* It was a perfect venue for our golden wedding anniversary party in 1969 organized by our children with all our friends and family around us. To our surprise and delight, messages and flowers arrived from friends abroad who had been invited to the party by the children. We felt very blessed.

It's been a happy house for us. Prakash was able to have the garden she always wanted; our prayer room looking out into the garden with numerous trees planted by Prakash, and a large lawn for me to practice my golf and keep on working on my swing!

---

* It was a house which some years later was showcased in a Festival of India in Paris when the architect, Ram Sharma, won the prize for the outstanding residential design.

CHAPTER 47

As I come to a close of my memoirs, one of those moments in one's life take place which are all the more pleasant and exciting for being totally unexpected. Ethel Whitehorn, one of my oldest friends in England, sent me a cutting from *The Times* in London regarding a reception that was being hosted in June 1972 in London by the British Government to celebrate the Diamond Jubilee of British military aviation. All surviving members of the Royal Flying Corps and the Royal Naval Air Service were asked to inform the Defence Ministry if they wished to be invited. I replied immediately saying that I wanted to attend the reception as a Member of the R.F.C. in 1917, and I asked if the R.A.F. was going to sponsor travel for those who wished to attend from overseas.

I received a letter saying that as the number of people who wished to attend the reception exceeded the number the Government proposed to invite a ballot would be held and those who were successful would receive the invitation. The letter mentioned that there was a 50 per cent chance of winning the ballot. I was further informed that those who received the invitation were expected to find their own way to London.

I was very disappointed as I had no intention of spending the large sum of money involved just to attend one reception! However, just about that time we happened to have dining with us our Chief of Air Staff, Air Chief Marshal Pratap Lal, a close and dear friend. When he heard about this he said since I was the first and only surviving Indian member of the Royal Flying

Corps, I must go and attend this historic event. If the Royal Air Force would not fly me, the Indian Air Force would certainly do so. Pratap said he would have a word about this with the Defence Minister. A couple of days later he telephoned to say that the Defence Minister was happy to give his approval to both my wife and I being flown in an R.A.F. plane to London and back!

In the meantime I also received a letter from the Defence Ministry in London enclosing an invitation to the reception. So we were flown out by the Indian Air Force. And so, at the reception there was a mini-reunion of 28th Squadron, immortalized in a cartoon, which hangs in our home. We took the opportunity of this unexpected visit to England and spent almost two months there, mostly staying with old friends and were deeply moved by the love and affection we received. These special bonds which are so naturally and easily renewed sometimes after years of no contact add a glow to one's life.

During my visit to England I could not help drawing a contrast with the London I first knew as a youngster of fourteen—1908 to 1972, sixty-four years, not much in the life of man on this planet. And yet what vast changes, almost unbelievable, we see in every field of activity. Opinions vary widely on the significance of these changes. However, it is generally agreed that the nature of man has changed little despite the enormous advances in science, medicine, in the knowledge of nature's forces and man's capacity, in some measure, to control them.

Without the evolution of man's nature there is great uncertainty about the future. I ask myself, unless man's inner consciousness is aroused and strengthened, will we turn to destruction rather than construction? I believe, and have lived with the belief that only religion and faith can help man achieve spiritual development. I don't mean religion and faith in any narrow denominational sense, but both in their broader, encompassing aspect.

And now looking back on all these years, with all that they have brought me in the way of happiness, fulfillment, elation, excitement, balanced by sorrow and disappointments, at times even frustration, I cannot think of a better way of putting it all than in the words of George de Maurier which have been with me through many years:

A little work, a little play
To keep us going—and so good-day!

A little warmth, a little light
Of love's bestowing—and so, good-night.

A little fun, to match the sorrow
Of each day's growing—and so, good-morrow!

A little trust that when we die
We reap our sowing—and so—good-bye!

H.S. Malik
India's Grand Old Gentleman of Golf

By Dick Severino

Asian Golf Digest, March 1980

Again last year, as in other years while in New Delhi for the annual Indian Open on the Asia Gold Circuit, it was a renewed privilege and pleasure to play, talk and dine with H.S. Malik, who, at age 85, is India's beloved grand old gentleman of golf.

'H.S.', as he is known affectionately among his many friends in both and diplomatic circles, is a former Indian ambassador to Canada and France after having served as Trade Commissioner for India in the United States and Canada—which accounts for his diplomatic identity.

As for his golfing identity, well, here is a man who, never having played before, began golf as a student at Oxford University in England in 1912 at the age of seventeen, and, completely self-taught, using Harry Vardon's book *How to Play Golf* as his bible, worked his way down to a scratch handicap in one year. No lessons, just that book and practice, practice, practice, play, play, play,

whenever and wherever possible. Not bad for openers. Hardly!

From that beginning, this then young, bearded and turbaned Sikh went on to play his way indelibly into the history of Indian golf— Indian golf by Indians, that is.

The 'by Indians' qualification is important, for whereas golf has a long history in India, with the Royal Calcutta Golf Club, the oldest in the world outside the United Kingdom, dating from 1829, the game was largely if not exclusively the province of the British until the long era of the British Raj was terminated when India achieved independence in 1947. Against that background, H.S. Malik, one of the best of the Indian golfers, was the first of any prominence who went abroad and projected Indian golf outside his own country.

Over a delightful curry at his home in New Delhi, H.S. told the story of how and why he first became interested in golf.

'When I went to Oxford,' he said, 'in the summer of 1912, I went along one day with my British guardian's son to Royal Eastbourne, where he had a game. I had never hit a golf ball—cricket, football were my games in India—but he insisted I have a game.

'They had a lot of very good golfers at Eastbourne in those days, some players with plus-four handicaps. We watched two of them tee off in a threesome. After they hit good tee shots, the third player, a golf architect named Simpson, hit a bad shot. "Hellfire, damn, blast the thing!" said Simpson loudly. So I said to myself, "There must be something in this game to excite this kind of emotion." I was very impressed with the immaculate way the golfers dressed in plus-fours (pants, not handicaps) and jackets—no playing in just shirts in those days. I became fascinated with golf.

'I took it up at Oxford, bought Harry Vardon's book *How to Play Golf*, taught myself to play without lessons, and in one year got down to scratch and earned my Oxford Blue.

'Two years later, in 1914, a wealthy British friend of mine who knew the story, arranged for me to have a day playing with Harry Vardon, who was then the professional at South Herts Golf Club in the northern part of London. And Vardon said to me, "You know, it's the most extraordinary thing, but you have exactly the swing that I had when I was young. It's an exact replica of my swing as it was then."'

And that from a book!

With his beard and turban and Vardon swing, young Malik attracted considerable attention on the golf course whenever and wherever he appeared, the more so when it became increasingly evident that he was a player of promise. As for the beard and turban, traditional adornments of all orthodox Sikhs, H.S. has an amusing anecdote of a match he had with an English barrister named Tyndall Atkinson at Sunningdale near London in 1913, about the time he was getting down to scratch.

'Atkinson offered to play me in a top hat to "equalize" the match,' he recalled, 'but I declined the offer and beat him anyway.'

After finishing his studies at Oxford, H.S. eventually joined the Indian Civil Service and was sent back to Oxford for another year of study. It was during that year, in 1920, that his younger brother, I.S. Malik, came to Oxford and began golf with H.S. as his first teacher.

Though, unlike H.S., I.S. failed to earn his Oxford Blue, the younger Malik did develop into a very good player, thanks partly if not largely to training under British professional Archie Comston, and went on to become the first Indian ever to

win the Amateur Championship
of India. I.S. won that title several
times, as did his son and H.S.'s
nephew, Ashok Malik.

Thus, the Malik name, including
the initials H.S., though he never
won the Indian Amateur, is
prominent on the hallowed honours
board at the gold clubs in India.
This is especially so at The Royal in
Calcutta, which stands as the Vatican
of Indian golf, and at Gulmarg, high
in the Himalayas in Kashmir, where
they've played golf seriously since
the turn of the century.

Over brandy after dinner, he
spoke of his return to India in 1922
following his second time at Oxford.
'Then,' he said, 'I believe I was the
only Indian playing golf in our
country. There were very few golf
courses, and those worth playing
on could certainly be counted on
the fingers of one hand.'

One of those that could be
counted was at Gulmarg, and he
told of going there to play in the
Northern Championship. 'The
caddies at Gulmarg had never seen
an Indian playing golf, and when I
made it into the final, they went wild
with joy. My opponent in the final
was an Irish International golfer, a
Captain Martin, a very good player,
and the caddies all followed the
match and rooted rudely against
him. Whenever he missed a putt,
they cheered and shouted, "Kill
him!" in their Kashmiri dialect. It
was embarrassing, and I tried to

quieten them down, but it was no
use. Finally, I won, and you could
hear them all over Gulmarg, they
were so happy that an Indian beat
the British.'

H.S. won that championship
again three or four years later when
he beat his brother, I.S., 12 and
11, in the 36-hole final. 'I.S. was
really playing better golf than I was
then—it was 1925 or 1926—but
he'd just gotten married and was
too anxious to beat me, with his
bride and all the family watching.
After we halved the first hole in par,
he three-putted the second green
to go one down. That bothered
him, and after that I won hole after
hole. It was purely psychological
with him. He beat himself, but he
was really the better player.'

More than thirty years later the
brothers Malik were to represent
India in the World Amateur Team
Championship for the Eisenhower
Trophy. I.S. led the Indian team in
the inaugural Eisenhower Trophy
matches at St. Andrews, Scotland
in 1958, and H.S. was the non-
playing captain of the team in
the 1962 matches at Merion, near
Philadelphia, Pennsylvania in the
United States. Son and nephew
Ashok Malik was a player on both
those teams.

Long before that, however, H.S.
had projected his diplomatic and
golfing charm across the United
States, Canada, and Europe as he
served his country in the successive

posts of trade commissioner and ambassador.

He went to the United States as Trade Commissioner and to Canada in 1938 as the clouds of World War Two gathered ominously, and remained in that role until 1944. His office was in New York, and he lived nearby Greenwich, Connecticut, where he played golf at the Greenwich Country Club and was a member at Apawamis, an exclusive golf club at Rye, New York in adjacent Westchester Country.

His quasi-diplomatic status, combined with various letters of introduction, brought him many invitations to golf clubs in various parts of the United States and Canada, where his impressive game, combined with his gentlemanly manner, led to still more invitations to play at such exhalted bastions of golf as Pine Valley in New Jersey and Oakmont in Pennsylvania, to name only two of the many.

Typical of his experience as he worked and played his way around two North American countries, promoting trade for India, was the occasion when he was in Pittsburg to make a business luncheon speech on a Monday. He arrived in town in time to have a game with the professional at nearby Oakmont— one of the toughest courses in the country—on Sunday before the speech. Playing level, he beat the pro in a well-played match.

'When I was introduced at the luncheon on the next day,' recounted H.S., 'the gentleman introducing me said, "I don't have to introduce our speaker to you today, because you all know already who he is and what he's done." The story of my match with the Oakmont pro was in the Monday morning papers. I think that was 1939.'

When India became independent in 1947, H.S. was appointed as his country's first ambassador to Canada, in Ottawa, and remained there until 1949 when he was sent to Paris as India's ambassador to France. He was the ambassador in Paris until 1956.

During his seven years in France he played a lot of golf, and became very well known on the Continent, as well, of course, in Great Britain where he had swung his first golf club in 1912. 'One of the most interesting things about golf,' he says, 'is that you meet so many interesting people playing the game.' True enough, and being an ambassador with a good swing and low handicap makes the introductions so much easier.

When he reminisces about the many personalities he met, played golf with, and became friends of through the years, he treasures especially his memories of the Duke of Windsor and King Leopold of Belgium. His soft, cultured voice takes on a special tone of respect and affection when he speaks of them.

His feelings for the Duke of Windsor perhaps is best expressed in the answer he gave to the questions as what event, circumstance or happening in all his years playing golf ranks as the most memorable in his mind. After mulling over the question for a bit, he said, 'That's difficult to say, to pick up just one thing from all the games and all the places and all the people that have made my life in golf so memorable. But here's a special one. I was playing with the Duke of Windsor one day at Le Boulie near Paris. I think it was 1951. There's a difficult par-3 hole there, and the Duke of Windsor hit a three-wood shot one onto the green. When he saw the ball was on the green, he rushed over to me and embraced me, he was so happy. "That's the first time I've ever done that," he said, beaming. And I thought to myself, there really is something special about this game that makes a former King of England so happy to be on the green like this.'

H.S. says warmly that one of his dearest friends is King Leopold, whom he first met in Geneva after World War Two when Leopold, a keen golfer and a good one, lived temporarily with his wife in Geneva before eventually returning to Belgium. They became good friends, played golf together, and when subsequently H.S. was the

ambassador in Paris, he and his wife used to visit Leopold and his wife, stay at the royal palace at Lachen near Brussels, and play golf on the private course in the palace grounds.

This led to one claim to fame that H.S., essentially a modest man, likes to speak of. 'We were staying at the palace one time after Leopold had abdicated in favour of his son, who became King Badouin. After lunch on Sunday we went out to play golf—Leopold, King Bedouin, Leopold's wife, the Princess, and myself, as we often did. Usually, the gardeners carried the clubs, but this time all but the two of the gardeners were on holiday. So, the question was, who would carry whose clubs? The two gardeners carried them for Leopold and the Princess; and Badouin said he would carry mine. I said, 'No, you can't possibly do that. I'll carry my own, and carry yours,' but he wouldn't agree, and I was literally forced to let him carry my clubs. So I had a reigning monarch for a caddie. That was in 1952 or 1953, and I think I am unique in this respect.'

H.S. Malik is indeed unique, not only in that respect but far more widely as the man who projected Indian golf so charmingly around the world in places where, until he appeared on the tee with his own immaculate attire set off intriguingly with his beard and turban, they didn't know that golf was even played in India—except, of course, for the British who had been there. In that sense, he was not only his country's ambassador to Canada and France, he was concurrently and will remain forever India's first and best ambassador of golf.

He had the distinction of having played played with Harry Vardon, James Braid and J.H. Taylor, the great British Triumvirate in the early era of modern golf; who once engaged the great Bobby Jones of the United States in a hand-wrestling match to see who had the stronger wrists—that was in 1921 when Jones made his first trip across the Atlantic to play in the Open Championship, and as H.S. recalls, they both got so involved in the friendly test of strength in the clubhouse of one of the British gold clubs that they wound up on the floor and the match was declared a draw.

A man who played an exhibition match in Paris with the Duke of Windsor, American Air Force General Lauris Norsadt, then Commander of SHAPE, and none other than the mighty Ben Hogan of the United States. That was 1953, the year Hogan won The Open at Carnoustie in his first and only attempt at that prestigious championship. There is a picture of that fourball in the montage of fascinating photographs which cover the walls of H.S.'s study.

He has been on the golf course for 68 years from 1912 to 1980. That's a lot of putts! And, most important, there is a man—*the* man—whose example and dedication led the way in establishing Indians as a growing part of golf in India back when the British dominated the game in that country. India owes him a lot for that.

Sardar Malik

By Khushwant Singh

Hindustan Times, November 1958

Much has been written in the press of the passing of Sardar Hardit Singh Malik. Much more would have been written about him if he had gone at the height of his fame and popularity. For the last many years he had largely confined his activities to the golf course and not many people realized that he was still around. On the 23rd of November he would have celebrated his 91st birthday.

I don't know of many people who packed so much in their lives as he did: played cricket and golf for Oxford University; enlisted in the French Foreign Legion; was the first Indian to fly military aircraft and be shot down; got into the I.C.S.; became Prime Minister of Patiala; High Commissioner to Canada, Ambassador to France and one of the best golfers of India. Above all, he was as handsome a Sardar you could see, and the most immaculately dressed. He was a connoisseur of good wines, gourmet food and yet a devoutly religious man.

Malik was an ardent admirer of the Nehrus and Indira Gandhi. His loyalty to Nehru—Gandhi family was torn apart by the storming of the Golden Temple by the Army. He was never the same man again. A mood of deep depression set in. By strange coincidence he suffered a stroke the day Mrs. Gandhi was assassinated. At great risk from marauding gangs out for Sikh blood, Mala Malik, took him to hospital. The family kept back from him the news of Mrs. Gandhi's assassination.

His funeral was as unique as his life. At his wife's behest raagis chanted hymns of joy and hope, not of mourning. In the room where his body lay Mrs. Prakash Malik sat alone with the tape recorder playing recitations from the Granth Sahib in Sardar Malik's own voice. When the funeral van moved out of his house, instead of crying there were triumphant shouts of Sat Sri Akal. When he was cremated, a golf club and a golf ball were placed beside his body. If there are good golf courses in Paradise, Sardar Malik should be playing at par with the best golfers of the world who have like him passed on.

Index